FACULTY REQUEST

Happiness and Greek
Ethical Thought

Continuum Studies in Ancient Philosophy

Happiness and Greek Ethical Thought

M. ANDREW HOLOWCHAK

Kutztown University
Pennsylvania

continuum
LONDON • NEW YORK

Continuum
The Tower Building, 11 York Road, London SE1 7NX
15 East 26th Street, New York, NY 10010

British Library Cataloguing-in-Publication Data
A catalogue record for this book is available from the British Library.

ISBN: HB: 0-8264-7472-1

Typeset by Aarontype Limited, Easton, Bristol
Printed and bound in Great Britain by MPG Books Ltd, Bodmin, Cornwall

Dedication

This book is dedicated principally to the ol' gang at the EMU library – Marsha, Bob, Stuart, Jesse, Keith, and Mike – who have adopted me as one of their own and who continue to honor me with the finest gift an 'itinerant' philosopher (or anyone!) can receive – friendship.

In addition, I would like to acknowledge four other singular people – Angela, Paul, Ru, and 'Whitey' – whose uncompromising friendship and love over the years has been and continues to be an illimitable source of happiness.

Contents

Preface

The Puzzle of Happiness

HAPPINESS HAS PERHAPS BEEN the focal point of and most seductive issue in philosophical discussions on ethics. While many, such as Aristotle and John Stuart Mill, take it to be the end of all human activity, almost all philosophers acknowledge that it is a valuable, if not essential, component of a good life.

On philosophical analysis, happiness proves as elusive as it is alluring. First, though most recognize its importance, philosophers disagree greatly about just what makes people happy. Among the early Greeks, Socrates, Plato tells us, believes that happiness is virtue, which he equates with knowledge. Aristotle defines it as virtuous activity, which has both a social and asocial dimension. Plato in *Republic* sees it as a form of justice. The Epicurean and Cyrenaic philosophers identify it with pleasure, but each school disagrees on what pleasure is. In more recent times, Sigmund Freud states that happiness is immediate erotic satisfaction. Immanuel Kant says happiness is a moral exercise of duty. John Stuart Mill links it to the freedom for self-determination.

There is also a second philosophical issue: Happiness for whom? Ought I to regard my own happiness above the happiness of others? If so, to what extent? If not, how does the happiness of others factor into how I ought to act?

These questions are themselves engaging, but they also invite serious philosophical discussion on a host of other intriguing issues such as, Ought I to be just?, Do I have a duty to help others?, What part does love play in a good life?, and even, Is happiness possible?

Finally, if happiness is an end of human activity, is it the sole end? If it is not an end, what role does it play in a good life?

In short, happiness is puzzling: All of us desire it, but there is widespread disagreement over what it is and how it is to be had. Happiness truly is as elusive as it is alluring.

In this book, one of my aims is to suggest a solution to the puzzle of happiness by looking systematically at what the ancient Greeks have had to say about it. Though different schools of thought existed and various solutions were proposed to the puzzle by these ancients, there was a common denominator to many, if not most, of these ethical systems: For many Greeks, happiness was a matter of psychical stability through right use of reason. This I use as the base for my own solution, as it slowly unfolds throughout each chapter of the book, to the puzzle about happiness.

Yet this work is more than just a casual stroll through ancient Greek literature to get at the nature of happiness. I also aim to give readers a detailed and readable critical analysis of some of the most significant ancient Greek ethical works and schools of thought as they pertain to happiness today.

This book comprises two parts. Part I examines four of the most prominent views on happiness in Greek antiquity – Platonism, Aristotelianism, Epicureanism, and Skepticism – each of which plays a prominent role in my solution to the puzzle of happiness. Part II makes the case that complete happiness, so far as it is attainable, consists of three nested levels of integration: personal, political, and cosmic. In laying out my argument, readers are introduced to Plato's Socrates, Diogenes the Cynic, Alexander of Macedon, the communitarianism of Plato and Aristotle, Stoicism, and Greek teleological thinking as it relates to ethics. I close the book with some final thoughts in my Postscript.

Overall, I believe the early Greek concept of the good life is in important respects much richer and more fulsome than our own. There is plenty we can learn from these early thinkers.

With these aims in mind, I have written *Happiness and Greek Ethical Thought* so that it is both accessible to casual readers who know little about the Greeks and Greek philosophy and helpful for students of philosophy who have likely had some exposure to both. As supplements, I have included two appendices: one of important figures (Appendix A), one of important, technical terms that are likely unfamiliar to most readers (Appendix B). In addition, at the beginning of this book, there is a key for abbreviations of important works that I refer to in many footnotes.

I introduce two translational concerns here. First, the Greek word that is customarily translated as 'happiness', *eudaimonia*, literally means 'blessed with good godliness'. Very early in Greek literature (beginning with Homer in the eighth century B.C.), to possess *eudaimonia* was to be fortunate, blessed, or favored by the gods, which was often, if not mostly, perceived to be a matter of circumstances outside of a person's control. Chance, it seems, played a large part in one's happiness. One has only to reflect upon how often the gods are seen to intervene in human affairs in Greek epic, tragedy, and even history. It is only with the advent of philosophy (beginning roughly in the fifth century B.C., but spelled out most fully by Aristotle in the following century) that *eudaimonia* came to be seen as something within one's control – at least, mostly so. Humans came to be seen as agents, responsible for their happiness or lack of it. With one's fortune no longer perceived to be mostly a matter of fate, *eudaimonia* took on a new, less fatalistic meaning. For Greek philosophers, happiness or *eudaimonia* is perhaps best grasped as the one-word answer to the question: What is the best possible life for a human being to live? It is exactly this sense of 'happiness' that I understand as I develop my thesis in *Happiness and Greek Ethical Thought*.

There is another Greek word that we shall frequently come across in various guises – *logos*. In philosophical texts, *logos* is often translated as 'reason'. In general, this is the best we can do, but for the ancient Greeks *logos* was a term pregnant with meaning. While it generally meant 'speech', 'word', 'order', 'report', 'reason', 'cause', 'end', 'explanation', and 'rule', among other things, it also meant 'proportion', 'measure', 'ratio', and 'value'. (For Christians, it was and still is synonymous with 'Christ'.) As such, this invites us to pause and reflect when we come across this word (and derivative forms of it) in Greek texts on ethics. For instance, when translating Plato's *to logistikon* as 'the rational' part of the soul, the notion that this part of the soul is essentially a ruling and harmonizing principle is lost.

Before ending, I have three cautionary remarks. First, this is a selective account of ancient Greek ethical thinking that focuses on Classical and Hellenistic thinkers, but extends into the second century A.D. Consequently, the conclusions I draw in developing my thesis are certainly not representative of all major ethical currents of thought over such a large span of time. Moreover, no conclusions from any particular school of thought should be taken to be representative of all members of that school, for many schools thrived for hundreds of years after being founded (e.g. Platonism, Stoicism, and Epicureanism) and were represented by many prominent members whose thinking on key philosophical issues, as we shall see in some cases, changed radically over time. Last, and along the same lines, the small size of this work gives readers little feel for the diversity of Greek ethical thought, both within and among schools, as well as the tension between rival schools. Nonetheless, I wish to show that ancient Greek ethical thinking was robust and integrative – that is it had a deep concern for problems that touched the everyday lives of everyday people. This, in large part, is why the Greek philosophers are still worth reading today.

There are always difficulties inherent in the study of cultures that are long past. These difficulties notwithstanding, there is the promise of substantial reward: As with the study of any different culture, past or present, the immediate payoff is a greater understanding of human nature through the common thread of our shared humanity.

In developing my thesis of happiness as integration, I hope to convince readers of the significance of the overall Greek contribution to the pursuit of happiness as we undertake it today.

Acknowledgements

I would like to thank all of my students throughout the years for their comments in my course on Greek Ethics. I would like especially to thank the students at Ohio University (Athens and Zanesville campuses, Spring Term 2002) for their many helpful suggestions on a draft of this book. I would also like to thank the many fine people at Thoemmes Continuum who made this book possible. Special thanks to Veronica Miller and Philip de Bary.

List of Figures

List of Abbreviations

Aristotle
An.	*On the Soul*
Cael.	*On the Heavens*
EE	*Eudemian Ethics*
EN	*Nicomachean Ethics*
GC	*On Generation and Corruption*
Metaph.	*Metaphysics*
Ph.	*Physics*
Pol.	*Politics*
Top.	*Topics*

Arrian
An.	*Anabasis* or *Campaigns of Alexander*

Cicero
Am.	*On Friendship*
Fato	*On Fate*

Fin.	*On Ends*
ND	*On the Nature of the Gods*
Sen.	*On Old Age*
Tusc.	*Tusculan Disputations*

Diogenes Laertius
Vit.	*Lives of Eminent Philosophers*

Epicurus
PD	*Principle Doctrines*
VS	*Vatican Sayings*

Epictetus
Ench.	*Enchiridion* or *Handbook*

Galen
Exper.   *On Medical*
   Med.   *Experience*
Sect.   *On Sects for*
   Intr.   *Beginners*
Subf.   *Outline of*
   Emp.   *Empiricism*

Herodotus
Hist.   *Histories*

Hesiod
Op.   *Works and Days*
Th.   *Theogony*

Hippocratic work
Art.   *On Craft*

Homer
Il.   *Iliad*
Od.   *Odyssey*

Lucretius
Nat.   *On the Nature of*
             Things

Plato
Alc.   *Alcibiades*
Ap.   *Apology*
Cr.   *Crito*
Euthd.   *Euthydemus*
Grg.   *Gorgias*

Phlb.   *Philebus*
Phdr.   *Phaedrus*
Prt.   *Protagoras*
R.   *Republic*
Smp.   *Symposium*
Sph.   *Sophist*
Thg.   *Theagnes*
Ti.   *Timaeus*

Plutarch
Vit.   *Parallel Lives*

Quintus Curtius Rufus
Hist.   *History of Alexander*

Sextus Empiricus
M.   *Against the*
             Professors
P.   *Outlines of*
             Pyrrhonism

Xenophon
Mem.   *Memorabilia*

Other Works
SVF   *Stoicorum Veterum*
             Fragmenta or
             Fragments of the
             Ancient Stoics
            H. von Arnim
            (ed.)

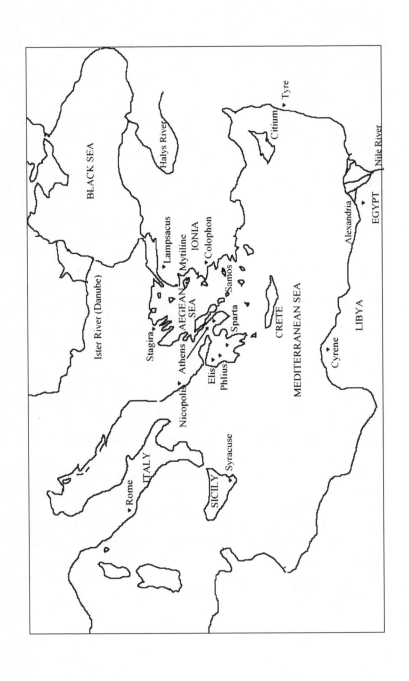

Introduction

Omnes actiones totius vitae honesti ac turpis respectu temperantur;
ad haec faciendi et non faciendi ratio derigitur.

Seneca, Epistula LXXVI

IN BOOK I OF THE *HISTORIES* of the fifth-century B.C. historian
Herodotus, the Athenian statesman Solon visits Croesus,
the wealthy king of Lydia. After giving him a tour of his
opulent empire, Croesus expects Solon to be awed by the
splendor and lavishness of his palace and by his lifestyle in
Sardis. Thinking himself the happiest and most blessed man
alive, he asks Solon who he thinks is happiest. The Athenian
tersely replies, 'Tellus of Athens', and goes forth to relate
the story of Tellus' own prosperity, his noble children, his
abundance of grandchildren, how Athens flourished during his life, and his glorious death in battle. Croesus, astonished that he himself was not chosen, asks Solon who he
thinks is happiest after Tellus (expecting himself, at least,
to have the second place). Solon answers him, 'Cleobis and
Biton'. He then goes on to relate the story of their matchless

strength and devotion to their mother. When their mother needed to be drawn in a heavy cart by oxen to a festival in honor of Zeus's wife Hera at Argos, the oxen were still in the field. The youths, wanting their mother to receive due honor, yoked themselves to the cart and pulled her for 45 stadia[1] and won the praise of all the Argives. While sleeping in the temple, the sons died that very night in response to their mother's prayer to Hera that the greatest good befall them, because of their extraordinary deed.

Having been overlooked a second time by Solon, Croesus now is doubly upset, for, seeing himself as a god among men, he takes himself to be the mortal who is most loved by the gods. The gods, however, notice and resent Croesus' own lofty self-appraisal (i.e. his hubris) and they are decidedly angry. Shortly after Solon's visit, by divine decree, Croesus's son, while on an ill-advised hunting expedition, is killed in a 'mishap'. Such was the price the Lydian king would pay for striving to rival the gods in happiness.[2]

This episode illustrates neatly the early Greek conception of happiness (Gr. *eudaimonia*). Happiness was no mere fleeting feeling, but it was determined by one's excellence of character (Gr. *aretē*) – a stable psychical attribute of an individual. In pre-Classical times, there were two views of excellence of character: the 'heroic' account and the 'Delphic' account.[3]

Heroic excellence of character is a matter of individual accomplishment through performing grand acts of heroism. Heroic excellence was exemplified by Tellus' glorious death on the battlefield and by Cleobis and Biton's brave show of strength in honor of their mother.[4] A heroic life was deemed preferable, more godlike, or 'happier' to a long life without such honors.[5] Consider as illustration the 300 Spartan soldiers, under King Leonidas, who went to their death willingly and courageously in 480 B.C. in defending the

Thermopylaean pass from an invading Persian force that may have numbered in excess of 200,000.[6]

In contrast, Delphic excellence of character was dictated by the ancient demands for justice (Gr. *dikē*) and self-control (Gr. *sōphrosunē*) in all affairs. These were reflected by two inscriptions on the Temple of Apollo at Delphi, the most famous Greek oracle in antiquity: *Know yourself* and *Nothing in excess*. The first inscription, early in Greek culture, was likely an injunction that meant each person should know his limitations as a human being – that is, no mortal should strive for godhood, as did Croesus of Lydia. With the influence of philosophical investigation somewhat later, it came to enjoin self-reflection and self-understanding. The second inscription states simply that moderation in all affairs is necessary for happiness, and this insight seems just as sober now as it must have seemed then. These two ethical prescriptions were famous in antiquity and characterized most of Greek ethics as early as Homeric times (eighth century B.C.). Classical (c. 500–300 B.C.) and post-Classical Greek ethical views, which are the focus of this undertaking, were an admixture of both precepts, with an emphasis on Delphic moderation.

In pre-philosophical literature, what unites the early heroic and Delphic models of happiness is religious apotropaism. Religious apotropaism – found, for instance, in Homer, Hesiod, Herodotus, Pindar, and Greek tragedy – has nothing to do with any objective standards of right or wrong actions, but is based on averting ill fortune through actions designed to appease the gods. As early Greek literature shows, Greeks believed that actions that appeased one god at one time might annoy either the same god at another time or a different god at the same time. Moreover, Greeks believed that even people who did all that they could do to win over the gods were not assured of divine guidance, succor, or justice. Consider, for example, what the Spartan king Menelaus, in an effort to avenge the theft of his lovely wife Helen by Paris of Troy, says to Zeus after his sword breaks on Paris' helmet:

> Father Zeus, no god curses us more than you. I thought Paris was going to pay for his crimes, and now my sword has broken in my hands, and my spear's thrown away: I missed the bastard![7]

Numerous instances like this show that religious apotropaism as a guide for securing happiness was a very arbitrary guide.

In the philosophical literature of Classical times, questions concerning happiness or good living tended no longer to be answered apotropaically, but by an appeal to reason. On the implicit assumption of some measure of control of one's own destiny, Greek philosophers sought to demythologize and to make a science of the right way to live one's life. While the philosopher Heraclitus (fl. 500 B.C.) noted all things are in flux and gave dryness as a material condition of wisdom, Socrates, years later, turned away from all material understanding of the cosmos and fixed his attention *exclusively* on human existence. Hereafter, Greek philosophers treated questions about good living as themselves worthy of serious philosophical exploration. Ethics as a branch of philosophy was born and the key issue concerning Greek ethics was happiness.

The early Greek notions of happiness differ substantially from ours. As I mention in the preface, the very word for happiness, *eudaimonia*, literally means 'blessed with good godliness' – that is, being fortunate or favored by the gods. This clearly has its roots in religious apotropaism, where happiness and good fortune were inseparable. In the main, however, Greek philosophers linked happiness with excellence of one's character, not fortune. Philosophers strove to show that happiness was chiefly, if not exclusively, within people's control, not due to the gods or fate. An account of human agency took root that placed a premium on responsibility for human actions. *Eudaimonia* became a matter of striving to live the best life possible and this meant more than having a perspective on right or wrong actions. Happiness was a rational and settled commitment to a particular way of life and the Greek way of life, especially during the time of Plato and Aristotle, was perceived to be essentially political[8] in nature.

Overall, using Greek philosophers as guides, I propose to take you, as readers, on a journey, of sorts. It is a far-reaching journey – one of cosmological scope – that begins, rather humbly, with the self (or perhaps, more precisely, *within* the self), and ends, strangely enough, just where it begins. Yet this is not to say that this journey takes you nowhere, for it is, I believe, the most important journey that you, if willing, will undertake in your lifetime.

> Speak, Memory, of the cunning hero, the wanderer, blown off course time and again after he plundered Troy's sacred heights. Speak of all the cities he saw, the minds he grasped, the suffering deep in his heart at sea as he struggled to survive and bring his men home.[9]

Notes

[1] One stade equals roughly 600 feet.

[2] *Hist.* I.30–4.

[3] Following Kahn here. Charles H. Kahn, 'Pre-Platonic Ethics', *Ethics,* ed. Stephen Everson (Cambridge: Cambridge University Press, 1998).

[4] The extent to which this ideal permeated Greek culture can be seen by looking at Sparta, Athens' great military rival in the fifth century B. C. Sparta was a city whose way of life was completely militaristic and wholly devoted to heroism through battle.

[5] MacIntyre says of this heroic view: 'If a human life is understood as a progress through harms and dangers, moral and physical, which someone may encounter and overcome in better and worse ways and with a greater or lesser measure of success, the virtues will find their place as those qualities the possession and exercise of which generally tend to success in this enterprise and the vices likewise as qualities which likewise tend to failure.' Alisdair MacIntyre, *After Virtue* (Notre Dame: University of Notre Dame Press, 2002), 142.

[6] Herodotus' account of the battle of Thermopylae occurs in Book VII (138–239) of *Histories*. Here he tells of an astonished Persian scout reporting back to the Persian king, Xerxes, that the Spartan soldiers were seen doing calisthenics and combing their hair prior to what would certainly have seemed to them to be imminent death.

[7] *Il*. III.388–91 (Lombardo's translation).

[8] Centered on the Greek city-state.

[9] *Od*. I.1–3.

Part I

FOUR VIEWS OF HAPPINESS

1

Happiness and Beauty

Platonic Eroticism in
Symposium

The love of the gods belongs to anyone who has given birth
to true virtue and nourished it, and if any human being
could become immortal, it would be true.

Diotoma to Socrates

ARISTOCLES OF ATHENS, better known as Plato,[1] son of
Ariston, tells us very little about himself in the many works
that he has left behind. The sole exception is a presumed
autobiographical *Seventh Letter*, yet the work is probably
spurious. In addition, his earliest biographers – Plutarch
(fl. 100 A.D.), Apuleius (second century A.D.), and Diogenes Laertius (third century A.D.) – write hundreds of
years after his death and are generally not historically accurate sources. Yet these biographies and scattered fragments in the ancient literature (especially the comments in
Aristotle's works) are all we have.

Plato was born in 427 B.C. On his mother's side, he
was said to have descended from the early sixth-century

Athenian statesman and reformer Solon. On his father's side, he came from a long line of distinguished Athenians, who claimed descent from the god Poseidon.

Plato's parents and grandparents lived through the height of Athenian political and military power, which fought off the mighty Persian army in the early fifth century. Plato was born during the Peloponnesian War (431–404 B.C.). With the affair of war, there were many challenges to the young democracy of Athens:[2] It agreed to oligarchic reforms in 411 B.C. (with the hope of gaining Persian aid to win the war) and, at the end of the war, it endured a short-lived, Spartan-backed tyrannical rule. In each case, democracy was fully restored. Yet it was ultimately a democratic Athens that put Plato's mentor Socrates to death in 399 B.C. Thus, Plato knew well uncertainty, intrigue, conspiracy, hardship, and suffering.

In 388 B.C., Plato traveled to Sicily and met Archytas of Tarentus, a Pythagorean philosopher, and Dion, the brother-in-law of the tyrant of Syracuse. At Syracuse, he was influenced by the Pythagorean love of mathematics and its application to real-world explanation. He would return to Sicily in 367 B.C. and 361 B.C., where he would try unsuccessfully to educate the new tyrant Dionysius II in philosophy.

Shortly after 388 B.C. in Athens, Plato founded his school, the Academy, where he taught and published most of his works. In 367 B.C., Aristotle joined the Academy and remained there until the death of Plato in 347 B.C., when Plato's nephew Speusippus took over the school.

Plato's works, many, if not most, scholars group into three periods, each of which is indicative of progress or change in his thinking. In his early works, Plato's focus is to give a picture of the historical Socrates. The topics Socrates discusses are virtue and virtuous living, and becoming virtuous is wholly an exercise of intellect. Plato portrays Socrates as one who wanders through the gathering places of Athens in search of people with whom he can talk in his quest for knowledge. Socrates is sometimes depicted as the paradigm of virtuous activity. Plato's manner of exposition in these early works is 'Socratic' in that elenctic dialogue, a method of cross-examination through question and answer conducted by Socrates, is the preferred literary device he employs.[3]

Socrates is also the focal point of the second group of Plato's works, his middle works, but in a different way. Here Plato, through Socrates, is interested not merely in ethical enlightenment through gaining knowledge, but a whole range of philosophical issues from epistemology, metaphysics, and education to politics and the possibility of life after death. No longer is a virtuous education mere intellectual training; Plato gives an account of human living that takes into consideration appetites, feelings, and even human spirit. In these middle works, Plato is coming out of the shadow of Socrates and, presumably, beginning to relate his own philosophical views.

Last, the third group of Plato's works is believed to belong to his later life. Here Socrates, when he is actually present in a dialogue, has a relatively insignificant role to play. In addition, Plato is often grappling with difficulties in the views expressed in the middle works. Strangely enough, some of these ideas he even seems to be rejecting outright.

Symposium, the focus of this chapter, is believed to belong to Plato's middle works. It is also a work that is not generally considered to be an ethical treatise, though I examine it here for its ethical content – more specifically, for what Plato has to say about the aesthetic dimension of a happy life.

Meeting the symposiasts

Symposium is one of Plato's most readable and enjoyable works. Here the philosopher artfully combines serious philosophical exposition on the nature of love in a setting that is playfully comedic. On the comedic side of the dialogue, the setting is a drinking party (Gr. *sumposion*) at which each of the participants (except Socrates), hung over from the heavy drinking of the prior night, have decided to eulogize the god *Erōs* (Love). On the serious side, *Symposium* gives us invaluable historical information on aspects of ancient Greek society such as sexual practices and entertainment, the historical Socrates, and Greek philosophical views concerning love. Most importantly, *Symposium* gives us an account of the importance of love for a happy and good life, concerned ultimately with the knowledge of Beauty and Goodness.

In the opening scene, a certain Apollodorus chances upon a Phalerian friend of his as the two walk toward Athens. The Phalerian man mentions a memorable symposium[4] in honor of a young tragedian named Agathon that occurred some years ago, and he asks Apollodorus whether he was then present. Apollodorus mentions that he was too young to have attended, but adds that he learned of this symposium from Aristodemus, who was in attendance. The remainder of the work is merely Apollodorus' recollection of the account that Aristodemus had related to him on a prior occasion.

The symposium occurs at the residence of Agathon, who one day earlier had just won an oratorical contest at Athens' Lenaian Festival in honor of Dionysus – a god representing merriment, abandonment, sexuality, and drinking.[5] Socrates was supposed to be at Agathon's home on the previous night, but he decided to delay his visit by one day in order to avoid the large crowd anticipated just after Agathon's victory.[6]

Plato begins his account of that memorable evening with Socrates' uncommon preparation for the party. Before leaving to see Agathon, Socrates bathes and even puts on sandals.[7] As he and Aristodemus walk to Agathon's place, Socrates loses himself to some philosophical problem and lags behind Aristodemus. Aristodemus, who was not formally invited to Agathon's home, can only uncomfortably press forward without Socrates. Aristodemus arrives and is invited inside to dine and revel in the second day of celebrating Agathon's victory. Socrates' absence is noticed, but the revelers, at Aristodemus' insistence, decide not to wait for him; they begin dinner without Socrates, who is fixed on the porch of a neighbor and lost in thought.[8]

Socrates arrives halfway through the meal and accept Agathon's invitation to take the most honored seat on the handsome youth's own couch. Those present, having drunk heavily at Agathon's on the previous night, decide against anyone presiding over the night's consumption of wine[9] so that they can guard against drinking to excess. The flute girl is also dismissed.[10] All of this suggests a more serious turn of events from the night before.

Of the group of celebrants, the physician Eryximachus proposes that everyone present honors one of the most neglected gods, *Erōs*, with a eulogy.[11] Eryximachus suggests that the order of presentation begins with Phaedrus, on the first couch, and ends with Agathon and Socrates, on the final couch. Everyone accepts Eryximachus' proposal.[12] In what follows, Plato gives us six eulogies on *Erōs* and then a soliloquy on love in praise of Socrates by a drunken Alcibiades, who enters late.

The first four eulogies

As the Greek word *erōs* itself intimates, the conversation will not be directed principally at love in any generic sense, but rather 'lust' or 'sexual desire' as it manifested itself in Athenian aristocratic society. Thus, the eulogies on *Erōs* concern male homoeroticism, specifically pederasty, and not sexual relations between a man and a woman. Yet before turning to the eulogies, I wish to say something on male homoeroticism in Greek society.

Male homoeroticism, practiced between a man and a pubescent boy, was part of Greek aristocracy beginning about 600 B.C., and was considered to be a more sublime form of love than that between male and female. Love between males was thought to be congruous with male values – military skill, courage, and male youth and beauty – and, as such, it was viewed as a sign of manliness. True homosexuality was rare,[13] though bisexuality was a way of life for many, if not most.

In terms of the actual relationship between men and boys, there was the 'lover' (Gr. *erastēs*) and the one loved (Gr. *erōmenos*). Male citizens under spell of *Erōs* would pursue a well-bred younger boy – between the ages of 12 and 20, with 16–17 considered prime years – with the hopes of consummating a sexual affair. Men looked for masculinity, beardlessness, bodily strength, and future socio-political prowess. The boy was expected to be coy and resistant, and his role, when won over, was completely compliant and passive. In return, the boy could expect some patronage for future political or social advancement. Nonetheless, prominently beautiful youths certainly did gain social status and glamour through coupling with the right lover.

Boys were accompanied by a guardian (*paidagōgos*) – a slave to keep away suitors as the boy traveled to and from school. Once a suitor won the approval of the boy's father, the courtship progressed through stages such as gift-giving, participation in sport, and, as is the case here, going to *sumposia*. Once the boy became bearded, he was expected to relinquish his former social identity and become a lover himself (for more, see Appendix B).

The first to eulogize the god *Erōs* is Phaedrus,[14] who focuses on *Erōs*'s genesis and his 'most important gift' to men. *Erōs*, Phaedrus argues, deserves special attention because he is a primordial god. Furthermore, he has given men the greatest good: the love between a man as lover and a young boy as one who is loved. He sums up, 'Love is the most ancient of the gods, the most honored, and the most powerful in helping men gain virtue and blessedness, whether they are alive or have passed away'. Overall, the speech is plain and uncomplicated, but it proves a fitting start for the rest of the speeches.

Pausanias follows Phaedrus. It is generally held, he states, that *Erōs* and Aphrodite are inseparable. Now, since there are two Aphrodites, Aphrodite All-Deme[15] (i.e. love common to all people) and Celestial Aphrodite[16] (i.e. love practiced by virtuous people), there must be two of *Erōs*, one common and one sublime.[17] When a relationship between a man and boy is common, then the love between the two is physical in nature. Such a love merely involves the gratification of the lover's sexual instincts at the expense of the boy's education.[18] Common love is worthless. Proper relationships between a man and a boy are sublime when the sexual gratification of the lover is balanced by concern for the ethical instruction of the boy. Sublime love is educative in that it confers upon the beloved stable and lasting ethical benefits. No actions of a lover are shameful, however scandalous they may appear, as long as he truly has the betterment of his beloved in mind.[19] In consequence, deeds themselves are only good or bad depending upon the type of love by which they are performed.

Following Pausanias' eulogy, we anticipate a speech from Aristophanes, but severe hiccups prevent him from eulogizing in turn. So, next is the eulogy of the physician

Eryximachus.[20] In keeping with the fourth-century B.C. practice of humoral, Hippocratic medicine, Eryximachus defends the thesis that *Erōs*, properly apprehended, is a harmonizer of opposites. Agreeing with Pausanias, he says that there are two kinds of *Erōs*, one common and one sublime, but this is not to say that love is simply the attraction people feel toward physical beauty. *Erōs* is much more than this: It affects matters throughout the whole cosmos. Just as in medicine, where the careful physician preserves a harmony between opposite material elements in the body (e.g. hot and cold, bitter and sweet, and wet and dry), sublime *Erōs* is the force that preserves the universal harmony of opposing elements. In contrast, common *Eros*, like disease, strives to destroy balance and harmony wherever it exists.[21] Through sublime *Erōs*, Eryximachus says, we behave moderately and maintain proper relations with the gods. Common *Erōs*, in contrast, inclines us to immoderation, thereby destroying the balance between opposites and our connection to the gods. In sum, like Eryximachus, *Erōs* is a practicing physician.

Critics generally acknowledge that the next eulogy, that of Aristophanes (which deliberately occurs out of turn), marks a major turning point in the encomia.[22] No longer are the speeches directed principally at the benefits of *Erōs* as a god, Aristophanes directs us to the very nature of love as we, as humans, uniquely experience it. His speech begins with an account of the nature of human beings at a time 'long ago'. What follows is a myth that gets at the very heart of the psychology of love.

Long ago, he relates, humans were of three distinct and complete sexes – males (the most godlike and offspring of Sun), females (offspring of Earth), and an androgynous sexual type (offspring of Moon). Every body was circular and, like its parent, moved circularly.[23] In addition, the parts of every type were doubled, even sexual organs.[24]

At one point, these early humans began to act maliciously toward the gods, and Zeus decided to split each person into two and to separate the halves so as to put a stop to the insolence.[25] This resulted in the type of humans that exist today. In consequence, all of people today, as halves, continually yearn through love for their other half.

As described by Aristophanes, *Erōs* is no longer a god, but a process – all persons' mostly fruitless erotic search for their other half, a vain striving for sexual completeness. Striving for sexual completeness, people usually settle for a temporary satisfaction of erotic urges with someone who does not complete them. Complete sexual satisfaction, Aristophanes states, only comes with the finding of and merging with our other half.[26]

Sophistry versus Socratic dialectic

The eulogies of the last three symposiasts – Agathon, Socrates, and Alcibiades – are of considerable importance. That they occur in the order that they do is essential for Plato. Socrates' speech is, as we shall see, wedged between the colorful drivel of the orator Agathon and the riotously drunken outpourings of Alcibiades. Plato's intent here seems to be to set up at least two different types of contrast: one, concerning the proper method of eulogizing (sophistry versus Socratic dialectic (Gr. *elegchos*), Socratic dialectic versus Platonic 'eroticism'); another, concerning character (Socrates versus Alcibiades). I examine first Plato's treatment of sophistry through the mouth of the youthful Lenaian victor, Agathon.

Following Aristophanes, Agathon proposes to disclose both the nature of *Erōs* as well as his gifts. *Erōs*, he says, is the youngest and the most fluid and supple deity. He is a delicate god with a lovely complexion.[27] Judged by his appearance, Agathon has described the perfect young boy of the man-boy coupling.

Then he goes on to describe the deeds of *Erōs*. *Erōs* deals fairly with gods and men. He acts with moderation. He is courageous and brave. He is even wise.[28] *Erōs*, now, seems to be the perfect lover – the man in the man-body coupling. The tension (and confusion) here seems obvious: Agathon has visually described *Erōs* as youthful object of homoerotic affection, but then says that his gifts to men are the gifts of a lover instead of one who is loved.

Overall, it may be that Agathon, in praising *Erōs*, is simply praising himself. For it is *Erōs*, like Agathon, who 'calls gatherings like these together'.[29] Moreover, like *Erōs*, Agathon is young and beautiful, and presumably he possesses virtue much beyond his years (for he has just won an oratorical contest). In addition, the narrator Apollodorus declares that Agathon had given a eulogy 'so becoming to himself and to the god . . .'.[30]

In addition, it is possible that there is a theme of seduction underlying the confusion. In describing *Erōs* both as lover and beloved, Agathon's eulogy might not be about *Erōs* as god, but rather *Erōs* as the love between himself and Socrates.

When Agathon finishes, those present loudly applaud. Socrates openly and abundantly lauds Agathon, but Plato makes it clear that Socrates is mocking, not praising Agathon. Socrates suggests that the speech of Agathon, modeled sophistically, is a feast for the ears but nothing to stir the soul to see the true nature of love.[31] Sophistry, having no concern for truth, is mellifluous verbiage. As Socrates, just prior to his own speech on *Erōs*, tells Agathon in mocked praise:

> [Y]our description of him (*Erōs*) and his gifts is designed to make him look better and more beautiful than anything

else – to ignorant listeners, plainly, for of course he wouldn't look that way to those who knew. And your praise did seem beautiful and respectful. But I didn't even know the method for giving praise (i.e. the Sophistic method); and it was in ignorance that I agreed to take part in this. So 'the tongue' promised, and 'the mind' did not. Goodbye to that! I'm not giving another eulogy using that method, not at all – I wouldn't be able to do it! – but, if you wish, I'd like to tell the truth my way. I want to avoid any comparison with your speeches, so as not to give you a reason to laugh at me.[32]

Socrates' insistence on telling the truth, of course, has nothing to do with any fear of others laughing at him. Socrates merely has repugnance for sweet-sounding drivel. He has, instead, a desire to know the truth. Plato here is describing the historical Socrates.

What follows, then, is no speech at all, but typical Socratic in-your-face dialectic that is cunningly orchestrated to show the very impotence and emptiness of Agathon's eulogy. Socrates persuades Agathon (and perhaps everyone else) of two things. First, *Erōs*, desiring beauty, must himself be unattractive,[33] since no one desires what he already has. Second, the god, since he desires good things, must not possess them.[34] Agathon is at a loss for words. Socratic dialectic, it seems, handily defeats sophistry.

Yet the success of Socrates' refutation through dialectic is partial and Plato demonstrates this in two ways. First, the dialectical phase, which runs only from 199c–201c, is an extremely small part of the overall work. This suggests that it is not Plato's aim in *Symposium* to showcase *elegchos* as it is in other dialogues. Second, and most importantly, the work of dialectic is unfinished. It functions sufficiently well to expose the confusion in Agathon's oratory, but it fails to disclose what *Erōs* is. To get at the nature of *Erōs*, Socrates himself had need of instruction. With the end of this dialectical phase of Socrates' eulogy, the one contrast of methodology is completed: dialectic triumphs over rhetoric, but the limits of Socratic *elegchos* are also disclosed. I turn to the second methodological contrast.

Socrates' initiation

Socrates goes on to eulogize *Erōs* through a discussion, he tells us, that he had some time ago with a Mantinean priestess by the name of Diotima, who taught him the real nature of *Erōs*.[35] The language throughout is that of the rites of passage from the religious irrationalism that flourished in the mystery cults of late fifth-century Greece, especially during the Peloponnesian War, and it suggest Socrates' own initiation into the 'mystery' of love. Socrates then gives a summary of what Diotima taught him in the rest of his eulogy.

Erōs, Diotima told Socrates, is not attractive, but this does not imply, as Socrates had said it did, that *Erōs* is unattractive. In reality, *Erōs* is neither attractive nor unattractive, but lies somewhere between the two.[36] She also argues that *Erōs* cannot be a god and is not a mere mortal. *Erōs*, occupying a middle ground between gods and men, must then be a spirit that mediates between them and makes the cosmos one and whole.[37]

Consistent with the theme of mediation, *Erōs*, conceived on the birthday of Aphrodite, is the child of Poverty (f.) and Plenty (m.). He is a vagrant, with tough and dry skin, who is without shoes and a bed. *Erōs* seeks what is beautiful and valuable – such as knowledge, courage, resourcefulness, education, and magic. What is beautiful is what *Erōs* loves, she said, and wisdom (Gr. *sophia*) is what is beautiful. Therefore, *Erōs* loves wisdom. So, *Erōs* is a lover of wisdom (Gr. *philosophos*) – a philosopher.[38]

Then she tells Socrates that we desire good things to make us happy and that happiness is an end in itself. Thus, the love of good things, which is common to all people, brings about happiness. This love of good things is the true sense of 'generic love'. Since all people love goodness, they want to possess it always. It follows that '*Erōs* is wanting to possess the good forever'.[39] Wanting to possess the good forever, then, brings about happiness, and happiness is inseparable from goodness and love.

Diotima then compares *Erōs* to a midwife. All people, she says, are physically and mentally pregnant – that is, all people desire to give birth. This is as close to immortality as mortal creatures can get and this is only possible in a beautiful medium. Beauty, therefore, is an indispensable part of birth. So, *Erōs* aims at 'reproduction and birth in beauty'.[40]

If we conjoin the two arguments, it follows that lovers desire to possess the good forever and they desire to do so by giving birth through beauty. Thus, lovers desire immortality. Physically pregnant men (common men) desire immortality through procreation with women.[41] Mentally pregnant men (better men), in contrast, engage in the right sort of erotic relations with young boys and thereby contribute substantially to the boy's ethical education. 'And in common with him (the boy) he nurtures the new-born; such people, therefore, have much more to share than do the parents of human children, and have a firmer bond on friendship, because the children in whom they have a share are more beautiful and more immortal.'[42] It is these exalted erotic relationships[43] that give rise to such outstanding men as Homer, Solon, and Hesiod.

Finally, Diotima initiates Socrates into the rites of exalted eroticism, a series of steps to philosophical wisdom. I sum the steps as follows.

(S₁) A man develops an appreciation for the physical beauty of a young boy (210a).

(S₂) The man learns to realize that no one body is any more beautiful than and admits of love more than another, and thus he loves all bodies the same (210b).

(S₃) He comes to value mental beauty (customs, activities and laws) more than physical beauty, and he yearns to cultivate the former in others (210b–c).

(S₄) He turns to seeking knowledge and gives birth to many beautiful theories and ideas, until a unique kind of beauty is found (210c–d).

(S₅) Finally, he sees a singular beauty that is eternal, absolute, divine, constant and independent of particular beautiful things (211a–e).

In short, the initiation involves a series of progressive, ascending abstractions away from particular, sensible objects (here, love for beautiful boys) towards objects of thought, until one grasps formal reality itself (see Plato's Forms). *Erōs*, then, is a goad to proper ethical education seriatim.

Ascending and seeing what is ultimately responsible for all things beautiful, both physical (sensory) and mental (intellectual), one experiences true erotic liberation. Diotima elaborates:

> If you once see the Form, it won't occur to you to measure Beauty by gold or clothing or beautiful boys and youths – who, if see them now, strike you out of your senses, and make you, you and many others, eager to be with the boys you love and look at them forever, if there were any way to do that, forgetting food and drink, everything but looking at them and being with them. But how would it be, in our view, if someone got to see the Beautiful itself, absolute, pure, unmixed, not polluted by human flesh or colors or any other great nonsense of mortality, but if he could see the divine Beauty itself in its one Form? Do you think it would

be a poor life for a human being to look there and to behold it
by that which he ought, and to be with it? Or haven't you
remembered that in that life alone, when he looks at Beauty
in the only way that Beauty can be seen – only then will it
become possible for him to give birth not to images of virtue
... but to true virtue. ... The love of the gods belongs to
anyone who has given birth to true virtue and nourished
it, and if any human being could become immortal, it would
be he.[44]

One stands at the summit, as it were, of both knowing and
being. Driven by love, properly channeled through education into philosophizing, a lover's erotic impulses become
perfectly sated by Beauty itself. In such a way, a lover
attains immortality.

In all, the initiation begins a Platonic transformation
of the historical Socrates – one that is completed with the
eulogy of Alcibiades – into the immortal or ahistorical
Socrates. No longer does Socrates, as depicted for instance
in *Apology* (see Chapter 5), tirelessly seek wisdom at the
behest of the god; Socrates in *Symposium* becomes a god
or *daimōn* – or at least, as Alcibiades' depiction (below)
strongly intimates, a man of daemonic stature.[45] Moreover,
there is a sense in which Plato transforms himself in *Symposium*. For dialectic, which plays such a significant role in
many of Plato's 'Socratic' dialogues, plays a relatively insignificant role in this work. It functions adequately to expose
the weaknesses of Agathon's speech, but its real role is to set
up Socrates' instruction by Diotima – that is, Plato's own
transcendental account of love. In a word, Socratic dialectic, through the historical Socrates, mediates between rhetoric and Plato's own eroticism in his account of Socrates'
initiation. Having completed the second methodological
contrast, I now turn to the contrast of character (Socrates
v Alcibiades).

Alcibiades' eulogy of Socrates

Socrates' speech finishes to loud applause, but the applause is all too quickly interrupted by some boisterousness just outside of the door. In walks a drunken Alcibiades, an extraordinarily handsome man,[46] and all the symposiasts excitedly (and the excitation is likely sexual) invite him in to join in their celebration. It is, after all, a celebration of *Erōs*. Alcibiades enters and is wearing Agathon's own victory wreath − made from violets, ivy, and ribbons. Though no longer a youth, he is still quite handsome and perhaps looks like a drunken Dionysus himself.[47] Alcibiades goes right toward Agathon, whom he considers the best looking man in the room, and places the victory wreath on the orator's head. He then slumps down between Agathon and Socrates, without seeing the latter. When he does chance to see Socrates, who is seated right next to him, he suddenly shouts:

> Good lord, what's going on here? It's Socrates! You've trapped me again! You always do this to me − all of a sudden you'll turn up out of nowhere where I least expect you! Well, what do you want now? Why did you choose this particular couch? Why aren't you with Aristophanes or anyone else we could tease you about? But no, you figured out a way to find a place next to the most handsome man in the room![48]

Alcibiades then takes part of the wreath off the head of Agathon and places it atop Socrates' head. Socrates' unexpected appearance, like Alcibiades' unexpected arrival, is characteristic of the immediacy of being smitten by physical love.

Alcibiades now assumes the role of *sumposiarchos* and decides, consistent with the passion that he feels for Socrates, that the drinking is now to become immoderate. He orders not the largest drinking vessel, but a huge cooling jar, which he fills to the brim, then gluttonously drains. He then has it filled for Socrates, who, he derisively adds, has never been seen drunk regardless of how much he has consumed.[49]

Eryximachus tries to encourage Alcibiades to say a word or two concerning *Erōs*, but Alcibiades, so smitten by Socrates' beauty, pledges to praise no one else, not 'even a god', as long as Socrates is around. All agree that Alcibiades may eulogize Socrates instead of *Erōs*.[50] Just as true lust has turned out to be nothing other than wisdom, the true god of love turns out to be none other than Socrates himself.

Alcibiades' eulogy clearly betrays the ambivalence of a scorned lover. He compares Socrates to a satyr.[51] Yet unlike a satyr, Socrates' erotic music comes not from pipes but from words[52] (Gr. *logoi*). His words alone take possession of all people and transport them to ecstasy. The effect that they have on Alcibiades is erotic: they tear at his very soul. 'The moment he starts to speak, I am besides myself: my heart starts leaping in my chest, the tears come streaming down my face, even the frenzied Corybantes seem sane compared to me . . .'. Try as he might, Alcibiades cannot pull himself away from Socrates, and his whole life seems to be one constant effort to escape him. 'Sometimes, believe me, I think I would be happier if he were dead. And yet I know that if he dies I'll be even more miserable. I can't live with him, and I can't live without him! What *can* I do about him?'[53] Alcibiades, who all along should have readily been pursued by Socrates (as boy is by lover), is himself in pursuit of Socrates.

Alcibiades goes on to relate in drunken fashion his own efforts to seduce Socrates. He often found himself alone with Socrates. In all such cases, Socrates would converse with him, but then leave as if uninterested in sexual fulfillment. Sometimes they would wrestle[54] in the gymnasium, which seemed an ideal situation to prompt a sexual encounter. Again, nothing sexual would happen. Once they even spent the night together. Though they slept beside each other, nothing happened. Just as Socrates in his quest for truth shunned money, fame, and political ambition, he also shunned Alcibiades' renowned beauty. Thus, the only means by which Alcibiades could have seduced Socrates, his physical beauty, had proven dismally ineffective for the handsome young man. Alcibiades drunkenly and mawkishly sums his utter frustration, 'I had no idea what to do, no purpose in life; ah, no one else has ever known the real meaning of slavery!' Thus, the 'wisdom' that Socrates had to give Alcibiades in return for the latter's extraordinary physical beauty turned out to be a real 'gold-for-bronze exchange'.[55]

At night's end, it is Socrates as a lover – more specifically, as a lover of wisdom – who becomes the one who is loved. Alcibiades ends by stating, 'He (Socrates) has deceived us all: he presents himself as your lover, and, before you know it, you're in love with him yourself!'[56]

Given his frequent exposure to the charms of Socrates, Alcibiades' failure to escape the desire for particular beauty – his insistence on consummating a physical relationship with Socrates – seems quite inexplicable. He is doggedly intent upon giving Socrates a physically erotic exchange for a share of the philosopher's reputed wisdom, which Socrates willingly gives freely to all that want to discuss philosophy.[57] He fails to see that, if Socrates should accept any exchange for the 'gold' he has to offer, then what Socrates would really have is not gold, but mere fool's gold. Appropriately enough, Alcibiades' eulogy of Socrates ends with laughter, not praise. Alcibiades' madness is after all not the result of excessive imbibing, but rather the consequence of torturous pangs of unrequited love.[58]

Nonetheless, Socrates is not without influence on Alcibiades. Though Alcibiades probably has not gained self-knowledge, he certainly has gained some recognition that his character is defective, even if he cannot or does not want to put what he has recognized to use for personal betterment.

In spite of the obvious ethical shortcomings of Alcibiades as a person, Alcibiades the eulogist in a straightforward sense gives the speech that wins the day. After all, as Plato depicts him, Alcibiades does in part represent Dionysus himself. Moreover, his speech, unprepared and unrehearsed, is from the heart (more appropriately, from the cooling jar). In consequence, though it betrays the pangs of unrequited love, it is nonetheless a eulogy that praises the true god of love: Socrates.[59] This also explains in part why Socrates cannot give a speech of his own at the symposium, but merely relates what Diotima has told him. For Socrates, like *Erōs*, is not the fount but the messenger of divine wisdom.

At the end of Alcibiades' eulogy, a large drunken group of men enter Agathon's domicile and the drinking, as if to mimic Alcibiades' behavior, gets chaotic. Some of the participants, such as Eryximachus and Phaedrus, leave the revelry. The storyteller, Aristodemus, falls asleep.

Upon waking at the break of dawn, Aristodemus sees Aristophanes, Agathon, and Socrates still drinking and conversing. Socrates is making a point that dramatists ought to be able to write comedy as well as tragedy.[60] Shortly, Agathon the dramatist and Aristophanes the comedian suffer the effects of fatigue and drink, and fall asleep. Socrates alone remains wakeful and leaves Agathon's house with Aristodemus. The latter relates that Socrates spent the remainder of the day as he did always and then, with night, went to sleep.

Overall, the contrast between Socrates and Alcibiades functions as an illustration of how reason and eroticism fit into Plato's mold for a happy life. In *Symposium*, these two seemingly antithetical elements, through proper mediation, become interrelated. From all of this, only one who, like the Socrates of *Symposium*, is prodded by anticipation of a vision of Beauty can be happy and live a good life. As Alexander Nehamas aptly sums, 'Sexual desire, properly channeled, leads not simply to gratification but to the good life'.[61] Uncultivated, it remains mere lustful desire. Thus, Beauty, as mediator, leads to the Good.[62]

Furthermore, in showing how Beauty can be a medium for the Good, Plato links ethics with what today is regarded as aesthetics. What is Plato's purpose for this? *Symposium*, a work centering on the form of Beauty, is essentially a work on living beautifully, and what is truly beautiful is philosophical living. In contrast to the life of the common person, the philosopher's life, exhibited by Socratic hardihood and zest for learning, is the most beautiful life, characterized by love of living through passion for learning, which, in *Symposium*, takes an erotic turn.

Relevance for today

What are we to make of *Symposium* as an account for how to live a good and happy life today? In what follows, I offer some suggestions.

One marked difficulty in seeing the relevance of Plato today is that the philosopher's overall aim in *Symposium* is to take us away from the transitory beauty of the ever-changing things in the physical world to the complete and unchanging beauty of things in the intellective realm of true reality – that is, Plato's world of Forms (see Appendix B). Diotima's instruction was designed to do just this. So, it seems no one is in a position to accept Plato's aesthetic views without also accepting his metaphysical views.

This obstacle notwithstanding, there are certain things we can extract from this Platonic work about how beauty relates to happiness that are relevant to us today.

First, Plato says that all of us desire immortality of some sort as a means of communion with what is eternal. For most of us, physical procreation is the best that we can do. So, we begin a family. Others of us 'give birth' to words, ideas, roads, buildings, and even gardens – each of which inspires still others to create (i.e. to seek what is good and perpetuate beauty). In short, through procreative or creative efforts, both of which are in the service of crafting beauty, we declare our immortality and affirm the eternality of beauty (which for Plato is beautiful not because it endures, but endures because it is beautiful). Through creating beauty, we link ourselves to both past and future and thereby transcend time, insofar as this is humanly possible. And when a creative activity is shared, the pleasure is redoubled. Writes philosopher John Dewey, '[O]ne of the elements of human nature that is often discounted in both idea and practice is the satisfaction derived from a sense of sharing in creative activities; the satisfaction increasing in direct ratio to the scope of the constructive work engaged in.'[63]

Second, Plato says that none of us can find true beauty and love in a complete erotic investment in any one particular object of affection. Thus, Platonic eroticism entices us to live as a lover who looks for beauty in all things, instead of just those things that have an obvious impact on us. Daily life offers countless 'erotic' opportunities – such as a spontaneous conversation with a complete stranger at a shop, a walk in the countryside, or even time spent on the telephone with an old friend – from which we often shut ourselves off. Yet in opening ourselves to experience beauty in all things, we open ourselves to experience life as a flow of events, not merely a series of disjoint episodes. We free ourselves to experience wholly and actively what lies before us in a Platonically erotic manner.[64]

Third, Plato teaches us in *Symposium* that intellectual activity and erotic affection, if we apprehend eroticism correctly, need not be antithetical as we generally assume they are. For Plato, true eroticism is a goad to intellectual activity – that is, complete happiness through knowledge of forms. In similar fashion, erotic affection today, properly in the service of an ethically driven intellect, can lead us to just those things that are quite possibly most enduringly conducive of happiness – things such as friendship, practical wisdom, generosity, and justice. Eroticism in the service of intellect leads to an unselfish sense of love that seeks happiness not so much in the fulfillment of individuals' own desires (as is characteristic of many ethical views today), but in the community of others.

Notes

[1] Literally, 'wide one'. He received the name because of his broad frame, the breadth of his brow, or the breadth of his interests. *Vit.* III.3.

[2] It was with Cleisthenes at the end of the sixth century B.C. that Athens became the world's first democracy.

[3] *Apology* and *Crito* (see Chapters 5 and 6) fall into this category of works.

[4] References to certain historical events, such as the Theban 'Sacred Band' and Spartan involvement in Arcadia, within the work enable us to date the writing sometime after 385 B.C. As to whether or not any such drinking party actually occurred, it seems unlikely.

[5] The year of Agathon's victory was 416 B.C.

[6] *Smp.* 174a.

[7] Socrates usual manner of dress is without shoes (*Phdr.* 229a).

[8] *Smp.* 175a–c.

[9] One elected to preside over the amount of wine consumed during the night's drinking was called *sumposiarchos*.

[10] *Smp.* 176a–e.

[11] The word 'eulogy' comes from the Greek prefix, *eu-*, meaning 'good', and the Greek word *logos*, meaning 'word' or 'account', among many other things.

[12] *Smp.* 177a–178a.

[13] E.g. Agathon and Pausanias, both of whom are symposiasts here.

[14] *Smp.* 177e–180b.

[15] In Homer, Aphrodite as the child of Zeus and Dione (*Il.* V.370 ff.).

[16] i.e. non-procreative, male-only love in Hesiod, insofar as Aphrodite was born from the severed genitals of *Ouranos* himself (*Th.* 190 ff.).

[17] *Smp.* 180c–e.

[18] *Smp.* 183d–e.

[19] *Smp.* 184b–e.

[20] *Smp.* 185c–e.

[21] *Smp.* 186a–e.

[22] After having read Plato's *Symposium*, some members of one of my classes played out the events that occurred in it in a presentation before the rest of the class. Recall that Eryximachus goes before Aristophanes, who cannot eulogize in turn because of severe hiccups (185c). The young lady, who played Aristophanes, proceeded to hiccup while the young man, who was portraying Eryximachus, was speaking. The effect was to direct the audiences' attention from Eryximachus to Aristophanes. In addition, one can also imagine the impact of Aristophanes' tickling himself with a feather and sneezing (189a). The total effect, which cannot come out in a reading of *Symposium*, must have been completely disruptive, almost laughably chaotic.

[23] The circular nature and movement of each is a clear reference that these early humans were godlike. Among geometrical objects, the circle held a special place for Greeks and circular motion was also privileged. Aristotle, for example, tells us that circular motion is complete and divine, since its starting point is its end (*Cael.* I.2

and I.9). Following Aristotle, Greek astronomers, hampered by an inability to see celestial motions as being anything but circular (and of uniform velocity), were limited in their models of the movements of celestial bodies.

[24] *Smp.* 189e–190b. Each person had two faces, four hands, four legs and two sets of genitals.

[25] *Smp.* 190b–c.

[26] *Smp.* 192e.

[27] *Smp.* 195a–196b.

[28] *Smp.* 196b–197b.

[29] *Smp.* 197d.

[30] *Smp.* 198a.

[31] *Smp.* 198b–199a.

[32] *Smp.* 199a–b. Nehamas and Woodruff's translation throughout. Plato, *Symposium*, trans. and comm. Alexander Nehamas and Paul Woodruff (Indianapolis: Hackett, 1989).

[33] This first proposition does not follow from Socrates' reasoning, as Socrates himself is forced to admit at 202a–b.

[34] *Smp.* 201b–c.

[35] This gives some reason to suspect that the words of Diotima are the words of Plato and not Socrates. Nehamas (1989) argues Socrates' confusion while Diotima speaks at 206b and 210a is further evidence. Against this is the fact that there is no hint of any confusion by Socrates as he now relates what Diotima had presumably told him.

[36] Cf. Aristotle's doctrine of the mean in Chapter 2.

[37] *Smp.* 202b–203a.

[38] *Smp.* 204b.

[39] *Smp.* 205a–206a.

[40] *Smp.* 206c–e.

[41] *Smp.* 208c.

[42] *Smp.* 209c. *R.* VI tells us that erotic love is neither lessened nor lost until one grasps the being or essence of each nature. Here one has intercourse with being and begets understanding and truth. Only after having given birth in this manner is one relieved of the pangs of childbirth. He now lives, knows, and is nourished (490a–b).

[43] Concerning *Erōs's* reproductive function and role as a messenger, if *Erōs* means giving birth to true virtue, not just images of virtue, then this is also probably why Plato has Diotima say that Love is a messenger who shuttles back and forth between humans and gods, between the mortal and the immortal, between the realm of things that are visible and the things that are intelligible (the good).

[44] *Smp.* 211d–212b.

[45] Hecht claims that Alcibiades' depiction of Socrates in the former's eulogy paints a picture of Socrates as an Odyssean figure. Jamey Hecht, *Plato's Symposium: Eros and the Human Predicament* (New York: Twayne, 1999), 95–6.

[46] *Protagoras* (309a–c) gives a good account of Alcibiades' renowned handsomeness. Xenophon tells us that he was hunted by both women and men of noble birth (*Mem.* I.ii.24). Plutarch says that his youthful good looks never left him throughout his life (*Vit., Alcibiades* 1).

[47] Alcibiades was also Socrates' most famous student. He later became an important Athenian general, who was charged with sacrilegious behavior in the mutilation of *hermae* (sacred statues representing the god Hermes) just prior to the Sicilian expedition during the Peloponnesian War. Such charges, perhaps trumped up by political rivals, led to his recall from the expedition. On his being recalled, he escaped and became a political ally of the rival Spartans, and later an ally of the Persians.

[48] *Smp.* 213c.

[49] *Smp.* 213e–214a.

[50] *Smp.* 214d–e.

[51] Satyrs were involved in mysteries, drunken orgies, and sexual licentiousness.

[52] That is, philosophy.

[53] *Smp.* 216c.

[54] Such exercise was customarily done while all parties were naked.

[55] *Smp.* 217b–219e. Following the levels of initiation, we see that Alcibiades, offering merely the physical beauty of one body, really has little or nothing to offer Socrates who desires to grasp the form of Beauty itself. The reference to this unfair gold-for-bronze exchange comes from Homer's *Iliad* (VI.232–6).

[56] *Smp.* 222b.

[57] Of course, Socrates never professes to have wisdom or knowledge of any sort, but he is always happy to exchange ideas with anyone with the hope of gaining knowledge. At *Apology*, Socrates states that he is wise in relation to certain others who claim to be wise only insofar as he recognizes that he knows nothing while they, knowing nothing, contend that they know what they do not know (20d–23b).

[58] *Smp.* 222c. As 213c–d clearly suggests, unrequited not in the sense that Socrates feels nothing toward Alcibiades, but only that, while Alcibiades is inclined to act on his feelings toward Socrates, Socrates is not at all disposed to act on his own feelings.

[59] The received view is that the eulogy of Socrates is the climax. See, for instance, Bretlinger 1970, 21.

[60] In *Smp.*, the philosophical dramatist, Plato, is also a philosophical comedian.

[61] Nehamas 1989, xxii. Plato, *Symposium*, 1989.

[62] *Smp.* 204e.

[63] John Dewey, *Freedom and Culture* (Amherst, NY: Prometheus Books, 1989), 34.

[64] I return to a similar point in Chapter 7.

2

Happiness as a Mean State

Aristotle's Nicomachean Ethics

Arguments and teaching surely do not prevail on everyone, but the soul of the student needs to have been prepared by habits for enjoying and hating finely, like ground that is to nourish seed.   Aristotle, *Nichomachean Ethics*

ARISTOTLE WAS BORN in Stagira of Thrace, when Plato was 43 years of age (384 B.C.), Diogenes Laertius tells us.[1] His father Nicomachus was then physician to the Macedonian king, Amyntas III, the father of Philip II.

Concerning his dress and mannerisms, Aristotle was foppishly intellectual. Diogenes states that Aristotle had fashionably short hair, slender calves, a lisp, and small eyes along with a sharp wit. In addition, he was an eloquent speaker, who was well dressed and who wore rings on his fingers.

At 17 years of age, upon the death of his father, Aristotle joined Plato's Academy. He remained there for 20 years, till the death of Plato in 347 B.C. While there, he was widely recognized as Plato's best pupil. It is at the Academy that Aristotle likely wrote his 'exoteric' works. These were highly polished treatises (e.g. 'Symposium', 'On Education', 'On Good Birth', 'On Moderation', and 'On Pleasure') that were written for the public at large and won him great praise.[2] Unfortunately none of these works survive.

After the death of Plato, Aristotle traveled to Ionia, where he lived from 347 to 343 B.C. At the city of Mysia, he settled with a small Platonic circle of friends and married Pythias, the adopted daughter of a local ruler Hermias, by whom he had a daughter also named Pythias. He left Mysia when Hermias was arrested and executed, and then he moved to Mytilene in Lesbos, where he met Theophrastus, his friend and successor upon his death. After the death of Pythias, Aristotle took residence with a woman named Herpylla and had by her a son named Nicomachus, the name of Aristotle's own father.

In Macedonia (343 B.C.), Aristotle tutored Alexander the Great (see Chapter 5), son of Philip II. This tutorial probably lasted about two or three years. The impact of Aristotle on Alexander is unclear, though it is likely that Aristotle's views on the inferiority of 'barbarians'[3] (i.e. non-Greeks) and his passion for discovery had a marked impact on Alexander and fueled his desire to conquer the East. There is also the story that Alexander's army, while laying waste to Persia and India, continually shipped back to Aristotle unique flora and fauna, discovered on the campaign.

After the death of Philip in 336 B.C., Aristotle removed to Athens to found his own school – the Lyceum. This school, resembling a modern-day university, enjoyed considerable status and Alexander the Great reputedly donated the extraordinary sum of 800 talents[4] to its development and upkeep. This enabled Aristotle and his followers to research numerous projects, such as the study of the 158 most important Greek constitutions,[5] and it helped him to acquire and keep hundreds of manuscripts and maps.

At the Lyceum, it is believed that Aristotle lectured on scientific and philosophical matters in the morning to a general audience, while he engaged smaller, more learned audiences with more perplexing concerns in the afternoon. He is said to have had a habit of walking around (Gr. *peripateō*, 'I walk around') as he lectured, and this is probably how his followers received the name 'Peripatetics'.

Aristotle composed most of his extant, 'esoteric' works, while at the Lyceum. Unlike his exoteric writings, the composition of these works indicates that they were probably not written for the general public, but for pupils at his school. Scholarly opinion is in general agreement that they were Aristotle's lecture notes, collected after his death and left unedited, since they are dense, redundant, often confusing, and sometimes without regard for consistency. Gaps in the notes were later filled in by pupils and interpolators, like Andronicus of Rhodes in the first century B.C. About one-fifth (around 30) of these esoteric works survive today. These works cover logic, physics, metaphysics, philosophy of science, psychology, meteorology, ethics, politics, art, and biology, among other things.

In the year of Alexander's death, 323 B.C., there was much anti-Macedonian sentiment in Athens. Aristotle withdrew to Macedonia in fear of his life, and he died the following year.

Breakdown of Aristotelian science

Of all the works in Greek antiquity, in none is the prescription for moderation in all things, typical of many Greek ethical systems, more evident than in Aristotle's ethical works,[6] especially his *Nicomachean Ethics* (hereafter, *EN*). As the title suggests, Aristotle's *EN* is either dedicated to his father Nicomachus or dedicated to or edited by his son of the same name. Before coming to grips with Aristotle's ethics, it is helpful to say something about his breakdown of the sciences.[7]

For Aristotle, there are three main branches of science: theoretical science (Gr. *theōretikē technē*), political or practical science (Gr. *politikē technē*), and productive science (Gr. *poiētike technē*).

First, theoretical science deals with things necessary and unchanging.[8] It is founded upon principles that are intuitively known to be true, and, from these, other truths that may not be as obvious are deduced through syllogism (see Appendix B). Theoretical science is the most perfect and divine science, as its objects of study, being necessary and unchanging (e.g. the nature of humans as opposed to the study of particular humans), are most god-like and choice-worthy. Consequently, the study of such objects is its own reward and not undertaken for the sake of some end (see Figure 2.1, below).

Next, political science studies what is good for city-states (Gr. *poleis*) and the people who inhabit them. This comprises both political science (in a narrower sense), concerning the good of a *polis* (s.) and ethics, concerning the right end of human activity. In contrast to theoretical science, political science is an inexact science. It begins by no appeal to intuitively known truths, but instead starts with premises whose truth is likely. Thus, what we conclude is not known to be true, only thought to be probable.[9] We engage in political science for the sake of activity (e.g. to decide what the best form of life for men is) and activity, Aristotle says, is an end in itself.

Theoretical science	Political science	Productive science
studies *things necessary* (ungenerated, indestructible, and unchanging, such as Deity, heavenly bodies, principles of being, and mathematics.	*concerning things contingent* (generated, destructible, and changing) that have a source of change in something else, that can be otherwise, that aim at successful intervention in the course of events.	*concerning things contingent* (generated, destructible, and changing) that have source of change in something else, that can be otherwise, that aim at successful intervention in the course of events.
reasoning is demonstrative: truth of conclusions is guaranteed by nature of reasoning (deductive and syllogistic) an by premises intuitively known to be true.	*reasoning is probabilistic:* truth of conclusions cannot be guaranteed by premises, as premises are only very likely true.	*reasoning is probabilistic:* truth of conclusions cannot be guaranteed by premises, as premises are suspect.
knowledge is for its own sake, the exercise of which is an end in itself.	*knowledge for the sake of non-productive action,* the exercise of which is an end in itself.	*knowledge for the sake of some productive end,* the exercise of which brings about that end.
Non-deliberative, but contemplative, since contemplation is its own reward.	*deliberative and contemplative,* since human action requires deliberation.	*deliberative and non-contemplative,* since production requires no contemplation.
three types of theoretical science: First Philosophy (also called Theology or Metaphysics), *Mathematics* (Geometry, Arithmetic, Astronomy, Harmonics, Optics, & Mechanics), and *Physical Science* (Psychology, Geology, Meteorology, Biology, Zoology, etc.).	*two types of political science: political science* (good of state) & *Ethics* (good of individual in state).	*some Examples of productive science: Poetics* (for education in the emotions), Rhetoric (for persuasion), Military Strategy (for victory), Household Management (for a good home), & Medicine (for health).

Figure 2.1   The three main branches of science

Last, productive science is the science of manufactured things. It too, using probabilistic reasoning, is inexact. Productive science is undertaken for the sake of what is produced (e.g. military science aims at victory and medical science strives for health).

Ethics, as part of political science, is not only subsumable under politics, it is also subordinate to it, for the members of a *polis* exist for the sake of the *polis*, not conversely. We are by nature, Aristotle often tells us, 'political animals'.[10] So, the well-being of its individuals is an indispensable condition for the well-being of a *polis*. Thus, the aims of ethics are a proper subset of those of politics. No questions concerning how a person ought to act are questions independent of questions concerning the good of the *polis* in which he lives.[11]

Since ethics concerns contingent things, it is not an exact science and exactness is not to be expected from it.[12] Conclusions are applicable in the main, not universally; its arguments cannot be demonstrative for the very premises from which we begin are suspect. We must start with what we know most readily, the particular circumstances surrounding an action, and then proceed to what is likely to be the case according to nature. Aristotle says, 'For while we should certainly begin from origins that are known, things are known in two ways; for some are known to us, some known unconditionally [but not necessarily known to us]. Presumably, then, the origin we should begin from is what is known to us.'[13] Thus, unlike theoretical concerns, practical matters do not admit of invariable rules, intuitively known to be true.

As with other treatises on non-demonstrative sciences, Aristotle begins by gathering learned opinions on ethical matters and then prunes away inconsistencies found within this collection. From what is left, he formulates a view on what is very likely to be true and then subjects these pronouncements to the test of proverbs and moral judgements of his time.[14] What remains unaffected by rational criticism, then, is likely to be the case.

The method outlined is a form of deductive argument that works by elimination. For example, Aristotle says at *EN* VI.6:

> [The states of the soul] by which we always grasp the truth and never make mistakes, about what can or cannot be otherwise, are scientific knowledge, practical wisdom, wisdom, and understanding. But none of the first three – practical wisdom, scientific knowledge, wisdom – is possible about principles. The remaining possibility, then, is that we have understanding about principles.[15]

Here he begins with four candidates for that faculty of the soul that secures the underlying principles of theoretical knowledge: scientific knowledge (ε), practical wisdom (ϕ), wisdom (σ), and understanding (v). After ruling out the first three, he is left with understanding (Gr. *nous*), and ends his investigation here.[16] Schematically (here I draw out the reasoning stepwise):

1) F is ε or ϕ or σ or v.
2) F is not ε.
3) F is not ϕ.
4) F is not σ.
5) So, F is v.

Clearly, the key to a sound argument here is whether our initial cluster of contenders in premise one happens to contain the correct candidate. Aristotle himself admits that we can never be absolutely sure of this. Then again, ethics is not an exact science.

The aim of human actions

The focus of his *EN* is *eudaimonia*, a Greek word, I have mentioned in the preface, for which there is no adequate English equivalent. *Eudaimonia* is not reducible to any subjective, internal state as is 'happiness'. *Eudaimonia*, consequently, should most often be taken to mean for Aristotle 'good (i.e. *ethically* good) living'. Difficulties notwithstanding, I stay with the standard translation of 'happiness' throughout.[17]

According to Aristotle, ethics studies what happiness is and the extent to which humans can achieve it. The aims of ethics, then, are both philosophical and scientific. Ethics includes normative reasoning (prescribing what we ought to do) as well as descriptive psychology (stating how elements of our psychological make-up can keep us from doing what we ought to do).

Happiness, Aristotle states, is not, like something produced, a product of action, but it is an end in itself or a mode of living. We do not live for the sake of bringing something about, but live for the sake of living. Happiness is, then, activity itself. Aristotle says:

> Our present discussion does not aim, as our others do, at study; for the purpose of our examination is not to know what virtue is, but to become good, since otherwise the inquiry would be of no benefit to us.[18] And so we must examine the right ways of acting; for, as we have said, the actions also control the sorts of states we acquire.[19]

In short, ethics principally aims not at mere knowledge of happiness, but rather at making men happy.[20]

Aristotle appeals both to commonly held views on happiness and his own observations of human behavior to initiate his investigation. Concerning what is commonly held, he states that all men agree that happiness is the aim of a virtuous life, yet not all agree on the nature of happiness: sensual men define it as pleasure; political men call it honor or excellence; and theoretical men regard it as contemplation.[21] Of these, though the pursuit of pleasure is basest and contemplation is the most estimable activity, Aristotle thinks each in some measure contributes to happiness.

The pursuit of happiness for Aristotle involves the acquisition and exercise of excellence[22] (Gr. *aretē*) at two distinct levels: one corresponding to excellence of thought, the other corresponding to excellence of character. Excellence of character (Gr. *ethikē aretē*), is a certain stable state of soul that comes about through being habituated to cultivate virtue and avoid vice – primarily under the guidance of virtuous laws. Excellence of thought (Gr. *dianoētikē aretē*), in contrast, comes about mostly through education over time and involves contemplation of eternal, ungenerated, and incorruptible things (the objects of theoretical science).[23]

Excellence of character

Aristotle's account of excellence of character begins at *EN* II. Excellence of character is not something that we have by nature, for if something in us is *due to nature*, we have an inherent capacity to do that thing and we actualize this capacity whenever we do that thing. For instance, stones by nature fall toward the center of the earth and not even 10,000 throws upward can change this. In contrast, if something is *due to habit*, then it is the exercise of this behavior that, through repetition, makes it part of our character. We become builders by building; we are not builders by nature, for then everyone would know how to build. Excellence of character, then, is like building: It develops habitually through actions over time. So, excellence of character is neither in us by nature nor against our nature;

we merely are of such a nature to be able to become virtuous or vicious in time, and this depends on the development of our habits and the correct use of reason.[24]

Aristotle next tackles the nature of excellence of character, and this leads him to an examination of the human soul. There are, he says, three qualities of the soul: passions (Gr. *pathē*: e.g. love, hate, appetite, longing, anger, etc.), capacities (Gr. *dunameis*: capabilities of feelings), and states of character (Gr. *hexeis*: what we have being well off or badly off with respect to our feelings). Ruling out the first two, he concludes that excellence must be a state of character.[25] But there must be more to the account than this, he thinks, for a state (the mere possession of excellence of character) is compatible with being asleep, and no one would consider calling one who slept the whole of his life a virtuous person. Aristotle states, 'And as in the Olympic Games it is not the most beautiful and the strongest that are crowned but those who compete (for it is some of these that are victorious), so those who act win, and rightly win, the noble and good things in life'. Thus, excellence of character is the exercise (Gr. *energeia*) of excellence, not merely the possession of it.[26]

How, then, does the exercise of excellence differ from craftsmanship (i.e. productive science)? First, for virtuous activity, one who acts excellently *knows that he is acting excellently*. Second, one who acts excellently *must choose virtuous activity because it is in itself desirable*. Last, one who acts excellently *must do so from a settled and unalterable state of character*. In craftsmanship, Aristotle thinks that only the first of these conditions (knowledge of what the craftsman is doing) is met.[27]

Aristotle spells out his catalogue of excellences and well-known doctrine of the mean in Books II–IV. Excellence of character comes through striving for the mean (Gr. *to meson*) between two vices: one of excess (Gr. *hyperbolē*) and one of

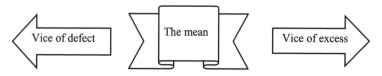

Figure 2.2   Aristotle's doctrine of the mean
Virtuous activity concerning any particular excellence is a matter of
steering clear of two vices: one of defect and one of excess

defect (Gr. *elleipsis*). Each excellence, then, is the intermediate between two vices (see Figure 2.2).

There follows a listing of particular excellences and their
corresponding vices at II.7.[28] There are, we find, excellences regarding attitude toward battles, pleasures and
pains, handling of money, honors, anger, truth-telling,
amusement, and attitude toward others.[29] Two examples
will suffice. Courage (Gr. *andreia*) is virtuous and it lies
between the vices of foolhardiness (Gr. *tharros*; vice of
excess) and cowardliness (Gr. *phoros*; vice of defect). The
courageous person will exhibit fear, but in the correct
amount and towards the right things. Yet he will also face
dangers if reason dictates, even to the extent of confront-
ing death.[30] Magnanimity (Gr. *megalopsuchia*), which he
describes at IV.3, is 'a certain ornament of the virtues'.[31]
Its vice of defect is pusillanimity (Gr. *mikropsuchia*), where
one regards himself as worthy of much less than he is, while
the vain person (Gr. *ho chaunos*; vice of excess) believes himself worthy of what is great when he is not.[32]

Not all (perhaps no) contrary vices are to be regarded
equidistant from their corresponding excellence.

Sometimes the vice of defect is farther from the mean.
For example, for magnanimity (see Figure 2.3), the pusilla-
nimous person (vice of defect) is more of an extreme than
one who is vain (vice of excess).[33] At other times, the vice
of excess is farthest from the mean, just as, with respect to

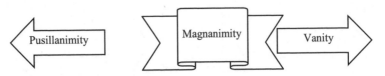

Figure 2.3   Excess less vicious
For magnanimity, the vice of excess, vanity, though vicious, is preferable to and less vicious than that of defect, pusillanimity

pleasure and pain, the self-indulgent person is more vicious than one insensible to pleasures and pains (see Figure 2.4).[34]

Consequently, in aiming for the mean in all excellent activity, we must first steer clear of the most contrary vice. Often this is the best that we can do in an effort to come as near to excellence as possible.[35] What guides us throughout is correct reason.[36]

What a person of excellent character deserves most is honor and honor is most befitting a person who surpasses others in one excellence in particular: magnanimity. The depiction Aristotle gives at IV.3 is too splendid to ignore. The magnanimous man appears a braggart to some, for he thinks that he is worthy of great things, but in truth he is no braggart, for he deserves such honors. So, he is an extreme with respect to his claims, since his claims are indeed bold, but a mean in that he rightfully deserves what he claims to deserve. He is not small-framed, for he is beautiful and small

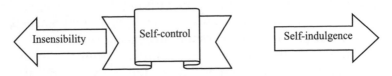

Figure 2.4   Defect less vicious
In the case of temperance, it is the vice of excess, self-indulgence, that is farthest removed from the excellence of self-control

people may be well proportioned, but they cannot be beautiful. He is moderately pleased at honors conferred by good men; honors from the lowly, he despises. In general, he is reluctant to receive benefits, because of his ethical superiority. While asking for nothing, he gives readily. Towards fortune, power, and wealth, he is moderate. He is open in his love and hatred, but love of truth is his chief concern. His life does not revolve around anyone but himself. He tends to overlook wrongs, does not gossip, and seldom gives out praise and blame, as it is seldom warranted. He walks slowly and has a deep voice and a measured utterance, for he is not easily excited or hurried.

In summary, as regards the particular excellences, happiness is a mean state that involves virtuous activity guided by correct reasoning at the right time, toward the right people, about the right things, for the right end, and in the right manner.[37] Book I.10 describes the man with excellence of character.

> For no human achievement has the stability of activities in accord with virtue, since these seem to be more enduring even than our knowledge of the sciences. Indeed, the most honorable among the virtues themselves are more enduring than the other virtues, because blessed people devote their lives to them more fully and more continually than to anything else – for this continual activity would seem to be the reason we do not forget them. It follows, then, that the happy person has the [stability] we are looking for and keeps the character he has throughout his life. For always, or more than anything else, he will do and study the actions in accord with virtue, and will bear fortunes most finely, in every way and in all conditions appropriately, since he is truly 'good, foursquare, and blameless'.[38]

Though virtue or excellence is the principal ingredient in a happy life and mostly up to us, he notes that external and bodily goods are also needed for complete happiness. First, an excellent person, like everyone else, will have his share of misfortunes, for chance, an external good, plays a part in every life. Nonetheless, the good person will dutifully bear misfortunes with equanimity and magnanimity.[39] Next, since lack of bodily goods can mar happiness even for one who is virtuous, these too are necessary for happiness, though they are avowedly goods of a lesser sort.[40]

Overall, the model of excellence as a mean is decidedly medical (in the humoral sense) and references to Greek medical practice are frequent. For instance, Aristotle says at II.3:

> First, then, we should observe that these sorts of states naturally tend to be ruined by excess (Gr. *hyperbolē*) and deficiency (Gr. *endeia*). We see this happen with strength and health – for we must use evident cases [such as these] as a witness to things that are not evident. For both excessive and deficient exercise ruin strength, and, similarly, too much or too little eating or drinking ruins health, whereas the proportionate amount produces, increases and preserves it. The same is true, then, of temperance, bravery, and the other virtues.[41]

This and numerous other references to medicine throughout *EN* indicate that the doctrine of excellence of character, as being in a mean state in relation to all particular vices of excess and defect, is medically modeled (see Hippocratic medicine, Appendix B). We should not forget here that Aristotle's father was court physician to the Macedonian king, Amnytas III.

Excellence of thought

Aristotle returns to the topic of happiness in the final book, Book X.6–8, after a lengthy account of friendship in Books

VIII and IX and a short exposition on pleasure at X.1–5. What he has to say here, however, goes beyond, even seems to contradict, his account of happiness in earlier books. If happiness is activity expressing excellence that is guided by reason, then complete happiness (Gr. *teleia eudaimonia*) will be *that activity which is most perfect and divine* — study or contemplation (Gr. *theōria*).

> Hence the gods' activity that is superior in blessedness will be an activity of study. And so the human activity that is most akin to the gods' activity will, more than any others, have the character of happiness. . . . Hence happiness extends just as far as study extends, and the more someone studies, the happier he is, not coincidentally but insofar as he studies, since study is valuable in itself. And so [on this argument] happiness will be some kind of study.[42]

Since the contemplative life actualizes what is most divine in us, for complete happiness, we must engage in contemplative activity as often as possible.[43]

All of this seems quite paradoxical. Aristotle's *EN* is a work on ethics and ethics essentially concerns matters that are political — that is, matters that relate to the well-being of the *polis* and the individuals in it. Yet the account of happiness at *EN* X.6–8 exhorts people with leisure to engage in contemplation, which seems to be essentially apolitical activity, as often as possible to be as happy as possible. Contemplation, as a private activity, seemingly has nothing to do with the well-being of the *polis* or even other people. Thus, ethics — which, by definition, is political activity — encourages us to engage as often as possible in activity that seems, by its very nature, self-centered and apolitical.

Perhaps recognizing this difficulty, Aristotle states that even contemplation is made better with friends, which suggests straightforwardly that pursuit of excellence of character (political excellences) and excellence of thought (contemplative activity) are not inconsistent.[44] It is also clear that the psychical calm that must result from contemplative activity better equips persons for measured political activity. And so, what seems problematic may be more apparently so than really so.

Is Aristotle's ethics relativistic?

There is another question that invariably comes up concerning Aristotle's doctrine that virtue is a mean state: is Aristotle's doctrine of excellence as a mean relativistic? The most relevant form of relativism here is Protagorean, which states roughly that what is right (here, right action) varies from person to person – that is, what is right for one person need not be right for another. For illustration, let us look at liberality, the excellence concerned with taking (or keeping) and giving (or spending) money. Aristotle states, 'The term "liberality" is used relative to a man's substance; for liberality resides not in the multitude of the gifts but in the state of character of the giver, and this is relative to the giver's substance'.[45] Clearly, no two men will be liberal in the same manner, since no two men are the same and no two men have the same resources. Each person has a distinct disposition toward liberality, a distinct personal history, and a distinct set of current circumstances. Consequently, no two people, however excellent, will strive for liberality to the same extent and in the same fashion. Moreover, they ought not. Thus, if Aristotle's doctrine of the mean is not relativistic, it certainly seems so.

Though we must concede that the degree to which each of us does (and ought to) strive for any particular virtue or excellence will necessarily vary, this in itself does not make the pursuit of excellence of character a relativistic enterprise. We need only to note that, for Aristotle, all humans who strive for excellence of character strive for exactly the same particular excellences. For example, each person wants to be courageous, though some will certainly be less capable than others due to physical peculiarities and past and present circumstances. Alexander the Great's capacity to strive for and actualize courage was certainly greater than that of the Persian king, Darius, who, outnumbering and fighting against the forces of Alexander, fled the scene of key battles (see Chapter 5). This is not to say that Darius did not strive to be courageous, for he did show up for battle. He was just no match for Alexander. Excellences themselves, for Aristotle, are not relative, though the extent to which each person pursues a particular excellence will always vary.

Moreover, relativism is not the same thing as subjectivism. Though for Aristotle *right actions vary from person to person* (a type of relativism), this is not to say *there is no truth to what constitutes right action for each person in a particular situation* (subjectivism). Aristotle describes finding the mean in a particular situation like finding the midpoint of a circle, which suggests quite unmistakably that there is a correct course of action in any given situation (though he acknowledges that this is practicably impossible and sometimes the best we can do is steer clear of the most contrary extreme).[46] Let me illustrate further with the following example. My own situation as regards the giving and taking of goods will depend on the number and quality of my own material goods at a particular time. For instance, at some time, my taking a gift of $1000 from a generous friend may not be the right thing to do. Perhaps my friend has been giving gifts too freely, without regard for his own well-being. Or perhaps I have been receiving gifts too freely of late, without due regard for the mean. In short, having circumstances determine right action makes right action circumstances-dependent – a type of relativism. Yet the overall situation demands a firm *rational* grasp of these circumstances prior to action for that action to be done virtuously and this would be the same for any agent in the same circumstances. For Aristotle, as with the Stoics (see Chapter 7), virtuous activity presupposes the clearest possible perception of the way things really are before acting and this, of course, rules out subjectivism.

Education

For Aristotle, ethics, as the word implies, concerns our habits over time and, in consequence, our character. Moreover, we have seen that it necessarily involves correct reason. Yet how, for instance, are we to reconcile the application of reason either to children's behavior, which is essentially irrational, or to those whose habits are so ill-formed that even their understanding of wrongdoing proves unavailing? Here is where Aristotle's keen observation of human behavior comes into play dispassionately and skillfully. Normative ethics merges with descriptive psychology as Aristotle proposes a solution to this prickly problem. The answer lies in education, and this, suitably, is the final section of the final book of the *EN*.

Aristotle has been telling us all along that happiness through excellent activity is an extraordinarily difficult task. At *EN* X.9, he says that, for those whose habits are long-in-place or hopelessly corrupt at a mature age (in other words, the many), argument is likely to have a limited impact. 'For it is impossible or not easy', he states, 'to alter by argument what has long been absorbed by habit; but, presumably, we should be satisfied to achieve some share of virtue when we already have what we seem to need to become decent.'[47] Feeling, not intellect, guides such people, since they neither listen to nor follow argument. Sometimes they aim at excellence, not because it is choice-worthy in itself, but because of fear of punishment. So, reason cannot persuade those under the direction of passion to lead an excellent life. In other words, such unthinking persons will not be able to attain complete happiness. At best, they can find some measure of happiness.[48]

For children of well-born status, however, the difficulty is tractable: education is the solution. By education, he does not mean teaching alone, for this, he acknowledges, has a limited impact on the very young, whose rational faculties are underdeveloped.[49] Ethical education consists principally in habituation guided by reason – that is, literally shaping behavior. Children, after all, are poorly disposed toward excellent behavior, and so their souls need nurturing through reason 'like ground that is to nourish seed'.[50]

Where does reason come into play if children themselves are mostly incapable of it? A father's instruction, like that of any individual man, is insufficient, for it lacks authority and the permanence required to guide a child throughout life. Moreover, children violently resist any authoritative individual who opposes their impulses, even if that individual has their best interest in mind. Children need a more authoritative, consistent, and powerful show of reason, which is law, for law is reason that springs from intelligence and understanding.[51] Consequently, we need excellent laws to cultivate excellence of character in our young.

Because of the status of law, it is incumbent upon communities, not individual fathers, to educate children. Yet where communities do not attend to the educative needs of children, then fathers themselves must attend to the education of their children.[52]

The problem now becomes how communal educators should proceed with education. Should education be conducted through what applies in general (i.e. through laws) or should it be conducted through attention to the needs of particular cases? Here again medical analogy offers a solution.

> [E]ducation adapted to an individual is actually better than a common education for everyone, just as individualized medical treatment is better. For though generally a feverish patient benefits from rest and starvation, presumably some patient does not. ... Hence it seems that treatment in particular cases is more exactly right when each person gets special attention, since he then more often gets the suitable treatment.
>
> Nonetheless a doctor ... will give the best individual attention if he also knows universally what is good for all, or for these sorts. For sciences are said to be, and are, of what is common [to many particular cases]. ... [S]omeone who wants to be an expert in a craft and a branch of study should progress to the universal, and come to know that, as far as possible; for that, as we have said, is what the sciences are about.[53]

Aristotle's solution seems wishy-washy, but it is not. Both the universal and the particular apply in proper education. Education, like sound medical practice, should include both individualized attention to children's needs as well as knowledge of what universally applies. The best educator will know the causes of becoming excellent and he will have a knack for catering a boy's education to his particular needs. The best educator, then, will both know what universally applies in the education of the young and have experience of particulars.[54]

In summary, if we should allow parents to educate their children, then we would expect that not all children would strive for the same things (or, at least, that most children would be poorly disposed to hit the mean). This is precisely what is most undesirable. So, to ensure that each will desire what is excellent and not what merely *seems* excellent, the best educator is the law. Yet since law cannot accommodate idiosyncrasies of each particular person's ethical upbringing, parents too must play a role. In this way, proper education involves both what is universal, laws, and what is particular, parental guidance.

Culpability

Following his penchant for covering a topic completely, Aristotle addresses responsibility of actions from *EN* III.1 to 5. First, he makes a distinction between voluntary acts and involuntary acts. Voluntary acts are those where the agent, being fully aware of the circumstances of an action, is the cause of the action. These receive blame when there is ignorance of the universal (what in general makes an action good), or praise.[55] In contrast, involuntary acts are those caused either by ignorance of the circumstances of an action or by compulsion. If forced, the agent is thus pained by such actions. If done on account of ignorance, the agent is pained only when his ignorance is disclosed. Others look upon him with pity or pardon.[56] The circumstances around such an action that determines whether it is done voluntarily or not are 1. who the agent is, 2. what the agent does, 3. about what or to what the agent acts, 4. what instruments are involved, 5. what result the agent obtains, and 6. the manner in which the agent acts. Ignorance of any of these conditions, especially the second and fifth, makes an act involuntary.[57]

What of forced actions, where a person knowingly performs some vicious action, but seemingly has no choice to do otherwise? Aristotle addresses this issue early. He says, 'What is forced has an external origin, the sort of origin in which the agent or victim contributes nothing – if, for instance, a wind or human beings who control him were to carry him off.'[58] This condition, though, contributes little toward clearing up difficult cases. Consider the tyrant who, having confiscated a man's parents and children, wants that man to do some opprobrious act upon the threat of death to his family. Such cases are difficult, Aristotle concedes, yet however much duress seemingly enters the scenario, the man still is literally capable of not doing the act, as he is not physically forced to do the act.[59] So, such cases are voluntary for Aristotle.

There is another difficult case to consider: acts not done *because of* ignorance, but done *in* ignorance. Here an agent acts but suffers no pain and no regret. An agent does such acts without knowledge of universal principles, for one who does not know the general rules of good conduct cannot be expected to suffer regret. Aristotle gives the examples of disreputable actions done while an agent is drunk or angry. Being ignorant of the universal, such cases are still cause for blame – though not pity or pardon – and are properly labeled 'voluntary',[60] since that person is ultimately responsible for getting himself into a state of anger or drunkenness.

To understand human culpability fully, we must look back to the causes of human actions. At *EN* III.2, Aristotle tells us, '[W]e first lay down the end, and then examine the ways and means to achieve it'.[61] It is clear that *choice* (Gr. *proairesis*) is responsible for our deliberate voluntary movements, for we act deliberatively by choosing what is perceived best among alternatives.[62] Prior to choice, however, is *deliberation* (Gr. *to bouleuesthai*) itself. We deliberate upon those matters where what is right is uncertain,[63] and we deliberate about how ends are to be met (and not about things that are not up to us).[64]

[A] human being would seem to be a principle of action. Deliberation is about the actions he can do, and actions are for the sake of other things; hence we deliberate about things that promote an end, not about the end.[65]

Prior to deliberation, there is *wish* (Gr. *boulēsis*), which too is for the end: some *good* or *apparent good*. Yet how do we know whether what we wish for is good or merely seems to be good? On this problem, Aristotle writes:

1. For those who say *the good* is wished, it follows that what someone wishes if he chooses incorrectly is not wished at all. For if it is wished, then [on this view] it is good; but what he wishes is in fact bad, if it turns out that way. . . . 2. For those who say *the apparent good* is wished, it follows that nothing is wished by nature. Rather, for each person what is wished is what seems [good to him]; but different things, and indeed contrary things, if it turns out that way, appear good to different people.[66]

Aristotle's solution to this problem is not entirely satisfactory. Here he appeals to the excellent person and again uses a medical analogy. For just as we judge what is sweet, bitter, hot, or heavy by appealing to the judgement of a healthy person, we must judge what is good[67] by appealing to an excellent person.[68] The excellent person, then, is a barometer of what is truly good. Aristotle does not address the further question *How can I pick out an excellent person?* His answer, I am sure, would be *The same way you pick out a healthy person*. The standard here, we must remember, is not infallibility, rather practicability.

Thus, we wind up with the following account of deliberative actions and human culpability. First, either the good or what appears good stimulates a wish for a particular end. Next, we deliberate about means to this end. Last, we choose one of these means as the right way to attain this end. In this manner, we initiate and are responsible for our own actions.[69]

Thus, with the Socratic claim that no one is willingly bad (see Chapters 5 and 6), Aristotle finds himself in agreement. Insofar as deliberative actions have their origin within us, we cause them and we are responsible for them. Therefore, we are deserving of the praise or blame that follows.

Ultimately, Aristotle's account of human culpability, like an insubstantial meal, leaves us wanting more. Something is not quite right. To illustrate, let us consider three types of person: one who chooses the good (i.e. some course of action) through habituation without reason (P_1), one habituated to act viciously who later comes to recognize his viciousness (P_2), and one habituated properly and who generally recognizes the good as good and chooses it because it is good (P_3). Now P_1 cannot be acting excellently, since he acts excellently *without knowing that he is acting excellently*.[70] He acts without reason and is, thus, not deserving of praise. In contrast, P_2 will in all likelihood not be able to become excellent, since his character is already mostly formed through bad habits learned early on. Seeing some action as good and doing that action is not sufficient for virtuous activity; there must be a habituative base. In addition, it seems difficult to fault one for a poor upbringing. Last, P_3 we recognize as the paradigm example of virtuous activity, where all three necessary conditions, listed at *EN* II.4[71] are met – to proper habituation, knowledge and right choice are added. Yet just what do knowledge and right choice add? In short, what precisely is the difference between the actions of P_1 and P_3? Aristotle writes:

> Arguments and teaching surely do not prevail on everyone, but the soul of the student needs to have been prepared by habits for enjoying and hating finely, like ground that is to

nourish seed. For someone who lives in accord with his feelings would not even listen to an argument turning him
away, or comprehend it [if he did listen]; and in that state
how could he be persuaded to change? And in general feelings seem to yield to force, not to argument. Hence we must
already in some way have a character suitable for virtue,
fond of what is fine and objecting to what is shameful.[72]

This and other passages in Book X suggest that proper
upbringing is a sufficient condition for virtuous *behavior* in
later life – that is, actions in accord with virtue – and a
necessary condition for *virtuous activity*.[73] In short, the realization that what is good is *really* good seems to add little, if
anything, to the habits acquired in one's formative years –
at least in terms of one's observable behavior. Presumably,
people must be lucky enough to have been habituated to
excellence from their earliest years or fortunate enough
to have a strong natural disposition to behave virtuously.
How, then, can people themselves be responsible for an
underdeveloped or vicious character?

This reading of Aristotle fails to consider the necessity and prominence of deliberation and choice in virtuous
activity.[74] Additionally, it neglects Aristotle's repeated
insistence in the latter chapters of Book I that – though
happiness comprises psychical, bodily, and external goods –
goods of the soul (i.e. excellences) are more responsible for
happiness than bodily or external goods, because virtue is
up to us.[75]

Consider also what Aristotle has to say about the repro-
bate.

Still, he is himself responsible for becoming this sort of
person, because he has lived carelessly. Similarly, an individual is responsible for being unjust because he has cheated,
and for being intemperate, because he has passed his time
drinking and the like; for each type of activity produces the
corresponding sort of person. This is clear from those who

train for any contest or action, since they continually practice the appropriate activities.[76]

Even the hopeless alcoholic was at least at one time free not
to develop such a vicious character, although he now
cannot voluntarily undo what he has done over time.[77]
Aristotle supplements this with the example of a thrown
stone. Once the stone is thrown, there is nothing the thrower
can do to bring it back. Still, it makes no sense to say that, if
it hits and breaks a vase, the thrower is not responsible,
as it was up to the thrower to throw or not to throw the
stone in the first place.[78] Here the act of throwing represents the choice linked with a particular action; the stone in
flight represents the seeming lack of freedom linked with a
person's character, once developed. In this manner, we are
in complete control over particular actions, since we can
have a full grasp of circumstances, but, over our character,
we have control only insofar we have control over the
beginning.[79]

What Aristotle fails to take into consideration here is that
the lion's share of everyone's character forms at a young
age, before the rational faculty is completely developed.
The disposition of the dipsomaniac to view alcohol as a
good is likely a product of his early years – perhaps his
family's acceptance of drunkenness as a way of life. It is
this defect that Aristotle does not directly address. The
only way to secure culpability for Aristotle is to deny that
proper habituation *early on* is a necessary condition for
happiness; it is instead a strong predictor of happiness.[80]
This leaves some room for humans to break away from
early habits, however strong, and develop the right sort of
habits over time later through deliberation and choice.
This, I believe, is Aristotle's view.

I end this section with two matrices (Figure 2.5, below) to
illustrate the interplay between habituation and reason as

	Good habits	Bad habits
Strong will	Strong will aligned with good habit (extremely frequent)	Strong will overcomes bad habit (infrequent)
Weak will	Good habits dominate weak will (extremely frequent)	Good action must be by chance (extremely infrequent)

Good action

	Good habits	Bad habits
Strong will	Bad action must be by force (extremely infrequent)	Bad habit prevails over strong will (frequent)
Weak will	Bad action by chance or quasi-forced (extremely infrequent)	Bad habits dominate weak will (extremely frequent)

Bad action

Figure 2.5 Reason and habituation
Here one can see the relationship between reason (i.e. will) and habituation as regards both good and bad actions

regards good and bad actions. As the various categories show (i.e. good v bad habituation and strong v weak will), these matrices are not meant to be exhaustive accounts of good and bad actions. I include them merely as a helpful heuristic.

Relevance for today

One of the greatest obstacles to overcome before any assessment of relevance is the view that the Greeks at the time of Aristotle had about their society and their role in it. In some ways, this view could not have been any more different from that of free societies today than it was.

Two of the main points of difference concern equality and liberty. These were concepts mostly foreign to Greek thinking. Nowhere, for instance, does Aristotle mention these or anything similar to them among his catalogue of particular excellences in his *EN*. This ought to seem very strange to us today, for we place great value on both. Yet, for the Greeks of Aristotle's day, almost all social, political, and commercial relationships (e.g. man and wife, master and slave, man and son, Greek and non-Greek) in and outside of a *polis* were based on inequalities of people's worth. Therefore, city-states, even democracies like Athens, were highly stratified social and political structures that were signally different from free societies today.[81] In addition, Classical Greek society had no true notion of liberty or freedom independent of some political institutionalization. People were believed by nature to be, Aristotle often said, a part of their *polis*, not free to be apart from it. Living for the sake of his *polis*, an individual's happiness was inconceivable outside of it. The closest concept Aristotle has to liberty is *autarkeia*, which for him entails the type of independence a dutiful person can find within a *polis*.

A second serious impediment to relevance concerns the non-egalitarian nature of Aristotle's ethical thinking as it relates to cultivating happiness – especially through political or contemplative activity. Both of these, especially the latter, presuppose two requirements: rationality and leisure. First, the requirement of rationality presupposes a fully developed rational faculty, which means for Aristotle that women, non-Greeks,[82] and boys cannot be happy, because of their defective or underdeveloped rational faculties. Next, the requirement of leisure presupposes wherewithal. Thus, happiness is attainable only for wellborn, Greek males who have money enough to pursue as fully as possible the finest and most divine thing – a virtuous (especially contemplative) lifestyle. Obviously, taken verbatim, Aristotle's ethical theory is untenable as it comes down to us.

Acknowledging these defects (and others referred to in the body of this chapter), we find that no strict application of the Aristotelian program is possible today. The question we need to consider is this: can we salvage anything?

I maintain that we certainly can and what we can salvage is quite substantive.[83]

First, Aristotle tells us that happiness involves knowledge of human psychology as well as ethical reflection. It begins with and crucially involves the slow and gradual development of a virtuous disposition through conditioning of the young. In short, conditioning involves having a primitive understanding *that* this is the way to act (i.e. the fact of the matter), without understanding *why* this is the way to act (i.e. the reason why the fact obtains). With maturation comes understanding, the capacity for truly excellent activity through recognition of what is good, and choice thereafter. Ethical maturation through habituation, understanding, and choice is, in a sense, convergence toward the *why*. Overall, no prescription for ethical lifestyle is possible, then, without the fullest grasp of the nature of human beings.

Second, Aristotle's notion that excellence of character is a mean between excess and defect, if true, gives us quite a practicable account of the happy or good life. If something is to be the right sort of action, we must avoid doing it excessively or deficiently. We must find the mean, which is no simple task. Each of us ought to have the correct amount of rational presence in all situations that involve virtuous activity – even personal or private actions. Each of us, for instance, ought to have the correct amount of temper in a situation that rightfully warrants anger. Each of us ought to show the correct amount of generosity in a situation that warrants generosity. Ethical activity requires deliberation and choice, and these are the warp and woof of each person's character. And so, each of us is ultimately responsible for the type of person we are.

Third, Aristotle's doctrine of the mean is at the same time an ethics of just desert, for excellence is to be judged in proportion to one's ethical worth. Overall, character is an admixture of action and intention, with an emphasis on the latter. One's ethical worth is not merely the sum total of one's actions over time, as this suggests that actions, not agents, are the key to excellence. Instead what one has done over time builds ethical character, and excellence of character, guided by volition, makes actions themselves either praiseworthy or blameworthy. To the most excellent people, we give the most divine gift: sincere praise. Others less deserving may receive money or other material items in keeping with baser actions. In short, the chief merit of Aristotle's ethics is its justness: all ought to receive in proportion to their due and ethical due varies from person to person. Since no two people are ethical equals, no two people ought to be treated alike.

Aristotle's notion of excellence seems so remote and perhaps even odious today primarily because, in contrast to other ethical or religious views, it is fundamentally judgemental and not sweepingly egalitarian. For example, Christians hold up faith, equality, humility, and forgiveness as prominent virtues, but these are noticeably absent among Aristotle's catalog of excellences. To the precept 'Love your neighbor', one would fully expect Aristotle to append '... only if he is worth loving'. Consider also how Aristotle's account of truth-telling and magnanimity would be received today in most cultures. A magnanimous person would seem arrogant should he speak freely, though plainly, of his excellence or of the defects of others. Yet this, for Aristotle, would merely be regard for truth and the perception of arrogance would be considered a misperception of reality. For many, such sobriety is just too cold.

Last, what is attractive about Aristotle's ethics is its emphasis that the good of all individuals is straightforwardly dependent on the good of their community (for Aristotle, their *polis*). Individuals in free societies today often prize autonomy to such an extent that regard for community, society, or country is almost meaningless. Yet regard for the good of a *polis* epitomized Classical Greek philosophical thinking. Aristotle, like Plato, went so far as to subordinate duty to oneself to duty to one's *polis* (called today 'communitarianism'). This, of course, seems to be taking duty too far. However, if we criticize Aristotle's communitarianism for placing the value of the city-state above any or all of the individuals in it, we must equally criticize the type of political liberalism or individualism today that asserts that the state exists only to satisfy the desires of each of the individuals in it. This is liberty taken too far, without regard for the community of individuals. The correct view, I believe, balances regard for individuals' self-expression with regard for duty to their state. This, more than anything, is what we might learn from Aristotelian mediation today.

Notes

[1] *Vit.* V.1.

[2] E.g. see Cicero's *ND* II.37 and 95.

[3] For Aristotle, non-Greeks, having little reason, were inferior by nature to Greeks. Thus they were naturally fit to be ruled and even called 'tools' of their master by Aristotle (*Pol.* I.6–7).

[4] One day's wage for the average working man was roughly six drachmae. One talent was equivalent to 6000 drachmae. If we assume the average working man's wage is today $100 per day, then the contribution was roughly $480,000,000!

[5] Only one, *The Athenian Constitution*, survives.

[6] Another work on Ethics, *Eudemian Ethics*, is generally regarded an earlier work and has three 'books' in common with *EN*.

[7] See *Top.* 145a14–18 and 157a10–11 and *Metaph.* 1025b18–26 and 1064a10–19.

[8] That which is unchanging as regards first philosophy (metaphysics), mathematics, and physics.

60   HAPPINESS AND GREEK ETHICAL THOUGHT

9 *EN* 1094b12–27 and 1098a26–35. As we shall see later, since ethics is about particular actions, there are difficulties in assuming Aristotle believed it could take the same form of argument as theoretical science. See Julia Annas, *The Morality of Happiness* (New York: Oxford University Press, 1993), 91–5.

10 *EN* 1097b12, 1169b19, *Pol.* 1253a3–4, 1278b20, and *EE* 1242a19–28.

11 In his *Politics*, Aristotle remarks that happiness is also one of the goals of the *polis*, for the happiness of the *polis* ensures the happiness of its individuals (VII.8, 9 and 13).

12 *EN* 1094b13–15, 1094b23–7, and 1104a7–12.

13 *EN* 1095b2–4.

14 *EN* 1198b9–12, 1095a17–21, 1179a17–23, and 1181b16–21.

15 *EN* 1141a3–8. Irwin's translation throughout. Aristotle, *Nicomachean Ethics*, trans. Terence Irwin (Indianapolis: Hackett, 1985).

16 Examples of this method are at *EN* II.5 (1105b19–1106a12), VI.6 (1141a3–8), and X.9 (1179b20–32).

17 Literally, *eudaimonia* is composed of the Greek prefix *eu-*, which means 'good', and the word *daimōn*, which means 'lesser god' or even 'destiny'. In *Republic* X, the Fates give each soul a *daimōn* or attending spirit, which enables the soul to fulfill its destiny (*daimōn*) (620e). See also *Phaedo* (107d–108c).

18 An obvious jab at Socrates, for whom knowing what virtue is is identical to being virtuous.

19 *EN* 1103b26–32.

20 *EN* 1104a26–30. See also X.9, 1179b1–4.

21 *EN* 1095b14–1096a5.

22 The standard translation for *aretē* in ethical affairs is 'virtue'. I prefer the broader term, 'excellence', which applies to physical superiority as well or even to the excellence of inanimate things.

23 *EN* 1103a14–17.

24 *EN* 1103a18–b25.

25 *EN* 1105b129–1106a14.

26 *EN* 1098b31–1099a6 and 1176b34.

27 *EN* 1105a26–33.

28 This is spelled out more elaborately and with some inconcinnities from III.6 to IV.7.

[29] The mean also figures crucially in political harmony. Those, he asserts, who push deviant forms of constitutions, such as oligarchies and democracies, to extreme, lose sight of proportion and lead toward what is no longer a constitution (*Pol.* V.9).

[30] *EN* III.6–9.

[31] *EN* 1124a1–2.

[32] *EN* 1123b8–13.

[33] *EN* 1125a33.

[34] *EN* 1109a1–5.

[35] *EN* 1109a31–b8.

[36] *EN* 1138b20.

[37] *EN* 1106b15.

[38] *EN* 1100b12–19.

[39] *EN* 1100b24–1101a8.

[40] *EN* 1098b13–18.

[41] *EN* 1104a12–20.

[42] *EN* 1178b23–30.

[43] *EN* 1177b32–1178a2.

[44] *EN* 1177a33–b2.

[45] *EN* 1120b7–10.

[46] *EN* 1109a25–35.

[47] *EN* 1179b17–19.

[48] *EN* 1179b5–29.

[49] *EN* 1179b32–3.

[50] *EN* 1179b26.

[51] *EN* 1180a1–24.

[52] *EN* 1180a29–32.

[53] *EN* 1180b7–22.

[54] Cf. *Metaph.* A.1, where Aristotle discusses the art of medicine from the knowledge of universal principles of medical health and from experience of many cases.

[55] *EN* 1109b31 and 1111a22–4.

[56] *EN* 1109b32, 1110a1–4, and 1110b13–18.

[57] *EN* 1111a3–20.

[58] *EN* 1110a1–4.

[59] *EN* 1110b1–18.

[60] *EN* 1110b18–1111a3.

[61] *EN* 1112b16.

[62] *EN* 1111b5–10 and 1112a3.

[63] *EN* 1112b8–12.

[64] *EN* 1112a31–34.

[65] *EN* 1112b32–5.

[66] *EN* 1113a17–23.

[67] The good Aristotle has in mind is the practicable good, for only this good can be otherwise (*An.* III.10; 433a28–30).

[68] *EN* 1113B25–35.

[69] Cf. *An.* III.10 and *Ph.* VIII.4–5.

[70] *EN* 1105a32.

[71] *EN* 1105a26–33.

[72] *EN* 1179b24–32.

[73] See also *EN* 1105a26–b5.

[74] *EN* 1105a32–5.

[75] E.g. *EN* IX.

[76] *EN* 1114a4–9.

[77] *EN* 1114a20–2.

[78] *EN* 1114a18–19.

[79] *EN* 1114b30–1115a3.

[80] This of course is not to deny what Aristotle says at *EN* II.4 – that an experiential base of habituation is a necessary condition of virtuous activity (1105a35).

[81] In Book I of his *Politics*, Aristotle outlines the different types of political relationships, all of which are based essentially on inequality. At the lowest level, that of individuals, there are the relationships between male and female (for the sake of reproduction, where the female is subordinate to the male) and ruler and ruled (master and slave, soul and body, male and female again, Greek and barbarian, for the sake of the preservation of both parties). At the next level, relationships within a family (which are for the sake of daily needs), we find property is subordinate to people, slaves are subordinate to free members, wife is subordinate to husband, and children are subordinate to parents). Finally, households are for the sake of the village and villages are for the sake of the *polis*. Aristotle even stratifies the various types of political units or constitutions: monarchies (virtuous rule of one) are best, aristocracies

(virtuous rule of the best few) are next, then polities (virtuous rule of many), democracies (corrupt form of rule of many; based on equality), then oligarchies (corrupt form of rule of few; based on wealth), and last tyrannies (corrupt form of rule of one). See also Books VIII and IX of *EN* for examples of inequalities in friendly relationships, especially VIII.7, where Aristotle nearly gives us an algorithm for unequal relationships (1159a24–9). Also recall inequality in sexual relationships delineated in Chapter 1.

[82] Aristotle goes so far as to claim that it is just to engage in war with those who are naturally fit, though unwilling, to be ruled (*Pol.* I.8; 1256b25–6). He certainly has here the Persians in mind.

[83] The seminal work of people like Elizabeth Anscombe and Alisdair MacIntyre has made virtue-based approaches to ethical issues significant alternatives to consequentialist or deontological approaches. G. E. M. Anscombe, 'Modern Moral Philosophy', *Philosophy* 33 (1958) and Alisdair MacIntyre, *After Virtue* (Notre Dame: University of Notre Dame Press, 2002).

3

Happiness and Pleasure

Epicurean Hedonism

He who says either that the time for philosophy has not yet
come or that it has passed is like someone who says that the
time of happiness has not yet come or that it has passed.

Epicurus

EPICURUS, SON OF NEOCLES, gives us a third approach to
happiness in Greek antiquity. More than the views of
Aristotle and Plato, Epicurean philosophy is chiefly and
irreducibly a way of life. When Epicurus does talk about
metaphysics and epistemology in what little remains of his
writings,[1] he does so principally because these philosophical
disciplines shed light on ethical issues. Philosophy, properly
guided by the principles of Epicurean metaphysics, leads
one to pleasure through attaining psychical calmness or
equanimity. This, for Epicurus, is the purpose of genuine
philosophical inquiry. Yet before proceeding with a sketch
and analysis of Epicurean hedonism, let me first say something about Epicurus himself.

Epicurus was a younger contemporary of Aristotle. His
chief biographer, Diogenes Laertius, gives us the following

account of his life.[2] Born in the third year of the 109th Olympiad[3] (341 B.C.), Epicurus was raised on the Ionian island of Samos (then an Athenian Colony) by his father Neocles and his mother Chaerestrata. Early on, he became a student of the Platonist philosopher Pamphilus.

In the year of Alexander of Macedon's death (323 B.C.), Epicurus moved to Athens to fulfill two years of compulsory military service. After this, he removed across the Aegean to the city of Colophon, near the Ionian coast. While at Colophon (321–311 B.C.), he studied under Nausiphanes of Teos, who exposed him to Democritean atomism[4] and taught him Democritus' notion of equanimity (Gr. *ataraxia*) as the goal of life. In 309 B.C., he moved to Mytilene on the island of Lesbos, where he founded his own school based on the principles of atomistic physics and philosophy. In 308 B.C., he traveled to Lampascus on the Hellespont to secure his school of thought by winning over certain influential disciples there.

In 306 B.C., Athens became the permanent home for his school, now called the Garden, which he bought for 80 *minae* (8000 *drachmae*[5]). Men, women, slaves, and citizens were freely admitted to the Garden to study Epicurean philosophy. (That slaves and women were admitted for study was, to say the least, quite unusual, perhaps even scandalous, for the time.) Here disciples quietly studied their master's principles and put into practice what they learned. They greeted and received each other intimately and cordially, and freely distributed their goods for the common welfare. Nonetheless, though the Garden was situated in Athens, Epicurus preached withdrawal from political life, for political activity, according to the philosopher, was deemed responsible for much of the disequilibrium in individuals' souls. Though Epicureanism was essentially apolitical, it had a broad appeal for many years and was tolerated, for the most part, by those who disagreed with its principles.

Epicurus died in the second year of the 127th Olympiad (270 B.C.).

Overview of Epicurean hedonism

Unlike Plato, whose philosophical views are unshakeably rationalistic,[6] Epicurean philosophy blends rationalism with empiricism. All knowing, he thinks, ultimately comes about through our experience of perceptible objects – what is apparent to us. From these, reason makes judgements about what is non-apparent to us – the unchanging realities behind the images of sensation. Epistemology, here, leads to metaphysics.

What reason tells us is that beneath the veneer of composite bodies that we readily see, there exist invisibly small 'uncuttables' or atoms (Gr. *atoma*) that move through void-space and make up all composite bodies. These atoms are the unchanging elements of Epicurus' metaphysics, and void-space is what makes their movement possible. A sure grasp of how atoms come together and form composites in void-space – i.e. of the principles of Epicurean metaphysics – is, however, needed to understand his ethics.

For Epicurean ethics, the ultimate goal or the highest good of life is pleasure (Gr. *hēdonē*), which he defines as the absence of pain or the privation of the fleeting pleasures that bring greater pain as a consequence. We strive for pleasure not in the direct sense of actively seeking it, but in the indirect sense of employing reason to avoid all pain, inasmuch as this is possible. Through the eradication of both bodily and psychical pain, we attain freedom from bodily disturbance (Gr. *aponia*) and peace or calmness of soul. All other contenders for the good life – even the most celebrated excellences such as courage, self-control, wisdom, and justice – are themselves desirable principally because they lead to pleasure. The chief agitators of psychical equanimity are mistaken beliefs about how the world works. People suffer mental agitation because they believe that the gods intervene in human affairs, that death is something to be feared, and that there are no limits to our desires.

In short, Epicurus deems epistemology and metaphysics worthy of serious study mostly insofar as they contribute toward the practical aim of psychical pleasure through the removal of unsettling, irrational beliefs. A true philosopher is really a practicing physician of the soul. In Epicurus' own words: 'Empty is the argument of the philosopher by which no human disease is healed; for just as there is no benefit in medicine if it does not drive out bodily diseases, so there is no benefit in philosophy if it does not drive out the disease of the soul.'[7]

In what follows, I begin with Epicurus' epistemological and metaphysical principles through a depiction of his cosmos,[8] and then turn to Epicurean ethics – the practical application of these principles through right reasoning for psychical calmness.

The Epicurean cosmos

The principles of Epicurean metaphysics and epistemology are spelled out in a surviving work called *Letter to Herodotus* or *Lesser Epitome*[9] that is handed down to us by Diogenes Laertius. The work begins with an appeal to the usefulness of a general outline on the most universal principles of nature. This appeal is also an exhortation: all must see that only a precise and careful employment of definitions and principles leads to correct understanding. Here I put down two procedural principles (PPs) that Epicurus at least implicitly uses throughout the letter.[10]

PP$_1$: The most incontrovertible epistemological and meta-physical principles must first be set forth.

PP$_2$: From the most incontrovertible principles, all other principles concerning natural things must be derived in stepwise fashion.

After his introductory remarks, Epicurus then says that it is through constantly studying nature that people achieve psychical equanimity in their life.[11] In the study of nature, what we know most readily is *what is apparent* to us – our sensory data. Assuming that what is apparent to us is true, we are in a position to draw inferences through reason about *what is non-apparent* (what reason tells us must be the case, given the truth of what is apparent).[12] Here we have two epistemological principles, which I state as follows:

EP$_1$: All sensory data are unmistakably true.

EP$_2$: What is non-apparent may be correctly inferred by reason from what is apparent (our sensory data).

EP$_1$, I note for now, should seem quite dubious and was certainly not the received view of his time, for it implies among other things that when a drunkard reports he sees pink elephants, he really does, in some sense, see them. EP$_2$ posits that reason allows us to penetrate beneath this veneer of changing things – the Temple of Poseidon, the table at the marketplace, the face of Socrates, and even the pink elephants of the drunkard – to the unchanging things behind them – ultimate reality. For ultimate reality, we need to appeal to reason.

Next, he proposes some metaphysical principles concerning what is non-apparent or the reality beneath appearances.

MP$_1$: Nothing is created from what does not exist.

MP$_2$: What passes away does not do so into what does not exist.

MP$_3$: The-All (Gr. *to pan*, or the totality of things) was, is, and always will be the same.

The source of these three metaphysical principles is unmistakably Parmenides.

What follows the three metaphysical principles is a barrage of cosmological claims – some posited alone, others with arguments on their behalf. The-All (i.e. the universe) consists of bodies, both simple (atoms) and compound ones, as well as void-space. That bodies of the second sort exist is clear through perception. That void-space exists is also evident, for such bodies exist and move and they need something in which to do both. The existence of atoms, he believes, follows from the metaphysical and epistemological principles (i.e. there must be something that is unchanging beneath the veneer of things that do change). Of the two kinds of bodies, atoms are invisibly small, unchanging, and eternal, while visible compounds, being made up of atoms, constantly change over time and have a temporal existence.[13]

In addition, at one extreme, The-All is limitless (Gr. *apeiron*) both in terms of its size and the number of bodies contained in it. At the other extreme, the number of kinds of atoms is not infinite, but unfathomably large, while the total number of atoms is infinite.[14] The extraordinarily large but finite number of kinds, he feels, is necessary to account for the great diversity of observed compound bodies.[15] In between these extremes, he tells us, there is an infinite number of worlds[16] (Gr. *kosmoi*[17]) that come into being and pass away and have different kinds of shapes.[18]

Next Epicurus tells us that atoms have shape, weight, and size.[19] Yet not every size exists, for then some would necessarily be visible, and not every mass exists, for what is limited in size is certainly limited in mass. Each body, then, is made up of a limited number of atoms and, since atoms are the limits of division, no body is infinitely divisible.[20]

The motion of atoms, caused by their weight, is continuous, without beginning, and without end. They move downward through void-space, because void-space offers no resistance to motion or weight.[21] This downward motion is 'as fast as thought' and occurs at equal velocity as long as nothing impedes it.[22] Composite bodies, as clusters of atoms, are formed through collisions of atoms that move at varying speeds.[23] These collisions, Epicurus thinks, are generated by random, uncaused swerves.[24] Were it not for these swerves, all atoms would simply fall in paths parallel to each other and none would, as it were, link up to form composites. The problem with positing uncaused swerves should be obvious: Epicurus violates his own Parmenidean axiom that something can come to be from nothing (i.e. a swerve can occur without a cause).

We have already seen at the outset that all knowledge for Epicurus crucially depends upon the truth of raw sensory data. Sensation is possible, he says, because extraordinarily tenuous film-like images (Gr. *eidōla*), responsible for perception, stream off objects and, maintaining a certain co-affection of their atoms, produce a faithful likeness of that object to a percipient. Here he also mentions spontaneous production of these films in the air as well as 'certain other ways' of production.[25] One such way may be the collision and entanglement of two or more streams of film-like images mentioned by the Epicurean poet Lucretius in the first century B.C.[26] Now since all such film-like images, while invisible in transit, are real images, their truth cannot be in doubt. In other words, the drunkard could actually be seeing a pink elephant when she claims to be seeing one.[27] Falsehood or error, then, must be the addition of some non-sensory internal motion – a false opinion concerning the image.[28]

The soul too is a physical body that comprises very fine atoms spread throughout body (vital wind, heat, and a third, even finer element). These 'psychical atoms', due to their fineness, travel easily throughout the body and enable us to perceive the films from the outside world during sensory perception. When the body is destroyed, so too is the soul, because the soul cannot survive without the body. Likewise if something should happen to the soul, the body loses its ability to perceive and it too perishes.[29]

Last, concerning the motions of heavenly bodies and meteorological phenomena in general, we must not assume that they are the craftsmanship of a creator god[30] or that they are blessed and immortal and think and act as humans do. Such bodies are not fiery masses that have acquired blessedness and choice.[31] None of these beliefs is consistent with divinity. Celestial objects[32] are completely regular and invariant, while gods, indifferent to the affairs of humans, are sublime and carefree. Thus, neither gods nor celestial bodies impact human affairs. All celestial phenomena have natural causes, and to think otherwise is to bring tumult to one's soul.[33] It is the task of natural science (Gr. *physiologia*), he adds, to understand such things.[34]

He ends the *Letter to Herodotus* by stating that the ethical ideal of psychical equanimity can be achieved only when the chief disturbers of the soul are removed. These again are our false views concerning the nature of things: that heavenly bodies or gods do influence human affairs, that death is something to be feared, and that there are no limits to the desires that are causes of confusion.[35]

Reason and human agency

The *Letter to Menoeceus*,[36] where Epicurus gives a concise summary of his ethical doctrine, is a very short work that begins with an exhortation for those who wish to be happy, both young and old, to take up philosophy.

> Let no one delay the study of philosophy while young nor weary of it when old. For no one is either too young or too old for the health of the soul. He who says either that the time for philosophy has not yet come or that it has passed is like someone who says that the time for happiness has not yet come or that it has passed. . . . Therefore, one must practice the things that produce happiness, since if that is present we have everything and if it is absent we do everything in order to have it.[37]

At this point, let us recall that for Aristotle the highest good for any person is contemplative activity through theoretical wisdom (Gr. *sophia*), whereas practical wisdom (Gr. *phronesis*), involved with deliberation for some good end (i.e. the political virtues or excellences), is deemed essential but subordinate to theoretical wisdom. For Epicurus, in contrast, human wisdom is exclusively of the practical sort, which concerns the health of each soul and body. Yet like Aristotle, Epicurus realizes that luck too comes into play in practical affairs. This is so because sometimes even the right choice has unforeseen, undesirable consequences. Still, this is no warrant to act mindless of reason. As with Aristotle, Epicurus thinks it is better to act rationally and experience unexpected misfortune than to act irrationally and chance upon pleasure.[38]

There is a problem for Epicurus' account of human agency. What do the principles of metaphysics, which describe the motions of atoms in void-space and the formation of composites, have to do with the employment of practical reason as an active guide to peace of mind? In other words, how does Epicurean metaphysics explain our capacity to deliberate and make rational choices, if we are nothing but atoms that have chanced to collect in just the right way to make a percipient human being?

Epicurus acknowledges the problem here, the Roman orator Cicero (106–43 B.C.) tells us, and proposes an answer at the atomic level. We recall that Epicurus states that random swerves of atoms (from their normal downward course of fall) enable them to collide and to form more complex bodies such as rocks, rivers, penguins, and people. In a completely deterministic universe (i.e. one in which random swerves do not exist), Epicurus realizes, people would not be responsible for their actions, for their actions would be completely reducible to and determined by the motions and collisions of atoms. One's behavior at the macro-level would be completely determined by what happens at the micro-level. So, by introducing randomness in the motions of atoms at the micro-level, Epicurus takes himself to have demonstrated that humans at the macro-level can freely guide their lives through choices that are themselves uncaused.[39]

This solution is wholly unsavory.[40] Epicurus is committing the fallacy of composition. This fallacy occurs when someone argues that if each of the elements that compose something has some particular property, then the thing itself that is composed of those elements also has that particular property. We can easily see the fallacy through the following illustration. Suppose I make a stew by adding only items that to me are very tasty. I add chunks of stewing beef, bits of Spanish onion, some Russet potatoes, some carrots and celery, and some peas. So far, things seem fine. Then I add two bottles of Russian Imperial stout, one cup of wheat flakes, the juice of twelve limes, some peanut-butter,

eight ounces of sharp cheddar cheese, some salted pista-
chios, two scoops chocolate protein powder, and so on.
It seems clear that I shall likely find that the stew, after
it is cooked up, tastes foul, not delicious, in spite of the fact
that each item that went into its composition, when considered by itself, is tasty to me. Similarly, even if Epicurus'
atoms could spontaneously swerve, this would not provide
sufficient warrant for asserting that the bodies made up of
atoms, here people, likewise act in such a manner (though
it clearly does not rule out the possibility). In short, Epicurus thinks that by introducing uncaused action at the
level of atoms, he is wholly warranted in assuming uncaused action at the level of composites. This does not
follow. What is worse, even if we should grant uncaused
action (i.e. spontaneous swerving) on the part of composite bodies, this would not give us free choice. It would
only show that some of our actions are without cause
and arbitrary, and this nowise allows for human agency and
culpability. This is as big a problem for philosophers and
scientists today as it presumably was for Epicurus.

This problem notwithstanding, Epicurus says that the
life of practical wisdom enables human beings – men as
well as slaves and women – to become as divine as possible:

> Practice these and the related precepts day and night, by
> yourself and with a like-minded friend, and you will never
> be disturbed either when awake or in sleep, and you will
> live as a god among men. For a man who lives among
> immortal gods is in no respect like a mere mortal animal.[41]

Like the Aristotelian philosopher who contemplates divine,
unchanging truths as often as possible, one who calms
himself through the study and application of Epicurean
principles becomes, as it were, a god among men.

Pleasure

So far we have seen that Epicurean philosophy is aimed at the study of metaphysical and epistemological principles for the sake of removing psychical disequilibrium. Such study, the *Letter to Menoeceus* says, purports to eliminate irrationality caused by mistaken beliefs that the gods intervene in human affairs, that death is not the end of existence, and that there is no limit to our desires.

That the gods exist, he says, is beyond dispute.[42] We must ascribe to the gods only those things that accord perfectly with their blessedness and indestructibility, instead of embracing the suppositions of the many. 'The man', he says, 'who denies the gods of the many is not impious, but rather he who ascribes to the gods the opinions of the many.'[43]

We must also believe that death, being the dispersion of the soul and the loss of sensation, is nothing to us. Consequently, we ought to remove the longing for immortality, a constant cause of distress, and take pleasure in the mortality of life. For what is there to fear about the absence of life? Death is not present in those who live, and when death is present, we no longer live. Concerning the length of life, Epicurus states that, just as we do not long for the greatest amount of food but the most pleasant, we do not wish for the longest life but the most pleasant.[44]

To get clear on the limits of our desires, we must delve into Epicurus' account of desires. There are two categories: natural (necessary and unnecessary) and vain desires (neither natural nor necessary). Of the natural and necessary desires, some are necessary for happiness, some are necessary for bodily freedom, and others are necessary for life (Figure 3.1, below). Understanding the natural and necessary desires (like want of simple food when the body is hungry) enables one to make choices that avoid

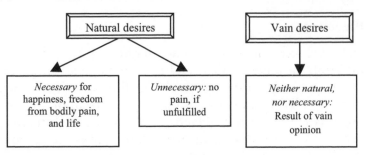

Figure 3.1   Epicurus' account of desires

pains, and thereby favor the health of the body and the equanimity of the soul. 'For we are in need of pleasure only when we are in pain because of the absence of pleasure, and when we are not in pain, then we no longer need pleasure.'[45] In contrast, the natural and unnecessary desires, like the desire for sex, are unneeded for continually happy living.[46]

Moreover, the vain desires, as a result of false beliefs, have no natural basis and, thus, are without any foundation whatsoever. It is the job of philosophy to free humans from their attachment to unnecessary and vain desires. Therefore, only in understanding the desires thus, he says, can pleasure be the starting point and end of a happy life.

What precisely is pleasure? It is not, he maintains, what sensualists or profligates would say. Those who continually drink and revel, indulge in sexual pleasures, or gormandize are not proper hedonists. Pleasure, instead, comes through sober deliberation of what to choose and what to avoid in order to bring about 'freedom from bodily pain and mental anguish'. Every pleasure is good and, conversely, every pain is bad. Yet what is pleasurable and what is painful may be different under different circumstances.[47]

Like others of his time, Epicurus distinguishes between katastematic and kinematic pleasures, each of which occurs in both body and soul. Diogenes Laertius, perhaps quoting Epicurus, has this to say concerning Epicurus' distinction: 'For freedom from disturbance (Gr. *ataraxia*) and freedom from suffering (Gr. *aponia*) are katastematic pleasures; and joy and delight are viewed as kinematic and active.'[48] Kinematic pleasures, it seems, are the result of mild motions in the blood, while kinematic pains are caused by violent motions within. Katastematic pleasure must, then, entail the removal of as many of the violent internal motions as possible, thereby leaving only smooth motions. In contrast, by actively or kinematically pursuing pleasure, people will likely find themselves suffering kinematic pain instead, for there is no limit to the active pursuit of pleasure.[49] Yet, for Epicurus, the worst internal pains are those caused by the soul, not those caused by the body, for the soul is troubled not only by present ills, but also by past misfortunes and those that have not yet come about.[50]

Epicurus' katastematic doctrine, that we arrive at pleasure through removal of pain, implies that pleasure and pain are exclusive and exhaustive states of affection – that is, there is no third state characterized by absence of both pleasure and pain. For Epicurus, the propositions 'I feel pleasure' and 'I do not feel pain' are themselves materially equivalent (as are 'I feel pain' and 'I do not feel pleasure'), for they describe precisely the same state of bodily affairs.[51] Real pleasure comes with sating our natural and necessary desires and doing so requires by nature that very little is done katastematically. To slake my thirst (remove a physical pain), I need only to drink that amount of water sufficient to compensate for my level of dehydration. What need have I of wine for this? Moreover, what need have I of water when I am not thirsty? To remove the psychical pain caused by thinking of the suffering of a loved one, who has recently died, might be experiencing, I need only to recall that such thoughts are vain, since death means nothing to anyone. In short, taking care of my natural and necessary desires is itself sufficient for pleasure. This entails that we must always be in some sort of affective state: When I meet my true needs, I am happy; when I do not, I feel the discomfort of pain. On such an account, there can be no intermediate state of non-affection or apathy.[52]

In some sense, what Epicurus is proposing is a calculus of pleasure and pain under the governance of reason.[53] Let me return to Socrates' decision to delay visiting Agathon by one day in *Symposium* (see Chapter 1) as an illustration. In applying an Epicurean calculus of sorts, Socrates would probably have had thoughts similar to these in his head. 'Should I congratulate Agathon today on his victory or wait until the next day? I am quite anxious to see the handsome and talented youth. If I should go out today, I would fulfill this desire, yet it is unlikely that I would be able to talk serious philosophy with anyone due to the heavy drinking after his victory and the general overcrowding of the immediate celebration. If I should go out tomorrow, I would have to stem my desire to see him today, but there will be a better chance to talk philosophy and less of a crowd.' For the sake of precision of illustration, let me assign numbers from '−10' to '+10' to each of the important circumstances that have a bearing on Socrates' reasoning. Let '−10' designate the maximum pain, '0' designate impossible to decide between pleasure and pain,[54] and '10' designate maximum pleasure. Schematically:

1. If I should go out today, *I would see Agathon* (+5), but *I would likely not be able to pass my time philosophizing* (−10).
2. If I should go out tomorrow, *I would have to wait to see Agathon* (−5), but *I would likely be able to pass my time philosophizing* (+10).

Socrates' decision, by the standards of Epicurean hedonism, would be clear: going to see Agathon on the day of the latter's victory, he will wind up with more overall pain than pleasure $(5 + (-10) = -5)$ in contrast to delaying his visit by one day $((-5) + 10 = 5)$. So, the pain of delaying his visit to Agathon's home, however, will be more than recompensed by his being able to philosophize all night long. As Epicurus himself says:

> And it is because this (pleasure) is our first innate good that we do not choose every pleasure; but sometimes we pass up many pleasures when we get a larger amount of what is uncongenial from them. And we believe many pains to be better than pleasures when a greater pleasure follows for a long while if we endure pains. So every pleasure is a good thing, since it has a nature congenial [to us], but not every one is to be chosen. Just as every pain too is a bad thing, but not every one is such as to be always avoided.[55]

The suggestion here and elsewhere[56] is that, in decisions regarding possible courses of action, all rational persons are obliged to consider *all of the available information that pertains to their decision.* When all of the available, pertinent information is taken into consideration, the route that is perceived to maximize pleasure through avoidance of pain is the only viable option for the Epicurean hedonist.

Hedonistic calculation for Epicurus can be summed as follows:

> From any range of possible alternatives for a course of action, choose the course of action which will likely result in the least disturbance of the soul and body over time.

We must bear in mind, however, that this construal must be taken with a grain of salt, since deliberative calculation is never undertaken merely to secure some particular episode of pleasure, immediate or otherwise; rather its long-term aim is happiness through the internal quiet that is characteristic of those who continually remove thoughts that bring about internal disquiet. In this manner, Epicurus looks more like Plato and Aristotle than he does a modern, calculating consequentialist.

Given its ethical focus, one of the most significant contributions of Epicurean philosophy to Greek thought is its redefinition of 'pleasure'. Epicurus' use of *hēdonē* marks a sharp conceptual break with common use of the term during his day (and even in ours). For instance, Epicurean hedonism has nothing in common with the pleasure-seeking practiced by Cyrenaic hedonists of his day, who advocated the active, unplanned, and immediate pursuit of the pleasures of the body, such as sex and drink.[57] Pleasure, for Epicurus, means psychical contentment or piece of mind, and this takes planning. For Epicurus, the Cyrenaic lifestyle would be one of constant painfulness.

Epicurean hedonism, then, is not a direct or kinematic prescription for pleasure, but one that indirectly or katastematically results in pleasure through striving to steer clear of all pain. And though complete katastematic pleasure, as the total eradication of pain, may be a conceptual ideal that is practicably impossible, it can serve as a measure of an individual's ethical progress.[58]

Justice

One of the main differences between Platonic and Aristotelian ethics and that of Epicurus concerns the notion of justice. Plato, in *Republic*, says that justice is matter of every part of a *polis* functioning for the good of the *polis* as well as every part of a person's soul functioning for the good of that person.[59] Aristotle says that justice is not only a matter of moral desert,[60] but it is also, in a manner of speaking, the complete virtue of an excellent person.[61] For both philosophers, justice is a real feature of both *poleis* and the individuals in them. In contrast, Epicurus thinks justice is not a fixed measure of order in persons and *poleis*, but a protean and slippery concept. For Epicurus' account of justice, let me turn to his *Principle Doctrines*.[62]

First, Epicurus acknowledges that there is a sense in which justice is the same for all and another sense in which it differs for all. He writes:

> In general outline justice is the same for everyone; for it was something useful in mutual associations. But with respect to the peculiarities of a region or of other [relevant] causes, it does not follow that the same thing is just for everyone.[63]

Similarly, Aristotle tells us that each person strives for the same virtues or excellences, but that the degree to which one person pursues one excellence will certainly differ from that of another and that the degree to which one person strives for one excellence at one time will likely vary at another. Virtuous actions depend on circumstances. Still, Aristotle's general ethical account steers clear of relativism in that those excellences each person ultimately strives for, such as courage and friendship, are precisely the same over time. With Epicurus, it is otherwise. At *Principle Doctrines* XXXVII–XXXVIII, he has this to say about justice:

> Of actions believed to be just, that whose usefulness in circumstances of mutual associations is supported by the testimony [of experience] has the attribute of serving as just whether it is the same for everyone or not. And if someone passes a law and it does not turn out to be in accord with what is useful in mutual associations, this no longer possesses the nature of justice. And if what is useful in the sense of being just changes, but for a while fits our basic grasp [of justice], nevertheless it was just for that length of time, [at least] for those who do not disturb themselves with empty words but simply look to the facts. If objective circumstances have

not changed and things believed to be just have been shown in actual practice not to be in accord with our basic grasp [of justice], then those things were not just. And if objective circumstances do change and the same things which had been just turn out to be no longer useful, then those things were just as long as they were useful for the mutual associations of fellow citizens; but later, when they were not useful, they were no longer just.[64]

Justice, Epicurus says, is relative and contractual – a matter of utility for citizens in their mutual associations. What is deemed just today, because a change in external circumstances may render it disadvantageous, may not be just tomorrow. Rational people agree to be just only because of fear that they too may suffer 'injustice' if they do not.[65] Stobaeus, quoting Epicurus, says, 'The laws exist for the sake of the wise, not so that they will not commit injustice but so that they will not suffer injustice.'[66] In short, there is no non-relative answer to questions concerning right and wrong action; justice itself must appeal to utility and all utility is done for the sake of pleasure. Justice is important insofar as and only insofar as it is instrumental for pleasure and there is no guarantee that the things that bring about pleasure today will continue to do so another day.

With Epicurus' view of justice, what is to prevent the following scenario from happening? In Book II of his *Republic*, Plato relates a tale of a shepherd named Gyges who finds a gold ring that makes its owner, upon wearing it and turning its setting in a certain manner, invisible. Gyges, being in service to the king of Lydia, eventually discovers the secret of the ring and is intrigued by the possibilities of undisclosed evildoing. He winds up seducing his king's wife, killing the king, and taking the place of the king next to the queen.[67] Plato introduces the tale here to entertain seriously the proposition, through the mouth of Glaucon, that anyone in a similar situation, even a 'virtuous man', would act likewise.

Given the Epicurean account of justice, what is there to keep even the best of people from committing the most egregious deeds in circumstances where it is very likely they, like Gyges, will escape detection?

Epicurus, however, can easily deflect this troubling scenario, as Epicurean hedonism is pleasure-seeking only inasmuch as it seeks pleasure katastematically, through avoidance of pain. Gyges, in seeking pleasure directly, is certainly no Epicurean and has committed himself to a lifestyle that is sure to bring him great pain.

Let us consider a different, more pertinent, scenario. An Athenian beggar, poor and sickly through a recent and unanticipated change in fortune, happens upon a wealthy merchant in discreet circumstances. The beggar realizes that he, without detection, can kill the merchant and take his money, and thereby readily meet his immediate needs. Knowing that the gods do not involve themselves in human affairs, he does not fear divine retribution. Knowing that death is the same for all, the end of existence, he does not fear what might happen after death. Knowing that he can find pleasure through eliminating as much pain as possible, he anticipates some pleasure in being able to gratify his bodily needs and see to his health. The beggar kills the merchant, takes his money, and escapes undetected. Since Epicurean justice seems to change 'with the winds', who is to say that the beggar behaves irrationally or unjustly?

This example seems problematic for Epicurus, but the philosopher anticipates such a scenario and offers a response. People, he argues, live according to an unwritten law of respecting the wellbeing of others. Fear of the consequences of violating such a law keeps many would-be transgressors from harming others. He says:

> Justice was not a thing in its own right, but [exists] in mutual dealings in whatever places there [is] a pact about neither harming one another nor being harmed. Injustice is not a bad thing in its own right, but [only] because of the fear produced by the suspicion that one will not escape the notice of those assigned to punish such actions.[68]

Thus, people who commit such acts against others will be perpetually plagued by the suspicion that they will someday be punished for their actions. Such fear of retribution itself is a ponderous source of psychical disequilibrium.[69] Therefore, considerations of just or unjust actions, though relative to circumstances, are not thereby arbitrary. They are claims about human organisms that face decisions, based on objective factors, concerning their own peace of mind. Any two people with exactly the same set of circumstances and the same life-history would at some particular time, if rational, come to the same decision about their own happiness at that time. Fear that someday the murder would be disclosed is a sufficient deterrent for any right-minded Epicurean never to consider committing such a deed in the first place. Thus, it is a 'fact' of human psychology and not any duty to a moral code that keeps people from unduly harming others.[70]

Still Epicurus' answer here seems unavailing and *ad hoc*. To see why, consider Maxim Gorky's short story 'Karamora'. In this piece, the antihero Karamora, after forcing a man by the name of Popov to his death, writes:

> I whipped myself up, trying to awaken a guilty reaction, which would declare resolutely: 'You are a criminal.'
> I realized with my brain that I was behaving in a low manner, but this realization was not confirmed by an appropriate feeling of self-chastisement, repugnance, remorse, nor even fear. No, I felt nothing of all that, nothing except curiosity, this curiosity became more and more corrosive and

almost restless, bringing forward questions like: 'Why is the passage from heroic gestures to meanness so easy?'

Gorky, of course, gives a view inconsistent with the Epicurean 'hero', for in Karamora there is a full grasp of the wickedness of his deed, yet no remorse (and even surprise at no remorse) upon completing the deed. Nor is there much worry over reprisal. Gorky's own insights into human psychology call into question what Epicurus takes to be a fact of human psychology.

Gorky's insights notwithstanding, the example of the Athenian beggar, for the true Epicurean hedonist, is unreasonable. Epicurus keeps reminding us that our immediate needs, satisfying our natural and necessary desires, are easily met. Who would need to rob another to handle one's hunger when some bread will do, and this is readily available to even the dullest of beggars? The act of robbing and killing another would prove that the very desires one is attempting to satisfy through such an action are unnatural or unnecessary. Who, grasping sufficiently that the proper use of reason is to dispel irrational beliefs, would consider robbing and killing another? The act of robbing and killing another would show that the murderous agent has not sufficiently mastered the principles of Epicurean philosophy.

In summary, Epicurus propounds adherence to the principles of justice primarily as a mechanism for peace of mind and derivatively so that the wise will suffer no injustice. His general account of justice is relative, since what is deemed just at one time can change at another. Nonetheless, as a measure of maximizing utility (i.e. pleasure), there is nothing subjective about it, in that what serves to maximize utility in any particular situation is a matter of the objective circumstances of that situation. When all is said and done, justice, for Epicurus, is a necessary component of a happy, communal life.

Friendship

Part of the reason an Epicurean community functions so well together, I have shown, concerns the application of justice as it relates to equanimity within the Epicurean ethical framework. Another, generally neglected, part concerns friendship.

Friendship is perhaps the very cornerstone of an Epicurean community. In his *Vatican Sayings*, he writes, 'Every friendship is worth choosing for its own sake, though it takes its origin from the benefits it confers upon us.'[71] Nonetheless, in defining pleasure as the ultimate good, Epicurus is committed to a focus on friendship's utility for security (i.e. pleasure) for individuals, not on its intrinsic value. As Seneca states:

> Although a wise man is self-sufficient, he will still want to have a friend, if for no other reason, in order to exercise his friendship, so that so great a virtue might not go to waste; not for the reason which Epicurus gave in this very letter, so that he might have someone to attend to him when sick, and to help him when he is thrown into prison or is impoverished. ...[72]

Still, given his commitment to hedonism of the egoistic sort – that individuals ought to strive to maximize their own pleasure – Epicurus' own references to friendship in what remains of his works suggest an ambivalence with which no true egoistic hedonist should have been comfortable.[73]

In the *Vatican Sayings*, he tells us that we must be willing to run risks for friends[74] and that we must even be willing to die for a friend.[75] According to Diogenes Laertius, Epicurus states that one ought always to speak well of friends, whether they are present or not.[76] *Principle Doctrines* XXVII tells us that friendship is declared to be the greatest inducement to happiness.[77] *Vatican Sayings* LXXVIII says, 'The noble man is most involved with wisdom and friendship, of which one is a mortal good, the other immortal.'

These additional passages highlight the difficulty. Epicurean hedonism, aiming at self-gratification, is primarily egoistic. Friendship, in contrast, is as much based on another's benefit as well as one's own. How, then, can friendship, which aims at gratification of another, be in any way responsible for binding a community of individuals whose chief goal is self-gratification?

In *On Ends*, Cicero notices this problem and relates three solutions proposed by later Epicureans. First, he relates, some Epicureans defend their master's principles by retaining a staunch, egoistic position on friendship. They argue that consideration for a friend's pleasure is subordinate to that of one's own, but a friend's pleasure brings about one's own pleasure and so one should treat a true friend as a second self.[78] Second, some Epicureans argue that, while friendship begins wholly because of considerations of pleasure, it matures in time to altruism.

> People first meet, pair up, and desire to form associations for the sake of pleasure, but that when increasing experience has produced the sense of a personal bond, then love flowers to such a degree that even if there is not utility to be gained from the friendship the friends themselves are still loved for their own sake.[79]

Last, there are other Epicureans who defend friendship contractually. Cicero writes, 'There are also those who say that there is a kind of agreement between wise men, to the effect that they will not cherish their friends less than themselves.'[80]

There are problems in trying to square each of these views with Epicurean hedonism, and so I shall not broach

this here. What is important however is Epicurus' insistence
that friendship, like justice, must occupy a privileged position if any community of rational beings is to live together
peacefully and happily while essaying to satisfy their
immediate needs.

Wisdom

For Epicurus, happiness is twofold: that of the gods, which is
absolute and cannot be further intensified, and that of
humans, which is determined by the perceived pleasure
and pain associated with certain avenues of activity.[81]
Human happiness, unlike divine happiness, is not guaranteed, but it is freely available to all who study Epicurean
philosophy. It requires that we develop and employ practical reasoning to eradicate pain. Those who follow this
course are the wise. Thus, Epicurean wisdom, unlike that
of Aristotle, is wholly practical. As such, unlike Aristotle,
the complete contemplative activity of the gods is not an
ideal to be approximated as fully as possible in order to
maximize happiness.

Diogenes Laertius gives an account of an Epicurean wise
person at Book X.117–21 of his *Lives*.[82] Such a person,
guided chiefly by reason and delight of contemplation, is
the picture of equanimity. He will marry and father children, yet not out of love, but only insofar as circumstances
require these. He will take care not to be held in contempt.
He will shun civic life, be a trusted friend, and drink will not
make him boisterous. Though he will feel pain, he will be
happy (even when tortured on the rack!). While choosing
not to write poetry, he will be an expert critic of it as well as
of music. Love of learning, not ostentation, will compel him
to set up a school. He will hold on to opinion firmly, though
he will be grateful when corrected.

Epicurus fills out this picture of the wise person in scattered fragments in other extant works. Some examples will suffice. Since the wise person uses rational calculation in all of his decisions, chance generally plays a small part in his life.[83] The wise person will also have greater regard for truth than the praise that comes from telling the common people what they want to hear. 'Employing frankness in my study of natural philosophy, I would prefer to proclaim in oracular fashion what is beneficial to men, even if no one is going to understand, rather than to assent to [common] opinion and so enjoy the constant praise which comes from the many.'[84] A wise person finds pleasure in keeping good memories fresh and bad ones out of mind.[85] He also finds pleasure in the anticipation of future pleasures.[86] In short, a wise person will do all that he is capable of doing to secure freedom from bodily and psychical disturbance.

Epicurus' own wisdom and quiet disposition of soul are themselves evident in a letter, written prior to his death, to his friend Idomeneus:

> I write to you while experiencing a blessedly happy day, and at the same time the last day of my life. Urinary blockages and dysenteric discomforts, which could not be surpassed for their intensity, afflict me. But against all these things are ranged the joy in my soul produced by the recollection of the discussions we have had. Please take care of the children of Metrodorus in a manner worthy of the good disposition you have had since adolescence towards me and towards philosophy.[87]

Relevance for today

Like love and beauty, pleasure too has an important role in a good life. The chief merit in Epicurean ethics lies in his recognition that, if we accept pleasure as an important ingredient in a good life (in the sense of directly seeking out things that are pleasurable), we are likely to suffer more pain than pleasure. Here it is limit that is important. There is no limit to the things that we find pleasurable and so, by taking pleasure itself as an end to which we directly aim, we continually strive for greater, more intense pleasures until pain is almost certainly guaranteed.

Epicurus is, of course, giving us an important insight into human nature. The gambler who goes to a casino with $1000 dollars and the aim of making as much money as she can with it will always come back penniless. For there is no limit to the amount of money she can make, and so she, if winning, will almost certainly keep playing until she loses everything. On the other hand, there is a limit to what she can lose: $1000. When she loses this, she *must* stop playing. In a similar manner, the active pursuit of pleasure, since it is limitless, can only end in pain, according to Epicurus. In contrast, the indirect pursuit of pleasure through avoidance of pain does have a limit: the eradication of all pain.

Comparisons are commonly made between Epicurean hedonism and Utilitarianism, of which there are several varieties today. Utilitarianism is a theory propounded by Jeremy Bentham and made famous by his pupil John Stuart Mill[88] in the nineteenth century. The theory proposes that each person behave such as to maximize happiness, goodness, or pleasure. The crux of Utilitarianism is the principle of utility, which may be summed up as follows:

> So act as to produce the greatest happiness (pleasure or good) for the greatest number of people.

Utilitarians, employing an ends-directed calculus of sorts, weigh each possible avenue of action by the perceived consequences of that action. If pleasure is the aim, then an action is valued insofar as it promotes the pleasure of the majority of all impacted people.

The cardinal difference between Epicurean hedonism and contemporary Utilitarianism is that the former, though it places great value on friendship and community, is ultimately egocentric, while the latter is ethnocentric. For the utilitarian, right action, determined by the greatest good for the greatest number of people, may come at the very expense of an agent. For Epicurus, right action always takes into consideration the expense of an agent, since its focus is the agent. Nevertheless, Epicurean hedonism placed a premium on loving others, if only because this is perceived to contribute mightily toward one's own pleasure. Both views, however, place heavy emphasis on rational calculation and weighing all of the relevant information before making a decision that relates to some future state of affairs. Both views, then, are consequentialist.

A second difference is the appeal to equanimity that is characteristic of Epicurean hedonism and lacking in hedonistic versions of Utilitarianism. For hedonistic Utilitarians, persons are judged by their actions, not intentions. A well-intentioned agent whose actions result in harm to others is deemed immoral because of the consequences of his actions. As such, results, not intentions, are responsible for persons being labeled good or bad over time. This is not to minimize the role of deliberation in bringing about good ends, for it is unlikely that anyone could maximize pleasure over time without proper attention to prior deliberation. In contrast, Epicurean ethics, similar to that of Plato and that of Aristotle, is goal-directed in a different way. A rational commitment over time to a particular style of living, here Epicurean simplicity, results in a changed person – one who is less troubled by false beliefs. This change in person, then, makes a continued commitment to Epicurean principles easier by facilitating self-sufficiency and self-sufficiency frees people from the exigencies of fate. Thus, there is a more straightforward relationship between action and intention for Epicurean hedonism that is not evident in Utilitarianism. Moreover, for Epicurus, the focus is not on particular episodes of moral decision-making as they arise; rather the focus is holistic — that is, on committing to Epicureanism as a way of life. As Epicurus himself says, 'Natural philosophy does not create boastful men or chatterboxes or men who show off the 'culture' that the many quarrel over, but rather strong and self-sufficient people, who pride themselves on their own personal goods, not those of external circumstances.'[89]

A third difference lies in contrasting notions of self-sufficiency or autonomy. For many, though certainly not all, modern Utilitarians, following Mill in part, autonomy is a matter of acting upon one's desires and thereby individuating oneself through free expression of those desires. Reason functions as an instrument to fulfill desires in a manner that avoids harming others. In contrast, for Epicureans, ethical self-sufficiency comes through rational recognition and adoption of the correct account of the way things work in the universe. Knowledge for Epicureans is truly what liberates. More than this, *only* through acquiring knowledge can people free themselves from pains that come about from false beliefs. Strictly speaking, both pictures are flawed. The former seems too unconstrained for a viable ethical notion of human agency. Reason is no longer a governing principle but an instrument of desires. It is not prohibitive in any significant, moral sense. The latter seems too uncompromising, presumptuous, and dogmatic. It is one thing to suggest that knowledge has a fundamental role in freeing people to live the best sort of life; it is quite another to say Epicurus' slant on the way the world works is correct. It is this type of dogmatic certainty by the different schools of philosophy in antiquity (and thus far we have seen three) that gave rise to the skeptical approach to happiness that we examine in Chapter 4.

In conclusion, even if we disagree with Epicurus' notions that pleasure is the sole end of life and is principally of the psychical sort, it seems plain that it is in some measure a needed part of a happy life. Moreover, the Epicurean redefinition of 'pleasure' as a commitment to a lifestyle free from as much pain as possible allows for an account of hedonism, in keeping with the Delphic precept of moderation in all things, that is practicable today and worth reconsideration. Finally, there is substance in Epicurus' notion that repeated consideration of the consequences of our actions over time is beneficial not merely because these consequences harm or benefit others, but also because such consideration over time will likely lead to a happier, more stable, person.

Notes

[1] Diogenes Laertius tells us that Epicurus was a very prolific writer who left behind over 300 scrolls, each of which contains no citation to any other author (*Vit.* X.26).

[2] *Vit.* X.1–16.

[3] The ancient Greeks measured time by the first recorded Olympiad in 776 B.C., roughly the date that we recognize as the emergence from the Dark Age and the beginning of the Archaic Period. Since the Olympics were held every fourth year after 776 B.C., we arrive at 341 B.C. for Epicurus' date of birth.

[4] Roughly the view that all that exists are atoms (or 'uncuttables') and empty space, and everything visible comprises atoms in void-space.

[5] Six drachmae were roughly one day's wage for an average sixth-century Athenian laborer.

[6] Plato's philosophy is generally regarded as maintaining that all knowledge comes through reason, which is independent of sensory experience. In other words, our senses play no part in the acquisition of knowledge. I showed in Chapter 1 that this might not be

quite right for Plato. *Symposium* strongly suggests that irrational factors also play a part in the acquisition of knowledge.

[7] *To Marcella* XXXI.

[8] The Greek word *kosmos* means more than the traditional translation, 'universe'. *Kosmos* implies order and a system that is rule-governed.

[9] *Vit.* X.35–83. Called *Lesser Epitome* because scholiasts, at places in the manuscripts, refer to similar points being made in works called *On Nature* and *Major Epitome* (e.g. *Vit.* X.39 and 40). Epicurus himself also tells us that his letter is a summary of much longer works on physics, which do not survive (*Vit.* X.35). This letter is part of a collection of three preserved by Diogenes Laertius in his account of Epicurus (*Vit.* X.35–135). The two other letters are *Letter to Pythocles* and *Letter to Menoeceus* (the latter containing a brief outline of Epicurus' ethical doctrine which we shall come to shortly).

[10] *Vit.* X.37–8. Following Sedley here. David Sedley, 'The Inferential Foundations of Epicurean Ethics', *Companions to Ancient Thought* 4: Ethic, ed. Stephen Everson (New York: Cambridge University Press, 1998), 129–50.

[11] *Vit.* X.37.

[12] *Vit.* X.38.

[13] *Vit.* X.39–41. An unresolved problem is the temporal existence of the gods. Epicurus unmistakably states the gods exist and they are *indestructible* animals (*Vit.* X.123). Yet, like all other existing things, they are also compounded of atoms. Being compounds, they must be changeable, since they too pass off films that we receive in dreams and during the day (Sextus, *M.* IX.25). Of course, being changeable and indestructible are not necessarily incompatible, but one needs a clear explanation from Epicurus why the gods have a permanent existence, while other compounded beings do not.

[14] A finite number of kinds of atoms and an infinite number of atoms implies that *at least* one of the kinds is itself an infinite set. It seems likely that what Epicurus has in mind is that each of the kinds is itself an infinite set. See Cicero (*ND* I.50) on Epicurus' use of the term *isonomia*, which suggests Epicurus believed that indescribably large or infinite sets (i.e. living beings v dead beings; constructive

v destructive forces) were equal to each other through a correspondence or equal distribution of their parts.

[15] *Vit.* X.41–2.

[16] *Vit.* X.45.

[17] Plural of *kosmos*.

[18] *Vit.* X.73–4. A scholiast has added that *On Nature* XII mentions different shapes, though not every possible shape.

[19] *Vit.* X.54.

[20] *Vit.* X.55–6.

[21] *Vit.* X.43–4 and 61.

[22] *Vit.* X.60–1. Inwood and Gerson's translation, unless otherwise indicated. Epicurus, *The Epicurus Reader: Selected Writings and Testimonia*, ed. Brad Inwood and L. P. Gerson (Indianapolis: Hackett, 1994).

[23] *Vit.* X.62.

[24] In stark contrast to the mechanical necessity of Democritus who believed that atoms moved in all directions in directionless, boundless space. For Democritus, motion was primary, not due to weight.

[25] *Vit.* X.46–8.

[26] *Nat.* IV.129–42 and 732–43.

[27] *Vit.* X.32.

[28] *Vit.* X.50–1.

[29] *Vit.* X.63–7.

[30] He is certainly thinking of Plato's divine craftsman in *Timaeus*.

[31] Directed at mythographers, such as Homer, Hesiod, and the playwrights.

[32] Generally considered divine in antiquity due to their perceived regular, circular motions.

[33] *Vit.* X.76–7.

[34] *Vit.* X.78.

[35] *Vit.* X.81–2. See also *PD* XI.

[36] *Vit.* X.121–35.

[37] *Vit.* X.122.

[38] *Vit.* X.133–5.

[39] Cicero's *Fato* XLVI–LXVIII.

[40] The ad hoc nature of this uncaused swerve was duly noted by Cicero (*Fin.* I.18–20, *ND* I.69–70, and *Fato* XXII–XXV and

XLVI–XLVIII). Epicurus' pupil, Lucretius, defends this swerve with three unconvincing arguments at *Nat.* II.216–50.

[41] *Vit.* X.135.

[42] See Cicero's *ND* I.43–56 and Sextus Empiricus' *M.* IX.25. Lactantius, in his *Wrath of God* (XIII.20–2), attributes to Epicurus a form of the problem of evil. If evil exists, then god 1. wants to eliminate it but cannot, 2. wants to eliminate it and can, 3. does not want to eliminate it and cannot, or 4. does not want to eliminate it but can. Lactantius suggests that Epicurus defends the last option.

[43] *Vit.* X.123.

[44] *Vit.* X.124–5.

[45] *Vit.* X.128.

[46] According to Diogenes Laertius, Epicurus states, 'Sexual intercourse never helped anyone, and one must be satisfied if it has not harmed' (*Vit.* X.118).

[47] *Vit.* X.129–32.

[48] The Anglicized adjectives, 'katastematic' and 'kinematic', are taken from the Greek words *katastasis* and *kinēsis*. The former means 'a setting down', 'a condition', 'a calming', and 'a settled condition or order', among other things. The latter means 'motion' or 'disturbance'. Thus, one sees clearly the superiority of katastematic pleasures over kinematic for Epicurus.

[49] The Epicurean program does not outright reject kinematic pleasures, but merely assumes the priority of katastematic ones.

[50] *Vit.* X.136–7. See also Cicero's *Fin.* I.55–6.

[51] One hedonistic school of thought, the Cyrenaics, argued that all pleasures are kinematic and that the absence of pain is not pleasure, but rather an intermediary state (*Vit.* II.89). For more, see Cicero's *Fin.* (I.37–8).

[52] The state for which the Stoic school of thought (see Chapter 7) strove.

[53] Of course Epicurus nowhere tells us to assign numbers to the pleasure and pain corresponding to the circumstances around each choice we make, and there are good reasons to believe that he would object to our doing so. See Julia Annas, *The Morality of Happiness* (New York: Oxford University Press, 1993), 85–6.

[54] I avoid the term 'neither pleasurable nor painful' because Epicurus, as we have seen, completely rules out the state of non-affection.

[55] *Vit.* X.129.

[56] See also Cicero's *Fin.* XXI.32–3, Cicero's *Tusc.* V.95–6, and Eusibius' *Evangelical Preparations* XIV.xxi.3.

[57] *Vit.* II.86–8. For a brief, but educative, look at differences among Cyrenaic hedonists, see Annas, *Morality of Happiness*, 227–36.

[58] Certainly not the complete eradication of internal motions, for this would result in death.

[59] *R.* IV.

[60] *EN* V.2.

[61] *EN* V.1.

[62] *Vit.* X. 139–54.

[63] *PD* XXXVI.

[64] *Vit.* X.152.

[65] The view of justice that Socrates' ornery interlocutor, Thrasymachus, details toward the end of Book I in Plato's *Republic*.

[66] *Anthology* IV.143.

[67] *R.* 359c–360d.

[68] *Vit.* X.150–1. (=*PD* XXXIII–XXXIV).

[69] Cicero correctly notes that this fear of retribution assumes undue incompetence on behalf of the wrongdoer (*Fin.* II.53).

[70] See also *VS* VII and Plutarch's *Against Colotes* 1127d and *A Pleasant Life* 1090c–d.

[71] *VS* XXIII.

[72] *Ep. Mor.* IX.8.

[73] See also *VS* XXXIV and XXXIX.

[74] *VS* XXVIII.

[75] *VS* LVI. Presumably because there is great pain in living out one's life without having helped a friend, while cessation of life is the absence of all pleasures and pains.

[76] *Vit.* X.118.

[77] *Vit.* X.148.

[78] *Fin.* I.66–8.

[79] *Fin.* I.69.

[80] *Fin.* I.70.

[81] *Vit.* X.121a.

[82] *Vit.* X.117–21 is a fragmented discourse on the wise person that is thrown in between Epicurus' *Letter to Pythocles*, which I do not discuss, and *Letter to Menoeceus*.

[83] *PD* XVI.

[84] *VS* XXIX.

[85] Cicero's *Fin.* I.57.

[86] Cicero's *Tusc.* V.96.

[87] *Vit.* X.22.

[88] Mill himself expresses his debt to Epicurus at the start of Chapter 2 of his book *Utilitarianism*.

[89] *VS* 45.

4

Happiness and Doubt

Greek Skepticism

> The person who entertains the opinion that anything is by
> nature good or bad is continually disturbed.
>
> Sextus Empiricus

THE THREE GREEK PHILOSOPHERS I have presented thus far
all have given reason a prominent role in the quest for happiness. Plato maintains that happiness consists principally,
if not exclusively, in the acquisition of knowledge. Aristotle,
reacting against Plato, argues that happiness is not merely
the having of knowledge, but its exercise – at the political
level, the use of practical wisdom through the various political virtues; at the theoretical level, the use of wisdom itself
through contemplative activity. Epicurus states that happiness aims at pleasure, and pleasure comes about through
the use of practical reasoning. Thus, Epicurean philosophy
concerns practical wisdom, not theoretical wisdom. And
though each philosopher gives a different account of happiness, each recognizes it as the true end of all human activity. Moreover, for each philosopher, it is reason, through

enabling us to see the way things really are behind the façade of appearances, that makes happiness possible.

A fourth approach to happiness in Greek antiquity, skepticism, was radically different. It came about as a response to and scathing criticism of the extant philosophical dogmatism of the day, which included Platonism, Aristotelianism, Epicureanism, and, mostly, Stoicism (see Chapter 7). Skeptics objected to there being so many schools of thought with so many radically different answers to philosophical questions. The very number of such schools was itself proof of profound disagreement among philosophers on difficult philosophical issues about which each school professed to have answers. For skeptics, dogmatic disagreement on such issues was a sign of philosophical confusion, not understanding. Skepticism professed to be an antidote to this confusion.

While we tend to link skepticism with doubt today, for Greeks, skepticism was primarily concerned with enquiry, not doubt. The Greek word *skeptikoi* literally means 'those who inquire', not 'those who doubt'. Greek skepticism was for ancient adherents fundamentally a way of life (Gr. *agōgē*) more than an epistemological tool. So, in this chapter, I draw from the Greeks and examine the skeptical lifestyle as an ethical ideal – principally through the writings of Sextus Empiricus, a philosopher and physician in the second century A.D. Through Sextus, I give a brief history of Greek skepticism as it appeared in three periods: the Pyrrhonic Skepticism of the fourth and third centuries B.C., the Academic Skepticism of the third and second centuries B.C., and the revival of Pyrrhonic Skepticism thereafter. Then, I turn to Sextus' rather technical exposition of skepticism as a way of life – with particular attention to how skepticism, properly understood, differs from philosophical dogmatism (of the sorts given in the first three chapters of this book). Next, I turn to the debate concerning skepticism and dogmatism in Greek medicine in an effort to show certain practical consequences of the philosophical debate. I end with some thoughts concerning the extent to which skepticism ought to be embraced in the quest for happiness.

Brief historical sketch

Pyrrho of Elis, son of Pleistarchus, was born c. 360 B.C. and died c. 270 B.C. We know very little about this philosopher, since none of his works are extant and there are only a few reliable references to him in antiquity, but we do know that many admired him and that he practiced skepticism as a lifestyle. Diogenes Laertius relates that Pyrrho maintained nothing could be said of anything with certainty, for each thing is 'no more this than that'. He adds that Pyrrho lived his life consistent with his skeptical attitude in that he took on whatever came his way without passing judgement. For example, while on a ship during a raging storm in which all passengers began to panic, Pyrrho pointed to a small pig, unperturbed, that kept on eating as if nothing was happening. This, he said, was the equanimity of a wise person.[1]

Timon of Phlius[2] (c. 320–230 B.C.), son of Timarchus, became a student of Pyrrho after a brief career as a stage dancer. While Pyrrho preached and practiced skeptical detachment (he took on things in skeptical fashion as they came to him), Timon preached and practiced skeptical involvement (he came to things and took them on in skeptical fashion). He loved money, wine, and gardens, and he seemed to delight in criticizing dogmatists. In his time away from philosophy, he would write poems of all sorts. These often took the form of lampooning dogmatic philosophers like Plato, Aristotle, and even a rival skeptic, Arcesilaus, whom I turn to next.

Plato's Academy, upon the headship of Arcesilaus (c. 315–c. 240 B.C.), son of Seuthes, rejected its extant dogmatism in favor of suspension of judgement and a different type of skepticism. Arcesilaus' main target of criticism was Stoic dogmatism (especially that of Cleanthes), with its insistence that certain perceptions were so manifestly clear that doubt concerning their truth was impossible. Aware of the potentiality of paralysis with skepticism (i.e. if we throw everything into doubt, what will serve as a guide for action?), he introduced a skeptical alternative to dogmatism that substituted probability for certainty as a guide to correct human action.

Carneades of Cyrene (c. 213–c. 128 B.C.), son of Epicomus,[3] was the next famous head of the Skeptical Academy and a philosopher of uncommon intellect and persuasion. Though his writings do not survive, we know much about him from his pupil and successor Clitomachus (head of Academy in 129 B.C.). For instance, in a surprising illustration of the method of skepticism, while on a mission in Rome, he fully persuaded an audience that justice was universal and natural on one day, and then wholly convinced another audience on the next day that justice is nothing but a useful expedient.[4] Carneades knew well the works of the Stoics – especially Chrysippus – and earned a great reputation through his continual attempts to refute them.

After a brief period of respite, there began a revival of Pyrrhonic Skepticism with Aenesidemus (of Cnossus?), whom we cannot securely date,[5] and Sextus Empiricus (fl. 200 A.D.). Aenesidemus is famous for formalizing the skeptical attack on dogmatism through his work on tropes (see below) and an epistemic distinction between indicative and recollective signs.[6] Sextus Empiricus, whose *Outlines of Pyrrhonism* is the focus of this chapter, was a physician and a pupil of Menodotus. Other than this, we know little about his life.

Sextus on skepticism and dogmatism

Pyrrhonic v Academic Skepticism

Sextus begins his *Outlines of Pyrrhonism*[7] by sketching out three different philosophical schools of thought: dogmatism, the skepticism of Plato's later Academy (Academic Skepticism), and skepticism proper (Pyrrhonic Skepticism). In doing so, he aims to show, first, that Academic Skepticism is essentially a type of dogmatism and, more importantly, that there are no sufficient grounds for entertaining dogmatism of any sort. So, of the three alternatives, only the last frees one's soul from the many troubles brought on by doctrinaire ethical reflection.

In his attack on dogmatists, Sextus has Plato, Aristotle, and Epicurus in mind, but his chief target is the Stoics – an important school of thought in Hellenistic times. To grasp the subtleties of Sextus' attack, it is necessary to give a brief sketch of the Stoic theory of knowledge that Sextus (and other skeptics) found so objectionable.

For Stoics, happiness (i.e. virtue) is essentially linked to the possibility of knowledge, because happiness is nothing more than knowledge. Unlike Epicurus, who maintains that all sensory impressions are true, the Stoics believe that only one type of sensory impression can be known to be true – that whose likeness to its object is so plain that we are literally forced to assent to it being true. This criterion of truth, the cognitive or kataleptic[8] impression (Gr. *phantasia kataleptikē*), is used as their standard of judgement for epistemic issues.

At *Against the Professors* VII.247–52, Sextus himself gives an account of the Stoic criterion of truth. He writes:

> A cognitive impression is one which arises from what is and is stamped and impressed exactly in accordance with what

is, of such a kind as could not arise from what is not. Since
they hold that this impression is capable of precisely grasping objects, and is stamped with all their peculiarities in a
craftsmanlike way, they say that it has each one of these as
an attribute.[9]

He goes on to emphasize that, for Stoics, the truth of a kataleptic impression is secured by its arising from what is,
its being isomorphic to what is, and its making a literal
impression (like a signet ring on wax) on a perceiver. Thus,
it is of such a kind that it could not arise from what it not.
A kataleptic impression 'all but seizes us by the hair and
pulls us to assent'.[10] Writes Cicero of the Stoic kataleptic
impression:

> For as a scale must sink when weights are placed in the bal-
> ance, so the mind must give way to what is self-evident. It is
> no more possible for a living creature to refrain from assent-
> ing to something self-evident than for it to fail to pursue what
> appears appropriate to its nature.[11]

In all, living virtuously for the Stoics is a matter of being
kataleptically disposed to the cosmos and everything in it.
Stoic wisdom comes only by assenting to those perceptions
that are kataleptic in nature and refusing to assent to all
others that admit of the least bit of doubt.[12] Therefore, a
happy life fully and exclusively concerns itself with the
acquisition of knowledge.

The Stoic sage and his notion of kataleptic impressions as
a basis for a theory of knowledge became the target of unre-
lenting criticism by skeptics of all persuasions. I give a much
fuller exposition of Stoic ethics in the last half of Chapter 7.
For now, I return to Sextus' general attack on dogmatism and his distinction between Pyrrhonic and Academic
Skepticism.

In Chapter 23 of *Outlines of Pyrrhonism*, Sextus distinguishes true Pyrrhonic scepticism from the skepticism of the New Academy (i.e. Carneades and Clitomachus). Academic Skeptics[13] assent to the proposition, *All things are inapprehensible*,[14] which itself is self-defeating dogmatism of a sort, since in doing so they are literally asserting that *Nothing can be known to be true* is itself true. This, quite plainly, defeats the purpose of skepticism. True skeptics, Sextus says, make no such flat assertion about the inapprehensibility of all things – that is, they always hold fast to the possibility of something being apprehensible.[15]

Although leaving in no grounds whatsoever for truth, Academic Skeptics did leave grounds for conviction of belief, based on a probability calculus for sensory impressions (Gr. *eulogon*, or 'what is probable'), and conviction based on probability, they maintained, was a suitable guide for action.

Sextus tells us of three types of probable impressions for Academic Skeptics. Of things probable, some are probable (and only probable), others are probable and tested, and others are probable, tested, and irreversible.

> For example, there is a certain length of rope lying coiled up in a dark room. When a man enters suddenly, the sense-impression he gets from it is the simply probable one that it is a snake. But when a person has looked round carefully and investigated all the circumstances, for instance that it does not move and that its colour is such and such, and so on, it appears to him, in accordance with his probable and tested sense-impression, a rope. One which is irreversible is like the following. ... [W]hen Alcestis had died, Heracles brought her back again from Hades and showed her to Admetus, who received a sense-impression of Alcestis that was probable and tested. However, since he knew that she was dead, his mind was distracted from giving its assent and inclined towards disbelief.[16]

By using degree of conviction based on the probability of an impression's truth as a guide for action, Academic Skepticism developed a probability calculus for right action. This account contrasts greatly with that of Pyrrhonic Skepticism, which maintains that one yields to and acts according to those impressions that seem plain without any judgement of probability concerning the truth or falsity, rightness or wrongness, of them. Yet, since the Academic Skeptics manifestly reject the possibility of knowledge, theirs is a species of dogmatism, not skepticism. Only Pyrrhonic Skepticism, since it takes no stance on the possibility of knowledge, is true skepticism.

The meaning of 'Skepticism'

Sextus tells us that Skepticism (I shall use 'Skepticism' hereafter to refer to Pyrrhonic Skepticism exclusively) is a mode of life that is searching, suspending, doubting, and Pyrrhonic. Of its method, he writes: 'Skepticism is an ability[17] to place in antithesis, in any manner whatever, appearances and judgements, and thus – because of equality of force in the objects and arguments opposed – to come first of all to a suspension of judgement (Gr. *epochē*) and then to mental tranquility'[18] (Gr. *ataraxia*). Consider, for example, the surface of a wall. To the eyes it appears smooth, but to the hands it feels rough. So, there is nothing our senses can do to decide the issue. When we place these two perceptions in antithesis, this leads to a suspension of judgement and then to peace of mind. Nothing is immune from argument. Skeptics oppose appearances to appearances, thoughts to thoughts, and appearances to thoughts. To say of a tower that it appears round at a distance and square from up close is to oppose appearance to appearance. To say that providence exists because of celestial harmony with the notion that good people often fair poorly while bad ones prosper is to oppose thought to thought. To argue against the observed whiteness of snow by noting snow is frozen water and water is black is to oppose appearance to thought.[19]

Though Skeptics subject anything to argument, Sextus states that it is not true to say that Skeptics deny everything. While a Skeptic cannot claim to know anything, Skeptics do not deny what is apparent to everyone's eyes. He writes:

> Those who say that the Skeptics deny appearances seem to me to be ignorant of what we say. . . . [W]e do not deny those things which, in accordance with the passivity of our sense-impressions, lead us involuntarily to give our assent to them; and these are the appearances. And when we inquire whether an object is such as it appears, we grant the fact of its appearance. Our enquiry is thus not directed at the appearance itself. Rather, it is a question of what is predicated of it, and this is a different thing from investigating the fact of its appearance itself.

He uses the example of the sweetness of honey. No Skeptic denies that honey appears sweet, because it affects almost everyone similarly. A Skeptic merely guards against predicating sweetness of honey in any unconditional sense.[20] Likewise a Skeptic, when feeling warm, would not say, 'I feel cold'.

The extent of a Skeptic's doubt is complete. Unlike an Academic Skeptic who assents to the proposition *All things are inapprehensible*, a Skeptic even doubts this proposition and others that are similar — Skeptical formulae such as *No more one* (i.e. *This appearance is no more likely to be true than that one*) and *I determine nothing*. Thus, *No more one* applies even to itself and cancels out itself. The same applies to the other formulae.[21]

Does this method constitute a system? Sextus says this in reply:

[I]f one defines 'system' as 'an adherence to a set of numerous dogmas which are consistent both with one another and with appearances', and if 'dogma' is defined as 'assent to a non-evident thing', then we shall say that we have no system. But if one means by 'system' a 'discipline which, in accordance with appearance, follows as a certain line of reasoning, that line of reasoning indicating how it is possible to seem to live rightly ('rightly' understood not only with reference to virtue, but more simply), and extending also to the ability to suspend judgement', then we say that we do have a system.[22]

Unlike the Stoic criterion of truth (the cognitive or kataleptic impression), the criterion upon which this system is based is not a standard for judging sensory impressions, but instead a standard for regulating human activities.[23] Skeptics practice philosophy not to disclose truth, which according to their view is still possible, but instead to avoid the paralysis of inactivity that they believe follows from any dogmatic form of skepticism.

Chiefly as a way of life, Skepticism is fundamentally end-directed. Like Epicureanism and, to a lesser extent, Platonism and Aristotelianism, equanimity is the aim of Skepticism. To show how this is possible without lapsing into dogmatism, Sextus states that a Skeptic initially strives to pronounce judgements on appearances, but doing this leads to a realization, a discovery, that each argument has a contradictory argument of equal merit (or nearly so). Reason, if it is to function with integrity, is compelled to suspend all judgements on appearances. In suspension of judgement, a Skeptic then *chances upon* calmness of mind. In and only in this sense does a Skeptic discover that calmness of mind attends upon suspension of judgement. Thus, he can claim that the latter is the end of human activity. To speak otherwise would be to lapse into dogmatism.[24]

In stark contrast to a person who refuses to pass judgement on things is the person who readily passes judgement.

> For the person who entertains the opinion that anything is by nature good or bad is continually disturbed. When he lacks those things which seem to him to be good, he believes he is being pursued, as if by the Furies, by those things which are by nature bad, and pursues what he believes to be the good things. But when he has acquired them, he encounters further perturbations. This is because his elation at the acquisition is unreasonable and immoderate, and also because in his fear of a reversal all his exertions go to prevent the loss of the things which to him seem good.[25]

None of this is to say that a Skeptic is wholly free from disturbance. A Skeptic cannot avoid what is unavoidable, such as the pangs of thirst when he is thirsty or the sense of loss at the passing of a loved one. What he can avoid, however, are pronouncements about the goodness or badness of things unavoidable (e.g. that thirst and death are bad things). So, where the common person suffers from feelings and judgements, the Skeptic suffers only from feelings.[26]

Skeptical formulae

From chapters 18 to 28 of *Outlines of Pyrrhonism*, Sextus examines several commonly used Skeptical formulae to illustrate both the method of opposing argument to argument and Skeptical detachment. Sextus' manner of exposition makes it likely that these functioned for Skeptics as mantras of sorts (Gr. *chiai*) – serviceable and repeatable reminders to themselves that happiness lay in detachment, not judgement.

The first formula is the famous elliptical phrase *Not more one* (Gr. *Ouden mallon*), which means, when fleshed out, *This appearance is no more likely to be true than that one.* Just as one cannot reasonably pass judgement that one body is heavier than another when they are evenly balanced on a scale, in a like manner, one cannot reasonably pass judgement on contrary appearances. And this utterance, he reminds us, is itself not asserted as true.[27]

Concerning possibility, there are several formulae: *Perhaps* and *Perhaps not*, *It is possible* and *It is not possible*, and *It admits of being* and *It does not admit of being*. Again, these are indicative of non-assertion.[28]

Next, there is the formula *I hold off from judging* (Gr. *Epechō*) for the credibility or incredibility concerning appearances at a given time. It is the equal force of contradictory judgements that compels suspension of judgement.[29]

There is also the formula *I determine nothing* (Gr. *Ouden horizō*), which concerns bringing forward and assenting to a view about what is non-evident. Sextus elaborates, 'My state of mind at the present is such that I make no dogmatic affirmation or denial of anything falling under the present investigation.' This is more a reported claim about how one feels than an assertion. So, the formula itself does not determine itself.[30] Similar to this is the formula *All things are undetermined* (Gr. *Panta estin aorista*). Here 'all things' pertains to non-evident matters that dogmatists assert one way or another and 'are' must be taken in the watered-down sense of 'seem to be'.[31]

Sextus gives *All things are ungraspable* (Gr. *Panta estin akatalēpta*[32]), *I do not grasp* (Gr. *Akatalēptō*), and *I do not apprehend* (Gr. *Ou katalambanō*) as the next formulae. These too must be understood elliptically. Fleshed out they translate *In all the dogmatic investigations I have inspected, the non-evident things they speculate about appear to me ungraspable.* Again this is more of a report of a Skeptic's state of mind than it is an assertion about the way things are.[33]

Last he mentions *To every argument an equal argument is opposed*. This too is elliptical. It literally means *For every argument which I have examined and which seeks to establish a point dogmatically, it appears to me that there is another argument opposed to it which seeks to establish a point dogmatically and is equal to it in point of credibility and incredibility*. He adds that other Skeptics renounce hortatory formulations (i.e. *let us oppose* ...) in favour of infinitive formulations (i.e. *to be opposed*), for the latter is more in keeping with peace of mind.[34]

Overall, these formulae are not to be uttered in the sense of assent or denial, but are to be employed with indifference and looseness. As always, they can even be used to cancel themselves out. Sextus elaborates with the analogy of purgative medicines:

> In regard to all Skeptic formulae it must be understood in advance that we make no assertions to the effect that they are absolutely true. We even say that they can be used to cancel themselves, since they are themselves included in those things to which they refer, just as purgative medicines not only remove the humors from the body but expel themselves together with the humors.[35]

All Skeptical formulae must be taken relatively, since they say nothing about the nature of the things to which they refer. In other words, they have referential, but no assertorial force. Yet this seems problematic. In stating that the words apply to themselves and cancel themselves out, this certainly suggests that they do have assertorial force. The Skeptical position seems patently inconsistent and untenable. The Skeptic would counter, I suppose, by stating such criticism is focused too much on words. Skepticism is not about words, but about living with one's mind disposed indifferently to any dogmatic concerns that might trouble it.[36]

The ten tropes

In chapter 14 of *Outlines of Pyrrhonism*, Sextus says that the number of tropes for suspension of judgement, according to the older Skeptics, is ten.[37] Here we find perhaps the most cogent justification for Skepticism as a way of life.

The first trope concerns differences in animals. Noting that different animals have different origins and different bodily structures, one can conclude *The same objects do not produce the same impressions in different animals*. As some animals are generated by sexual union, others are generated asexually, and this must make for differences in their capacities to perceive. Moreover, who would believe that thorny animals, hard-shelled animals, fleshy animals, feathered animals, and scaly animals each have the same sensitivity to touch? The same applies to the other senses. It is noteworthy here that for Skeptics, unlike Stoics, human sense-impressions have no privileged position in the world of animals.

The second trope concerns the differences in humans. *The same objects do not produce the same impressions in the same animals*. Different peoples have varying bodily types and constitutions, which in turn extend to psychical differences. Scythians differ from Indians, he notes, and these differences are likely due to differences in physical dispositions within the body.

Third, there are the differences in the senses. *The same objects do not produce the same impressions in different senses*. Perfume delights olfaction while it disgusts taste. The juice of the spurge pains the eyes, but harms none of the other senses. Olive oil soothes the skin, but bothers the windpipe and lungs.

A trope about circumstances is fourth. *The same objects do not produce the same impressions in different circumstances*. These include natural and unnatural states, want and satiety,

waking and sleeping, loving and hating, drunkenness and
sobriety, confidence and fear, and so on. For instance, those
possessed by a god (unnatural state) seem to hear divine
voices, while most others (natural state) do not. One with
bloodshot eyes sees a yellowish-orange coat that does not
appear thus to another without bloodshot eyes. What is
worse, we cannot even be in a position to privilege our waking sensory impressions, since, when asleep, our waking
impressions seem just as unreal as dreams do to one awake.

The fifth trope concerns position, distance, and place.
The same objects do not produce the same impressions in or at different
positions, distances, and places. A portico from either end seems
tapered, though from the middle it seems symmetrical.
Lamplight seems dim when the sun shines, but not when it
is night. An oar appears to be broken in the water but
straight when pulled out.

The trope of admixtures is the sixth trope. *The same objects*
do not produce the same impressions because they always seem to be
mixed with other things. Each perceptible thing seems never
to be seen singly, but always together with some other
thing. Skin, for instance, takes on a different color in different temperatures of air, so it seems impossible to say what
the color of skin is. The same sound seems different when it
is heard in dense or rarefied air.

The seventh trope concerns the quantity and composi-
tion of external bodies. *The same objects in different quantities or*
because of differences in composition do not produce the same impres-
sions. Concerning quantity, sometimes medicines are beneficial in small amounts and injurious in larger doses.
Concerning composition, small filings of a goat's horn
seem to be white, but the horn itself appears black.

The argument from relativity is the eighth trope. Here
Skeptics maintain the relativity of all things in the Pyrrho-
nic manner of *All things have the appearance of being relative.*
Sextus goes on to say that anyone who denies the relativity

of all things proves it, for in opposing it, he is placing it opposite to itself, which makes it relative to what it opposes.[38]

The ninth trope is about frequency of occurrence or its
lack. *Objects produce different impressions because of the frequency
or infrequency of their occurrence.* Many believe that comets
are divine omens, while the sun, which greatly exceeds
any comet in its brilliance, is taken for granted due to
its frequency of brilliance. Water, were it rare, would
appear much more valuable than all other things now
considered valuable, while gold, were it common, would
seem unimportant.

The final trope concerns cultural variances. *Differences in
disciplines, customs, laws, mythology, and dogma produce differences
in impressions.* Sometimes we oppose one of these to itself or
one to another. For instance, Ethiopians tattoo their babies,
while Greeks do not. Indians view public intercourse with
women without shock, while other people do not. Discipline
is opposed to law when law forbids the hitting of a free man,
though pancratiasts[39] and gladiators strike and sometimes
kill in contest.

The etiological tropes

The dogmatic confusion of Stoics, Platonists, Peripatetics,
and Epicureans, according to Sextus, was etiological confusion – that is, confusion concerning causes. Thus, as all
true Skeptics practice tropes for suspension of judgement,
as a way of life, Sextus relates that some Skeptics practice etiological tropes to expose the confusion and arrogance of Dogmatists.

In chapter 17 of *Outlines of Pyrrhonism*, Sextus gives the
Eight Etiological Tropes of Aenesidemus. The first concerns etiological speculation in general. Etiological speculation is futile, since, in going beyond appearances, it

cannot be confirmed by them. Second, etiologists often limit themselves to one causal account of something, when there are many accounts that accord with appearances. What guarantee, then, do they have of the truth of their account? Third, they assign random causes to orderly phenomena (e.g. movements of planets). Presumably, the criticism here is that the causes should not only explain movement, but order also. Fourth, in giving an etiology of appearances, they often mistakenly assume they know how the cause itself came about (and that this is similar in manner to how appearances came about). This, he says, may not be the case. Fifth, there is no universally agreed-upon methodology of etiologists. Instead, each is constrained by unique assumptions about how things work. Thus, each etiologist will have a different, perhaps contradictory, account of how things have come to pass. Sixth, etiologists often select only from appearances that agree with their speculations, while they ignore those that disagree. The criticism here is that all appearances should accord with the correct causal account. Seventh, they sometimes give causes that conflict not only with appearances, but also with their own assumptions. Eighth, when the difficulties in appearances are great, these difficulties expose great problems in the etiological framework assigned to the appearances. Overall, many of the causal problems listed here are problems that philosophers still grapple with today.

In chapter 15, Sextus then employs the later Skeptics' Five Tropes − disagreement, infinity, relativity, assumption, and circularity − to refute the etiologists. His argument goes as follows. The cause given to something either will be in harmony with all sects of philosophy, Skepticism included, or it will not. From all the discord, harmony seems impossible, so not being in harmony (i.e. *disagreement*) is probable. If it is not in harmony with all the sects, then there must be some cause of its lack of harmony. If an etiologist assigns an apparent cause to an appearance and remains at the level of appearance, he will fall into an *infinite regress*. The same follows if he assigns a non-apparent cause to something non-apparent. If he assigns an apparent cause to something non-apparent or a non-apparent cause to something apparent, he *reasons in a circle*. If he stops at any place, he relegates analysis to a certain set of circumstance and introduces *relativity* or stops on account of some unwarranted *assumption*.[40]

Skepticism and dogmatism in Greek medicine

Medical schools of thought

The skeptical attack on dogmatic philosophy was paralleled by an attack of dogmatism in the sister science of philosophy, medicine, as early as the fifth century B.C.

Early Greek secular medicine had begun to take root in the late fifth century B.C. through a group of doctors known as 'Hippocratic' physicians. Many of the writings of these physicians survive and, through them, we have learned much about early medical practice and theory.

When we turn to these works, what we find is factionalism concerning just how medicine ought to be practiced. There were the Dogmatists (or Rationalists), who purportedly crafted medical practice to accord with their views on etiology of diseases, and there were the Empiricists, who cast aside all causal speculation in favor of an approach based on past observation, other physicians' reports, and even guesswork.

Dogmatists maintained that proper medical therapy was guided by knowledge of both internal and external causes behind the veneer of experience. The Dogmatist who

wrote *On Craft* says, 'Every phenomenon will be found to
have some cause, and if it has a cause, chance can be no
more than an empty name.'[41] Dogmatic physicians, from
certain pre-established principles (Gr. *dogmata*) and a comparative method, would use reason to work backward from
symptoms to causes. The same author adds, 'What escapes
our vision we must grasp by mental sight, and the physician,
neither being able to see the nature of the disease nor to be
told of it, must have recourse to reasoning from the symptoms with which he is presented.'[42] Dogmatist physicians
often referred to imbalances in bodily humors (e.g. bile,
black bile, blood, and phlegm) and/or bodily elements
(e.g. hot and cold, wet and dry, and/or sweet and astrin-
gent) and used therapy to restore balance. By the end of
the fifth century B.C., there were numerous etiological
accounts of disease.[43]

Empiricism emerged in the third century B.C. in
response to the many different Dogmatic schools with their
many different etiological accounts of disease.[44] Empiricists
relied chiefly on past observation – that is, experience (Gr.
empeiria) of like circumstances – and memory to guide therapy. They refused to speculate about causes or anything else
that could not be seen. In a sense, Empirical physicians
looked upon dogma itself as a disease.[45]

By the first century B.C., there were numerous schools
of secular medicine, many of which were allied to schools
of philosophy. Asclepiades founded a school based on the
principles of Epicurean atomism. Cure for disease, in keeping with the principles of Epicureanism, was not based
on the imbalance of humors, but instead physicians used
mechanical, hygienic, and regimentic methods in an effort
to restore a patient's normal movement of bodily atoms.

Asclepiades' pupil, Themiston of Laodicea (fl. 50 B.C.)
founded Methodism. Methodism worked on the assumption that there were two classes of disease, those where the

pores are open and those where the pores are closed. Physicians were trained to 'see' these differences and their treatments accorded with methods to relax constricted pores and constrict relaxed pores.

Another prominent school was linked to Stoicism. For this school, *pneuma* (a type of vital air) was deemed the vital principle of an organism. As air was drawn in from the lungs into the left side of the heart, it was converted to both natural and psychical *pneuma*. Natural *pneuma* would then be distributed to the arterial or pneumatic system, while psychical *pneuma* would go to the brain to be distributed to the nervous system.

Other physicians, like Galen and Rufus of Ephesus (both fl. second century A.D.), were eclectic.

Galen on medical factionalism

It is through Galen that we get evidence that the factionalism in medicine between Dogmatism and Empiricism was even greater in the second century A.D. The three Galenic treatises from which I draw for evidence of this are *On Sects for Beginners*, *Outline of Empiricism*, and *On Medical Experience*.

In spite of the factionalism, Galen observes that Dogmatist and Empiricist medical *practices* were virtually indistinguishable. For instance, let us consider how Galen depicts a physician from each school dealing with memory loss. A Dogmatist may argue that *memory loss is the result of swelling of the cerebral membrane and any kind of motion is bad for a swollen membrane, so no one should talk to someone with memory loss*. In contrast, an Empiricist would merely note that *since all observed cases of speaking to a patient with memory loss worsened his condition, no one should talk to someone with memory loss*.[46] The main difference between these conflicting schools, according to Galen, lies not in the remedies themselves, but in the Dogmatists' insistence on an etiological grounding for all remedies. He elaborates:

> And, to speak quite generally, the dogmatics and the empiricists draw on the same medicines for the same affections. What they disagree about is the way these remedies are discovered. For, in the case of the same manifest bodily symptoms, the dogmatics derive from them an indication of the cause, and, on the basis of this cause, they find a treatment, whereas the empiricists are reminded by them of what they have observed often to happen in the same way.[47]

Whereas Empiricists were guided solely by their collections of past experience, Dogmatists strove for a causal understanding of such experiences – that is, general principles to guide medical practice. Empiricists aimed to remove symptoms; Dogmatists aimed to treat the cause of the symptoms.

For Empiricists, Galen says, experiences were formed in different ways. Some were viewed as spontaneous visual perceptions that occurred by chance (e.g. when someone ill drinks cold water and feels better) or by nature (e.g. when someone ill breaks into a spontaneous sweat and feels better). Some were extemporaneous, as when someone is led on by a dream to try some remedy and, when he does, he feels better. Others were imitative, as when something has been observed to work in a certain manner, though the number of observations is not compelling, and the physician imitates what he has observed.[48] Each of these can be the result of one's own perception, a report of a perception, or a type of analogical reasoning that guides novel cases – *epilogismos*.[49]

Experiences were then collected according to similarity into theorems such as 1. what always happens, 2. what usually happens, 3. what happens as often as it does not, and 4. what rarely happens. The empirical principles that guided empirical practice were *Similar remedies for similar affections* and *If a remedy proves ineffective after some time, try its contrary.*[50]

In Dogmatic medicine, in contrast, the manner of procedure was through indication (Gr. *analogismos*) – a rational method that allowed inference from a symptom, as an observed sign, to an unobserved underlying cause. According to Galen, Dogmatists cataloged three types of indication. In order to establish α a as the cause of τ, a Dogmatic physician needed to know primary indications (the nature of the human body), secondary indications (e.g. the strength of the patient, his nature, and his age), and tertiary indications or auxiliary factors that causally play a less direct role (e.g. climate, waters, occupation, foods, and habits). This web of causes was intricate and physicians needed to know how to factor in all indications in order to achieve diagnostic and therapeutic success.

Against Dogmatic physicians, Empiricists argued that other craftsmen – helmsmen, farmers, wine-growers, and others – practiced their crafts remarkably well without a knowledge of causes.[52] Additionally, since the methods for diagnosis and treatment of diseases, according to Galen, were roughly the same for both schools, Empiricists argued that adding a causal explanation was superfluous and vain. They also made much of Dogmatists' disagreement on etiological conclusions. For example, while Empiricists and Dogmatists alike agreed that *vinegar aids digestion*, one Dogmatist might assert that *this was due to its warmth*, while another might contend that *this was due to its capacity to pulverize food*. Therefore, Empiricists argued, the method of indication was unavailing.[53]

Against Empirical medicine, Dogmatists claimed that the alphabet, geometry, and music were founded on reason, not experience. Additionally, they noted that observation was insufficient to guide treatment, since there must be a means of separating symptoms into different kinds and judging how their observed order impacts illness. Furthermore, since the storehouse of circumstances surrounding any single case is unimaginably large, reason was deemed necessary for disentangling the many supposed etiological factors and ascertaining true causal relevance. Otherwise, investigation would be arbitrary.[54]

Sextus on Skepticism and medicine

What precisely is the relationship between Medical Empiricism and Skepticism according to Sextus? One might be tempted to think that, with the name Sextus Empiricus, this physician was a practicing Empiricist or at least one with great sympathy for Medical Empiricism. Astonishingly, however, Sextus states baldly that a Skeptic would do better in renouncing Empiricism in favour of Methodism. At *Outlines of Pyrrhonism* I.34, he writes:

> This (Methodism) is the only one of the schools in medicine which seems not to involve itself in reckless and arrogant speculation about the apprehensibility or non-apprehensibility of things in the sphere of the non-evident. On the contrary, in conformity with the Skeptics, they follow the appearances and take from these whatever seems expedient. For ... everyday life ... is fourfold. One part consists in the guidance of nature, another in the compulsion of the feelings, another in the tradition of laws and customs, and another in the instruction of the arts. Now just as the Skeptic, in accordance with the compulsion of the feelings, is guided by thirst to drink and by hunger to food, and in like manner to various other objects, so also the Methodic physician is led by the feelings of the patient to the corresponding remedies. By constipation he is led to the remedy of relaxation, just as the contraction due to intense cold causes a person to

take refuge in a warm spot. By a flux he is led to the suppression of it, just as persons in a hot bath, dripping all over with sweat and becoming faint, see that they must put a stop to it, and hence seek the relief of the cold air.

What is more, like true Skeptics, Methodists use (medical) terminology with indifference. 'For just as the Sceptic employs the formulae *I determine nothing* and *I apprehend nothing* without prejudice . . . so also the Methodic uses the terms *generally* and *pervade* and the like without any subtlety of meaning.' His renunciation of Empiricism is not categorical, but relative: Skepticism has more in common with Methodism than with other schools of medical thought.[55]

Relevance for today

It perhaps seems somewhat misleading to introduce skepticism in a book about happiness that features Greek philosophers. After all, this book is a quest for happiness, and skepticism seems to suggest that this search is itself in vain or, at least, greatly misguided.

Yet ancient skeptics of all persuasions, were they around to reply to this objection, would probably have strongly disagreed. They too spent much time in thoughtful analysis of the same questions that dogmatists examined concerning the best possible manner of living. For skeptics, the difference was that skeptical analysis showed that such questions did not admit of unambiguous answers. Still, through skeptical analysis, skeptics gave an answer to the question *How ought I to live my life to be happy?* The Pyrrhonic Skeptic's answer (again, hereafter Skeptic), for instance, was to live in a way that maximizes peace of mind.

This, of course, is the same answer that Epicurus gives, and though there are express differences in how Epicureans and Skeptics would go about securing equanimity, there is something sensible about both answers. Both Epicureans and Skeptics recognize that much of our unhappiness is due to psychical anxiety that is the result of embracing unwarranted or false views of the way things work. For Epicureans, remedy consists in adopting Epicurus' own brand of metaphysical dogmatism. For Skeptics, remedy consists in renouncing all dogmatism (even the Academic Skeptics' assertion of the inapprehensibility of all things).

Still, if the best one can do through philosophical argument is to show that for any argument another contradictory argument can be equally well supported, then why would anyone take up philosophy in the first place? Why would anyone think that philosophy could be a guide to happiness?

It is here that Skeptics, like Epicureans, would remind us that happiness is just a matter of mental tranquility through eliminating mental unrest. If we buy into this – and this does not seem to be so unpalatable to deserve outright rejection – then it seems reasonable to ask whether this skeptical lifestyle is the only or the best way to secure equanimity. Here we recall the Epicurean's assertion that only the correct understanding of the way things work (the right dogmatic view, not doubt) can bring about peace of mind. Why, then, should we think that doubt, not certainty, leads to tranquility and removal of unrest?

According to Sextus, a Skeptic can give no other assurance than that of chance and experience. He writes:

> His initial purpose in philosophizing was to pronounce judgement on appearances. . . . In doing so, he met with contradicting alternatives of equal force. Since he could not decide between them, he withheld judgement. Upon his suspension of judgement there followed, by chance, mental tranquility in matters of opinion.

He illustrates this point by the story of Apelles the artist, who being unable to depict a horse's foam on a painting, threw his sponge at the picture in frustration. In doing so, by chance alone, his airborne sponge created the foam he was all the while after. Similarly, Skeptics found by chance observation that mental tranquility follows suspension of judgement as surely as a shadow follows a body in sunlight.[56] In other words, experience shows what argument cannot: the Skeptical method brings about equanimity.

The Skeptical response, however, seems anything but empirically obvious. Still, let us assume for argument's sake that Skepticism does in fact lead from psychical unrest to psychical rest. Here we face a different problem: How can we prevent Skepticism from leading to *complete* rest? In other words, if everything can equally be cast into doubt, even doubt itself, what reason do we have for getting out of bed in the morning?

A Skeptic's reply is that he lives according to appearances. If argument shows that no one can surely predicate 'good' of, say, friendship or of lime juice, a Skeptic, who finds the taste of lime juice appealing and who enjoys having friends, will still flavor food with lime juice and enjoy his friends. His practical life will not change; what will change is his cognitive commitment to things in life being good or bad. He may come to doubt everything, even doubt itself, but he will make no fundamental changes in his manner of living.

This is a strange reply however. It presupposes that people will be *most* at ease when they realize that, for every reasoned action they undertake, there is (at least in principle) an equally good argument for not taking that action. However, such a presupposition seems unlikely to bring about human happiness. And so, what is the motivation to take up Skepticism as a way of life? At the political end of matters, a true Skeptic, who fights to right an apparent injustice, cannot justify any of his actions on behalf of his cause. What is worse, he cannot begrudge anyone who tries to prevent him from acting. Given these problems (and even acknowledging the defects of dogmatism), why should anyone find Skepticism an attractive alternative to dogmatism?

In response to a philosophical position of complete doubt, the twentieth-century philosopher Ludwig Wittgenstein correctly noted, 'A doubt that doubted everything would not be a doubt.'[57] To make any sense, doubt must hinge upon something that is beyond doubt. Otherwise there *is* no reason for getting out of bed in the morning.

In spite of this criticism of complete scepticism, Wittgenstein's own (later) views on the possibility of knowledge are very much like those of Skeptics. However, unlike Skeptics, for Wittgenstein philosophy seems to perpetuate more harm than good. He argues that philosophical problems stem from misuse or abuse of words within a linguistic community. Words function well enough by themselves, but problems arise when persons begin to scrutinize them analytically (i.e. when philosophers start philosophizing). In an attempt to penetrate through critical analysis, we lose sight of what is obvious and fall into confusion. In *On Certainty*, Wittgenstein likens this confusion to his seeing a painting from an appropriate distance and then trying to understand it more precisely by moving on top of it − as if this would give him some deeper understanding of it.

> It is as if I were to see a painting (say a painted stage-set) and recognize what it represents from a long way off at once and without the slightest doubt. But now I step nearer: and then I see a lot of patches of different colors, which are all highly ambiguous and do not provide any certainty whatever.[58]

Wittgenstein believes that philosophical analysis is profuse and needless. Essaying to clarify through analysis, it perverts everyday language, which functions fine the way it is. In short, he believes that it is vain to practice philosophy.

Skeptics, though, need not maintain that philosophical practice is vain, as they do not commit themselves to the impossibility of knowledge. Yet Skepticism does not commit itself to the possibility of knowledge either. Thus, the following objection seems harmful: if Skepticism is a method that does not commit itself one way or another toward the possibility of knowledge, it does not seem to show any *methodological* promise of ever disclosing knowledge. After all, to the claim *Knowledge is possible* one could always place against and argue equally as well for the claim *Knowledge is not possible*. And this seems to take us nowhere. Skepticism, as Sextus presents it, cannot be taken on board as is as a suitable guide for happiness today. Does doubt at all have a role in a happy life?

Perhaps part of our present-day reluctance to embrace skepticism of any sort stems from our underlying fear concerning its destructive potential. Philip Hallie writes:

> It (doubt) can be used to strengthen a position, or it can be used to destroy all positions. The positive, constructive powers of reason that Plato, Aristotle, the Stoics, and the Epicureans extolled and exemplified are not potentially so omnivorous as doubt. Perhaps an awareness of its great dangers is one of the reasons why of all the great movements of antiquity that we have been mentioning Skepticism has been the least carefully understood and the most despised. Galileo's critics refused to look into his telescope not only out of laziness, but also, perhaps, out of fear; and the critics of Freud attacked him without reading him for other reasons than merely a lack of time.[59]

Yet for all of its destructive capacities, there is sincerity and honesty in doubt that is lacking in dogmatism.

In many circumstances and on many issues, reason tells us clearly that certainty is disingenuous.

The key issue, as Wittgenstein noted, is the extent to which we, as rational beings, ought to be skeptics. For whichever way you go about it, complete skepticism in philosophical disputation makes philosophy futile as a guide for right living.

Nonetheless, as John Stuart Mill recognized, the power of doubt can extend beyond destruction to discovery. Unlike Skeptics, who used reason to show that any view could be argued just as well as another, Mill believed that reason could function for disclosure of truth in political, religious, and philosophical issues that were presently in doubt. He stated that if an opinion could withstand vigorous criticism over time, it would likely be correct or, at least, the best we could possibly do to attain certainty on such an issue.[60] In contrast, any attempt to impose some view as true − whether by one, some, or the majority − without an exhaustive exposure to debate was flatly declared to be a type of unwarranted and unhealthy tyranny.

To work toward truth in practical affairs unsettled by reason, Mill believed that debate from all sides was essential.

> Truth, in the great practical concerns of life, is so much a question of the reconciling and combining of opposites that very few have minds sufficiently capacious and impartial to make the adjustment with an approach to correctness, and it has to be made by the rough process of a struggle between combatants fighting under hostile banners.[61]

He also astonishingly maintained that opposition to opinions that are universally accepted (or nearly so) should even be manufactured, if they do not exist.[62] Mill's continual desire to challenge views that were believed true was historical: history shows, he says, that neither is the received view entirely true nor is the silenced view entirely false. Truth, more often than not, lies somewhere between the two[63]

It is perhaps this Millean sense of skepticism, one that does not cast into doubt all concerns whatsoever but merely those issues unsettled by reason, that seems to be what we can best extract from ancient skeptical attitudes. This is not a foolproof method for arriving at truth in undecided cases – for in many such cases, truth may not even be the aim or a possibility – but it is one that embraces diversity, creativity, energy, open-mindedness, cooperation, and fallibility in its never-ending quest for resolution and understanding.

We are, as Aristotle often noted, curious animals, which derive great pleasure through some measure of understanding ourselves and the world around us. Doubt, as a measure of our ignorance, is an indispensable goad for furthering our understanding and liberating us from the manacles of our ignorance. Where dogmatism thrives to the exclusion of doubt, free enquiry is prohibited and learning becomes impossible. In such an oppressive atmosphere, humans, as rational beings, can never be happy.

Notes

[1] *Vit.* IX.61–108.
[2] *Vit.* IX.109–16.
[3] Or Philocomus. *Vit.* IV.62–6.
[4] Sextus Empiricus, *Selections from the Major Writings on Scepticism, Man, and God*, ed. Philip Hallie (Indianapolis: Hackett, 1985), 20.
[5] All we know is that he came after Pyrrho and before Sextus Empicirus.

6 Indicative signs signal the essence of a thing and are said to resemble that thing (e.g. bodily movements are indicative of an underlying soul), while recollective signs signal experiences that get linked together (e.g. smoke brings a recollection of fire or a scar brings a recollection of a prior wound). *P.* II.10.

7 I use Etheridge's translation throughout, unless otherwise indicated. Sextus Empiricus, *Selections from the Major Writings on Scepticism, Man, and God*, ed. Philip P. Hallie (Indianapolis: Hackett, 1985).

8 'Kataleptic' indicates grasping.

9 Long and Sedley translation here. A. A. Long and D. N. Sedley, *The Hellenistic Philosophers*, Volume 1 (New York: Cambridge University Press, 1990).

10 *M.* VII.255.

11 Long and Sedley translation.

12 The Stoics thought that such perceptions had propositional content.

13 Sextus means Plato's Academy, which took a skeptical turn shortly after his death. He mentions the Middle Academy (Arcesilaus and his followers) and the New Academy (Carneades, Clitomachus, and their followers). He also mentions later Academics (under Philo, Charmidas, and Antichus), which turned back to dogmatism.

14 i.e. there is no criterion of truth.

15 The type of skepticism that continually drove Socrates in his pursuit of knowledge.

16 *P.* I.33.

17 Not in the Aristotelian sense of a capacity in objects, but a capacity in us to achieve equanimity of mind through the skeptical method.

18 *P.* I.3–4.

19 *P.* I.13.

20 *P.* I.10.

21 *P.* I.7.

22 *P.* I.8.

23 *P.* I.11.

24 For a good discussion of these difficulties, see Martha Nussbaum, 'Epicurean Surgery: Argument and Empty Desire', in *The Therapy*

of Desire: Theory and Practice in Hellenistic Ethics (Princeton, NJ: Princeton University Press, 1994), 300–6.

[25] *P.* I.12.

[26] *P.* I.12.

[27] *P.* I.19.

[28] *P.* I.21.

[29] *P.* I.22.

[30] *P.* I.23.

[31] *P.* I.24.

[32] *Akatelēpta,* literally, non-kataleptic or non-cognitive.

[33] *P.* I.25.

[34] *P.* I.27.

[35] *P.* I.28.

[36] Nussbaum writes, 'Strictly speaking, Skeptical argument opposes only that which has been asserted and believed – and the Skeptic tells us that he asserts nothing. So Skeptical arguments do not oppose themselves in exactly the way in which they oppose dogmatic arguments – just as purgative drugs do not need to loosen themselves while they are loosening the rest of the contents of the digestive system. They need to oppose themselves only to the degree that the pupil, being human, is inclined to rely on them as she proceeds. This degree of reliance will weaken over time, as the pupil's detachment becomes greater across the board' (Nussbaum, *Therapy of Desire*, 311).

[37] Aenesidemus is likely the reference here.

[38] There is a glaring equivocation of 'relative' here. The first sense is 'non-absolute' and the second is 'opposite'.

[39] The pancratium was an especially violent and popular athletic event in antiquity that combined elements of boxing and wrestling.

[40] *P.* I.17.

[41] *Art.* VI.

[42] *Art.* XI.

[43] Michael Frede, 'Stoics and Skeptics and Clear and Distinct Ideas', in *Doubt and Dogmatism,* ed. Myles Burnyeat and Jonathan Barnes (New York: Oxford University Press, 1980), 228–9.

[44] Ibid., 228–9.

[45] M. Andrew Holowchak, *Ancient Science and Dreams: Oneirology in Greco-Roman Antiquity* (Lanham, MD: University Press of America, 2001), 9–11.

[46] *Exper. Med.* XXV.

[47] *Sect. Intr.* IV. Walzer and Frede's translation. See Galen, *Three Treatises on the Nature of Science: On the Sects for Beginners; An Outline of Empiricism;* and *On Medical Experience,* trans. Richard Walzer and Michael Frede (Indianapolis: Hackett), 1985.

[48] *Subf. Emp.* II.

[49] *Subf. Emp.* II–III.

[50] *Subf. Emp.* IX.

[51] *Sect. Intr.* III–V.

[52] *Exper.Med.* IX.

[53] *Exper. Med.* XI and XIII.

[54] *Exper. Med.* III–VII.

[55] *P.* I.34.

[56] *P.* I.12.

[57] §450. See also §625. Ludwig Wittgenstein, *On Certainty*, ed. G. E. M. Anscombe and G. H. von Wright (New York: Harper & Row, 1969).

[58] Ibid., §481.

[59] Philip P. Hallie, 'Classical Scepticism – A Polemical Introduction', in Sextus Empiricus, *Selections from the Major Writings on Scepticism, Man, and God,* ed. Philip P. Hallie (Indianapolis: Hackett, 1985), 4.

[60] John Stuart Mill, *On Liberty* (New York: Penguin Books, 1985), 116.

[61] Ibid., 110.

[62] Ibid., 99 and 111.

[63] Ibid., 108.

Part II

THREE LEVELS OF INTEGRATION

5

Happiness and Self-Integration

Are you not aware that if Heracles, my ancestor, had gone no further than Tiryns or Argos – or even than the Peloponnese or Thebes – he could never have won the glory which changed him from a man into a god, actual or apparent.

Alexander of Macedon

As COGNITIVE SCIENTISTS TODAY know fully, the human organism is psychically complex. One of the most recognizable models of our psychical complexity comes from perhaps the most lauded and criticized psychologist of our time – Sigmund Freud. In his most celebrated model of the mind, Freud breaks up our psychical apparatus into three parts: the id (our primal self and center for pleasure), the ego (our agency for delaying pleasure to accommodate reality), and the superego (our sense of conscience). For Freud, proper human functioning involves a harmony of tensions between the three parts that principally reduces to getting control over the inordinately strong hedonistic impulses of the id.[1] Notwithstanding the strength of our hedonistic impulses, Freud believed that we could learn to tame them with proper guidance. In *The Ego and the Id*, he writes:

> Thus in its relation to the id it [the ego] is like a man on horseback, who has to hold in check the superior strength of the horse; with this difference, that the rider tries to do so with his own strength while the ego uses borrowed forces. ... Often a rider, if he is not to be parted from his horse, is obliged to guide it where it wants to go; so in the same way the ego is in the habit of transforming the id's will into action as if it were its own.[2]

To many of his contemporaries, Freud's insights may have seemed to be astonishingly innovative for his time, but the complexity of the soul was recognized in Classical Greek antiquity as well in models that were remarkably intricate. In Book IV of *Republic*,[3] for instance, Plato develops a tripartite model of the soul, where the rational part, in a psychically healthy human being, controls the spirited and appetitive parts. Plato's pupil Aristotle, in *On the Soul*, gives an even more elaborate account of the human soul in which humans – having a psychically based capacity for nutrition, locomotion, appetite, reproduction, perception, and reasoning – are distinguished from other animals by their capacity to reason. For both philosophers, any account of living a good and happy life must deal with harmonizing the various, often discordant, parts of the soul, and maintaining this harmony. For both, the harmonizing principle is reason and the harmonizing agency is that part of the soul containing reason.

A recognizably important way of acquiring and maintaining accord among the different parts of the soul is through self-knowledge. One of the most celebrated rational principles for the ancient Greeks, *Know yourself*, which was inscribed on a wall at the oracle at Delphi, concerned just this.

This chapter is about personal integration – specifically, what the Greeks have to teach us today about self-knowledge and why it is an indispensable part of happiness. First,

I briefly sketch the different accounts of the soul that Plato and Aristotle give. I show how, for each, self-knowledge is a matter of functional, organic unity or true personal integration, where every part of the soul functions dutifully for the good of the organism as a whole. Next, I look at three celebrated examples of avowedly virtuous men in antiquity – Plato's Socrates, Diogenes the Cynic, and Alexander of Macedonia – and apply the standard of personal integration to each. Last, as always, I close with some thoughts on the relevance of these views for us today.

Platonic justice

Plato came to a conclusion concerning the human soul similar to that of Freud, yet his ideas antedated Freud's by some 2400 years. In *Republic*, on the analogy of the tripartite *polis*,[4] Plato mentions an appetitive soul (Gr. *to epithumētikon*), characterized by indulgence in such things as lust, food,

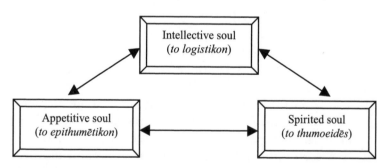

Figure 5.1   Plato's tripartite soul
Justice, essential to happiness, is a matter of internal harmony or stability between the discordant parts of the soul. Here it is the rational soul that effects moral stability. Note that the Greek word for reason, *logos*, means also 'relation', 'proportion', 'law', and 'rule'.

and drink; a spirited soul (Gr. *to thumoeidēs*), characterized by acts relating to war (courage, indignation, resolve, and boldness); and a rational soul (Gr. *to logistikon*),[5] characterized by regard for reason, law, moderation, wisdom, and truth. We learn that the spirited soul and rational soul naturally function amicably together, while these two parts of the soul are naturally antagonistic to the appetitive soul.[6]

To help us understand the interaction of these three, Plato in his *Phaedrus* offers an analogy similar to that of Freud. He compares the soul to a manned chariot with horses. There is the charioteer and two winged horses: one black and one white. The charioteer represents the rational soul and is chiefly responsible for the non-violent, orderly movement of the chariot. The white horse is noble and good and represents the spirited soul. In contrast, the black horse is of contrary character and represents the appetitive soul.[7] Plato's point here, like Freud's, is that the human soul is naturally complex and *naturally at odds with itself*. It is no small feat for the rational soul to get the other two parts of the soul working together for the betterment of any person. Often the best for which we can hope is not to stray too far from our intended goal.

There are naturalistic and normative points to consider here as they relate to human happiness. Regarding the former, what Plato, Aristotle, and, in our own day, Freud got right is that our psychical apparatus, whatever it consists of, is naturally complex and made of some elements that are by nature antagonistic. Given this, and here I turn to the normative point, it is easy to see why personal integration is so difficult to attain. There is a continual war within each of us that makes internal harmony difficult. The key to internal harmony for Plato and Aristotle is the proper cultivation of reason.[8] This concordance of soul Plato describes as a form of justice.

One who is just does not allow any part of himself to do the work of another part or allow the various classes within him to meddle with each other. He regulates well what is really his own and rules himself. He puts himself in order, is his own friend, and harmonizes the three parts of himself like three limiting notes in a musical scale – high, low and middle. He binds together those parts and any others there may be in between, and from having been many things he becomes entirely one, moderate and harmonious. Only then does he act. And when he does anything, whether acquiring wealth, taking care of his body, engaging in politics or in private contracts – in all of these, he believes that the action is just and fine that preserves this inner harmony and helps achieve it, and calls it so, and regards as wisdom the knowledge that oversees such actions. And he believes that the action that destroys this harmony is unjust, and calls it so, and regards the belief that oversees it as ignorance.[9]

Aristotle on the pleasure of being alone

A pupil of Plato, Aristotle too recognized the complexity of the human soul. At I.13 of *Nicomachean Ethics*, he speaks of two parts of the rational soul and two parts of the irrational soul. Concerning the parts of the rational soul, one part (Gr. *to epistēmonikon*) contemplates invariant first principles and the other part (Gr. *to logistikon*) contemplates things variable.[10] Of the two parts of the irrational soul, one (Gr. *to phutikon*) is responsible for nutrition and growth, while the other (Gr. *to epithumētikon*) seems both to fight against and obey reason.[11] Excellence of character for Aristotle involves getting the seemingly ambivalent part of the irrational soul to obey reason, not fight it. The good man, then, has the parts of his soul working in harmony toward what is good. Aristotle describes the personally integrated person:

Each of these features is found in the decent person's relation
to himself. ... [T]he excellent person is of one mind with
himself, and desires the same things in his whole soul.
Hence he wishes goods and apparent goods to himself, and
achieves them in his actions, since it is proper to the good
person to reach the good by his efforts. He wishes and does
them for his own sake, since he does them for the sake of his
thinking part, and that is what each person seems to be.
Moreover, he wishes himself to live and to be preserved.
And he wishes this for his rational part more than for any
other part. ... Further, such a person finds it pleasant to
spend time with himself, and so wishes to do it. For his memories of what he has done are agreeable, and his expectations
for the future are good, and hence both are pleasant. And
besides, his thought is well supplied with topics for study.
Moreover, he shares his own distresses and pleasures, more
than other people share theirs. For it is always the same
thing that is painful or pleasant, not different things at different times. The decent person, then, has each of these features in relation to himself.[12]

Base people, in contrast, are the complete opposite of virtuous persons. Such people are wretched and act, without
knowing why, first in one way and then in another. They
are so far from personal integration that they even shun
themselves. Again, I use Aristotle's own words:

[T]hey (i.e. base people) are at odds with themselves, and
have an appetite for one thing and a wish for another, as
incontinent people do. For they do not choose things that
seem to be good for them, but instead choose pleasant
things that are actually harmful. ... And those who have
done many terrible actions hate and shun life because of
their vice, and destroy themselves. Besides, vicious people
seek others to pass their days with, and shun themselves.
For when they are by themselves they remember many dis-
agreeable actions, and expect to do others in the future; but

they manage to forget these in other people's company. These people have nothing loveable about them, and so have no friendly feelings for themselves. Hence such a person does not share his own enjoyments and distresses. For his soul is in conflict, and because he is vicious one part is distressed at being restrained, and another is pleased [by the intended action]; and so each part pulls in a different direction, as though they were tearing him apart.[13]

It follows that good living, for Aristotle, involves stability of character and this entails a harmonizing of the discordant elements of the soul. Contrariwise, bad living is merely a symptom of internal discordance.

Having shown that both Plato and Aristotle believe that happiness is characterized by rational order in the human soul, I turn now to the second aim of this chapter – the application of the standard of personal integration to Socrates, Alexander of Macedonia, and Diogenes the Cynic. I begin with the Socrates of Plato's dialogues.

The trial of Socrates

One of the reasons that Socrates (469–399 B.C.), son of Sophroniscus, was a centerpiece of so many of Plato's dialogues was doubtless his stability of character. To have had such a profound influence over Plato, one of history's greatest minds, is itself testament to the breadth of Socrates' character. If the depiction of Socrates that Plato hands down is mostly accurate, then we can say that Socrates was truly a remarkable person with exemplary reasoning skills, a mordant wit, a penetrating intellect, and a singular devotion to the pursuit of truth.[14]

Plato's *Apology* (Gr. *apologia*, meaning 'defense') gives us the best characterization of Socrates' manner of living and love of philosophy. In 399 B.C., Socrates was on trial for his life on account of a handful of accusations, all of which were reducible to the charge that he was a corrupter of the young and a bane to Athens.[15] These charges were not without substance, as is sometimes assumed, for just a few years prior to Socrates' trial, Athens had just lost a protracted war with Sparta (404 B.C.) and some of the most suspicious Athenian figures (e.g. Alcibiades[16] and Critias[17]) were pupils of Socrates.

While defending himself, Socrates relates a story that attempts to explain much of the enmity directed against him in Athens. He tells of his recently deceased friend, Chaerephon, who had once gone to Delphi to ask the oracle, 'Is anyone wiser than Socrates?' The oracle responded that no one was wiser. Socrates, who constantly professed only complete ignorance in the most important matters pertaining to his avowed quest for virtue, was quite perplexed upon hearing this.

Not believing that the Delphic oracle could be taken to mean that he himself had any real wisdom, Socrates subsequently went forth in an effort to discover the meaning of this riddle by trying to find someone wiser than himself. In doing so, Socrates was, in effect, trying to show that the oracle could not be taken literally. First he went to certain Athenian politicians and found that they professed to know things that they really did not know. Thus Socrates became satisfied that he was wiser than the politicians, at least insofar as he did not profess to know things he did not know.[18] Afterwards Socrates visited the poets, tragedians, and other such people. To his astonishment, he found that these men seemed to understand their own works even less than those who listened to them.[19] Last, he went to the craftsmen. Socrates acknowledged that these people did indeed know many fine things (related to their crafts) that Socrates did not know, yet they also professed to know other, more important things too (presumably related to matters of virtue). And so Socrates again thought that he was wiser than they were, since they were unaware of their ignorance in the most important human concerns.[20] He ultimately concluded that the oracle could not have meant *Socrates is wisest*, but rather *Anyone, who like Socrates understands that his wisdom is nothing next to divine wisdom, is wise.*[21] Yet, in questioning some of the leading citizens of Athens, Socrates was turning some of the most important people in Athens against him.

Socrates then elaborates on the importance of the oracle and his service to the god in his continual quest for truth.

> So even now I continue this investigation as the god bade me – and I go around seeking out anyone, citizen or stranger, whom I think wise. Then if I do not think he is, I come to the assistance of the god and show him that he is not wise. Because of this occupation, I do not have the leisure to engage in public affairs to any extent, nor indeed to look after my own, but I live in great poverty because of my service to the god.[22]

In doing the bidding of the god,[23] Socrates takes himself to be tending to the well-being of his own soul and that of all others who are willing to participate in his pursuit of knowledge. Yet in specifically seeking out Athens' 'wise' men, who have little or no interest in conversing with him, Socrates is really saying that those who seem to be best qualified to know what a virtuous life entails appear to know less about such a life than those who seem less qualified. Why should this be so?

Socrates believes that those who professes to know what a particular virtue is (e.g. piety, courage, wisdom, moderation, or justice) should be able to give an account of this virtue that withstands all attempts at refutation. If they cannot do so, then they ought to seek out such knowledge before making judgements about or performing actions concerning the virtue in question. For example, in Plato's work *Euthyphro*,[24] a young man of the same name is in the process of prosecuting his father on the grounds that he (the young man) is an expert on piety. Yet Socrates' dialectical exchange with Euthyphro proves otherwise. With his ignorance exposed, the proper path for the young man seems clear: he should acknowledge his ignorance of piety and forestall his plans of prosecuting his father until such time, if ever, that he should acquire knowledge of piety. Euthyphro, through youth and stubbornness, does neither of these. Annoyed and firm in the belief that he knows what he does not know, he hastens away from Socrates.

Socrates' counter-examination of his main accuser in *Apology*, Meletus, takes precisely this path.[25] While engaging in dialectical conversation with Meletus[26] (who has charged Socrates with, among other things, corrupting the young), Socrates craftily goes on to show that Meletus himself does not know what it means to corrupt the young. Thus, lacking any such knowledge, Meletus has no business charging Socrates with corrupting the young. Of three arguments that Socrates puts forth against Meletus, the most philosophically illuminating one I give below.[27] I flesh it out from Socrates' own perspective.

(C_1) In my dialectical conversations with the young, I was either doing ill or I was not.

(C_2) If I was not doing ill, there is no need to prosecute me.

(C_3) If I was doing ill, I chose to do ill knowingly or I did it unknowingly.

(C_4) No one who knows what is ill will choose to do ill.

(C_5) So, I could not have done ill knowingly (C_3 and C_4).

(C_6) So, if I was doing ill, I must have been doing it unknowingly (C_3 and C_5).

(C_7) If I was doing ill unknowingly, then I should not be in court, but I should be instructed and freed of my ignorance.

(C_8) So, if I was doing ill, then I should not be in court, but I should be instructed and freed of my ignorance (C_6 and C_7).

(C_9) So, I should not be in court (C_2 and C_8).

(C_{10}) So, there is no need to prosecute me (C_9).

There is more. If Meletus, in charging Socrates with corrupting the young, possesses knowledge of what it means to corrupt someone, he must also know what it means to educate someone. Yet he has never attempted to instruct the 'ignorant' Socrates. Given this, it is fitting to conclude that Meletus has never given thought to what it means either to corrupt or educate the young. In other words, Meletus, clearly lacking the knowledge that he ought to have in order to prosecute Socrates, is not fit to prosecute Socrates. Socrates should not be on trial.[29]

After finishing with Meletus, Socrates, showing unexpected *sang froid*, addresses the jury with his closing statement on behalf of his acquittal. Instead of an emotional plea to the jurors that is designed at winning sympathy (which was not unusual in such cases[30]), Socrates tries to persuade the jury of his innocence through an assessment of the relevant facts and an appeal to reason.[31] Socrates, after all, has no cause to fear a decision that he be put to death. One should only fear evil, not what one does not know, he asserts, and no one knows whether or not death is an evil.[32]

In his defense, Socrates also gives an explanation for his withdrawal from political affairs. Politicians, his own experience has shown, do not act from any consideration of justice. Consequently, 'a man who really fights for justice must lead a private, not public, life if he is to survive for even a short time'.[33] For Socrates, true justice begins by turning inwards, toward the self.

Before the verdict, Socrates lets all in attendance know that he will never cease to practice philosophy, even if convicted, for this is what the god bids.[34]

When a verdict of guilty is reached, Meletus (as Socrates' accuser) proposes that Socrates be put to death.[35] Socrates, as if to mock the court, counters that a proper assessment for his 'crime' is free meals at the Prytaneum – a privilege afforded only a select few and one that he, more than many others who have been awarded the privilege, fitfully deserves.[36] Socrates then says that he can pay at most one *mina* of silver.[37] Plato's friends pool their resources and up the proposed fine to 30 *minae*. The jury, numbering 501 here, votes again and Socrates is sentenced to death by some thirty votes.[38]

On receiving the verdict, Socrates prophesies ill to those who voted against him.[39] He offers to stay and philosophize about what has just happened with those who voted to acquit him.[40] He also proposes that his 'condemnation' is in keeping with the designs of the gods. For Socrates' *daimonion*, which comes to and opposes him whenever he is about to do something wrong,[41] has at the moment of his condemnation failed to oppose him. This is itself a sure sign that what is generally construed to be the worst of evils, death, must itself be something good.[42] He adds that there is no reason for anyone to be afraid, for no good man can be harmed in life or in death.

Apology ends with Socrates saying: 'Now the hour to part has come. I go to die, you go to live. Which of us goes to the better lot is known to no one, except the god.'[43] Ironically, Socrates, who during his trial was accused of atheism by Meletus,[44] willingly accepts his death at the bidding of the god.

The conquests of Alexander

One of the most intriguing, dynamic, and puzzling characters in all of history is the Macedonian king Alexander the Great (356–323 B.C.). Like the Achilles of Homer, Alexander was handsome, greatly spirited, and full of ambition. Of this extraordinary man, one of his primary early biographers, Flavius Arrianus (Arrian), writes in *Conquests of Alexander* (Gr. *Anabasis*):

> [T]here has never been another man in all the world, of Greek or any other blood, who by his own hand succeeded in so many brilliant enterprises. . . . [T]his book of mine is, and has been from my youth, more precious than country and kin and public advancement – indeed, for me it *is* these things. And that is why I venture to claim the first place in Greek literature, since Alexander, about whom I write, held first place in the profession of arms.[45]

In 342 B.C., Philip II, Alexander's father, hired Aristotle to tutor the boy. Though the true extent of this tutorial is unclear, Aristotle probably instructed Alexander on such topics as the cosmos, biology, geography, ethics, politics, and logic.[46] Aristotle must have reinforced in Alexander the inferiority of non-Hellenic peoples, who were by their very nature fit not to rule but to be ruled,[47] as well as a great curiosity for exploration and scientific discovery.

As a dyed-in-the-wool Grecophile, Alexander's favorite reading was, not surprisingly, Homer's *Iliad*, which had an extraordinary influence on the development of Greek notions of excellence of character in antiquity. Plutarch in 'Life of Alexander' writes that Alexander would keep a copy of Aristotle's recension of Homer's *Iliad*, which he called the 'the *Iliad* of the casket', along with his dagger beneath his bed.[48]

Upon the untimely death of his father, Alexander assumed the crown of all of Macedonia at the early age of 21. King Philip was murdered just as he was about to embark upon a campaign against the Persians to punish them for their invasion of Greece in the battles from 490 to 479 B.C. Alexander, displaying uncharacteristic verve and pluck for one so young, proceeded to carry out his father's plans to invade Persia, perhaps for no other reason than this was his inheritance from his father.

Alexander's leonine courage and matchless ability to think quickly on his feet resulted in defeat for the Persians in battle after battle (though in most cases Alexander was greatly outnumbered).[49] With each victory, Alexander pushed his formidable army further eastward and beyond the Persian Empire into India. All the while, he was preoccupied and even consumed by a desire to explore, conquer, and prove his godhood through military deeds. Yet after years of battle, his troops grew weary and became rebellious. They finally coerced him to discontinue his eastward conquests and return them to Macedonia. He, however, took a southerly path homeward, before turning westward, in order to add to his conquests upon his return.

Was Alexander happy in his consuming quest to conquer other peoples? To answer this question, I take a closer look at Alexander the man through his ancient biographers.

Biographer Quintus Curtius Rufus says that Alexander was only happy in battle and while engaged in battle, his thirst for victory and glory was quenchless. Curtius relates the story of 20 Scythian ambassadors, who approached Alexander, one of whom spoke to Alexander as follows.

> Had the gods willed that your stature should match our greed the world could not hold you. You would touch the east with one hand and the west with the other, and reaching the west you would want to know where the mighty god's

light lay hidden. . . . Now you are stretching out your greedy, insatiable hands towards our flocks. Why do you need riches? They merely stimulate your craving for more. You are the first man ever to have created hunger by having too much – so that the more you have the keener your desire for what you do not have.[50]

In another instance, having attempting to rally for battle his worn and demoralized troops, Alexander outlined his plans for the remainder of his campaign. He proposed to vanquish the rest of India, then Libya, and then land as far as the Pillars of Heracles. In a speech to his men, he vaunts, 'And to this empire there will be no boundaries but what god himself has made for the whole world.'[51] What the god has designed, he suggested, was godhood itself. Alexander continued:

Stand firm; for well you know that hardship and danger are the price of glory, and that sweet is the savor of a life of courage and of deathless renown beyond the grave.

Are you not aware that if Heracles, my ancestor, had gone no further than Tiryns or Argos – or even than the Peloponnese or Thebes – he could never have won the glory which changed him from a man into a god, actual or apparent? Even Dionysus, who is a god indeed, in a sense beyond what is applicable to Heracles, faced not a few laborious tasks; yet we have done more: we have passed beyond Nysa and we have taken the rock of Aornos which Heracles himself could not take.[52]

In peacetime or leisure, he yielded increasingly to vice and dissipation. Incessant drinking and whoring filled most days. He eventually even took up Persian dress and many of their customs, so much so that his own soldiers claimed that he was no longer a Macedonian.[53]

Book VII of Arrian's *Anabasis* begins with several tales concerning sages who openly opposed Alexander's ceaseless quest for glory.[54] Arrian sums the ceaseless ambition of Alexander the person:

> One thing, however, I feel I can say without fear of contradiction, and that is that his plans, whatever they were, had no lack of grandeur or ambition: he would never have remained idle in the enjoyment of any of his conquests, even had he extended his empire from Asia to Europe and from Europe to the British Isles. On the contrary, he would have continued to seek beyond them for unknown lands, as it was ever his nature, if he had no rival, to strive to better his own best.[55]

Alexander's march across the virtually impassable Gedrosian Desert is further evidence of his desire for immortality. According to Arrian, he chose the march, which would take him 60 days, simply because no one had ever crossed the scorching sands successfully with so large an army. But even in choosing the impossible, he was not entirely insensitive to the suffering of his troops. He marched ahead of them to serve as inspiration for them. At one point, when the slightest bit of water was spotted, scooped up, and given to Alexander to drink, the king poured the water into the sand – an act that proved 'as good as a drink for every man in the army'.[56] Nonetheless, the march was foolhardy, as it resulted in the needless loss of thousands of his men as well as thousands of the women and children who came along with them.[57]

Alexander was no megalomaniac, at least not in the sense of having a grossly exaggerated notion of what he could accomplish, for he had proven himself quite capable of doing much more than he had set out to do. He and his troops[58] truly had exceeded mortal men in deeds on the battlefield; there was nothing left for which to strive but to match or exceed the achievements of the heroes and gods – like Achilles, Heracles, and Dionysus – of his day. Moreover, at various stages of his life (e.g. his visit to the

Temple of Ammon in Siwah, Egypt) he received oracular confirmation of his godhood.

On the other hand, that so many thousands of people had to die during and beyond his Persian campaign in his gory quest for personal glory is inexcusable. Of his brutality, Victor Davis Hanson writes:

> Too many scholars like to compare Alexander to Hannibal or Napoleon. A far better match would be Hitler, who engineered a militarily brilliant but similarly brutal killing march into Russia during the summer and autumn of 1941. Both Alexander and Hitler were crack-pot mystics, intent solely on loot and plunder under the guise of bringing 'culture' to the East and 'freeing' oppressed peoples from a corrupt empire. Both were kind to animals, showed deference to women, talked constantly of their own destiny and divinity, and could be especially courteous to subordinates even as they planned the destruction of hundreds of thousands, and murdered their closest associates.[59]

Like Icarus,[60] Alexander aimed too high. He sought not to be a leader of men and a principled ruler, but rather a conqueror of nations and a god among men. Driven by an unslakable thirst for conquest, his courage was at bottom foolhardiness. Lacking self-control, Alexander could not have been happy. Arrian himself sums the disintegrative character of the conquering hero.

> [T]he splendid achievements of Alexander are the clearest possible proof that neither strength of body, nor noble blood, nor success in war even greater than Alexander's own – not even the realization of his dream of circumnavigating Libya and Asia and adding them both to his empire, together with Europe too – that none of these things, I say, can make a man happy, unless he can win one more victory in addition to those the world thinks so great – the victory over himself.[61]

True to his mentor Homer, Alexander's sense of morality was expressly and exclusively heroic. Like his hero Achilles, Alexander was content with the prospect of a short, glorious life. Curtius sums Alexander's own life in the latter's words:

> I could have been content with my father's inheritance, and within Macedonia's bounds have enjoyed a life of ease as I awaited old age without renown or distinction (though even inactive men cannot control their destiny and those who believe that a long life is the only good are often over-taken by a premature death). But no − I count my victories, not my years and, if I accurately compute fortune's favors to me, my life has been long.[62]

Diogenes the dog

The Stoic philosopher Posidonius lists Diogenes (404–323 B.C.), son of Hicesius, as one noteworthy for his progress toward wisdom.[63] Diogenes was an older contemporary of Aristotle and a native of Sinope. Upon coming to Athens, he became the pupil of a reluctant Anthisthenes,[64] who himself was swayed by the ideals of Socratic hardihood and Hera-clean hard living.[65] From Anthisthenes, Diogenes learned to live simply, without ornament. Biographer Diogenes Laertius says that, from watching a mouse scampering about, Diogenes of Sinope learned not to seek pleasan-tries, not to be afraid of the dark, and to adapt to existing circumstances.[66]

For Diogenes, as for Epicurus, happiness consisted of simple living. While Epicurus thought that simple living would maximize pleasure through avoidance of pain, Dio-genes, in contrast, chose simplicity because of his abhor-rence of luxury, extravagance, and custom. He is said to have acquired the name 'cynic' because his manner of living emulated that of a dog (Gr. *kuōn*).[67]

Though Diogenes thought that true happiness came through living virtuously and virtuous living came through living simply, he sought simplicity to an alarming, perhaps inhuman, extent. Diogenes' detestation of human conventions reduced life to a test of endurance. To endure the exigencies of life, he believed, was all there was to living a virtuous and 'happy' life. Consequently, music, geometry, astronomy, and other such studies he considered useless.[68]

To endure rightly, the philosophical life involves training for hardship. Such training can be either physical or mental. One can, for example, arrive at virtue and happiness from the physical path of gymnastics, for both physical and mental training are both essential to proper human living and each is attained through the habit of toil.[69] Diogenes Laertius writes of this Cynic's approach to cultivating toil: 'Nothing in life, however, he maintained, has any chance of succeeding without strenuous practice; and this is capable of overcoming anything. Accordingly, instead of useless toils, men should choose such as nature recommends, whereby they might live happily.'[70]

As Diogenes Laertius relates, Diogenes the Cynic's manner of speaking was abrupt, rude, and directly to the point. I cite some examples. To Lysias the druggist, who asked Diogenes whether the gods exist, Diogenes replied that they must, as he, Diogenes, was looking right at a god-forsaken wretch (i.e. Lysias).[71] Again, Alexander the Great supposedly once came to Diogenes, who was then sunning himself. When Alexander asked the beggar what a king, such as he, could grant Diogenes, the philosopher responded, 'Stand out of my light'.[72] Moreover, when some person took Diogenes into a magnificent house and asked him not to spit in the house, Diogenes, saying that he could find no more suitable place, spat in the man's face.[73] Diogenes is also said to have masturbated openly in the marketplace and to have remarked afterward that he wished it were as easy to relieve hunger.[74] Last, after being scolded for drinking in a tavern, he remarked, to the one rebuking him, that he also gets his hair cut in a barber's shop.[75]

Diogenes preached that one could learn to find the greatest pleasure in despising pleasure, and this alone reveals much. Diogenes was disgusted with the ways of people. Thus, it seems unlikely that he could have found pleasure in the full retreat from human conventions that he espoused, but only pain or, at best, a smug sullenness. The 'simple life', for the Cynic, could not have been a happy life. Like Socrates, some probably found him amusing and many even found him to be enlightening. His many disciples and the high regard that many, the Stoics especially, had for him attest to this. Yet this is where the similarities end. Most, I am sure, found him annoying, if not disgusting. Unlike Socrates, despising his fellow human beings, it seems likely that he must have despised himself also. Following the model proposed earlier in this chapter, if happiness requires personal integration and personal integration is psychical equilibrium, then it seems fair to conclude, since his soul tugged mightily in contrary directions, Diogenes could not have been happy.

Relevance for today

As should be evident by now, the Delphic inscription, *Know yourself*, was at the very heart of Greek culture – so much so that most ancient Greek ethicists, perhaps beginning with Heraclitus and Socrates, advocated personal integration as the first step toward living a happy life. Following Plato and Aristotle, being personally integrated was a matter of all of the parts of the soul functioning, under the governance of the rational part, for the good of the soul as a whole.

For many philosophers today, the Delphic injunction is perhaps more relevant as a heuristic for self-help
approaches to psychology than as a precept of serious philosophical inquiry. This is symptomatic of the liberal/
empirical strain that permeates much of philosophy today,
starting with thinkers such as David Hume and John Stuart
Mill. For many contemporary philosophers, philosophical
practice has become purely a matter of describing what
they observe to be the case. Metaphysical systems are
claimed to be informative only insofar as they tell us about
what goes on inside of the heads of philosophers, not insofar
as they relate to reality. Social goods, including virtues, are
deemed good only because they happen to be desired by
people, not because these are themselves worth choosing.
Scientific investigation is seen as a problem-solving enterprise, not one that is truth-generating.

What is perhaps most insidious about the liberal/empiri-
cal trend in modern ethical philosophy is the segregation of
individuals and institutions – what I call the 'Great
Divide' – as it manifests itself in three divisive tendencies
in contemporary philosophy.

First, following the nineteenth-century empiricist John
Stuart Mill, there is the tendency today to separate the
public and private realms and relegate ethical speculation
exclusively to the former. According to Mill, morality only
concerns the effects of one's interactions with others, for
better or worse. Whatever harm anyone does in private,
so long as it is self-contained, has no bearing on morality.
This, in effect, amounts to a splitting of the self: There is
the public or moral self, whose actions must be socially sen-
sitive, and the private and amoral self, whose actions need
not answer to anyone. These two selves can be as dissimilar
as Jekyll and Hyde, so long Hyde never goes public with
his viciousness. This, of course, is just what seems most

absurd: that one could, at least in principle, cultivate and keep separate two radically dissimilar persons in two separate realms.

Second, in keeping with David Hume (eighteenth century) and the Positivists of the twentieth century, there is the tendency to separate claims of fact (i.e. *It is raining outside*) from those of value (i.e. *Socrates is wise*), and allow only the former, since they are straightforwardly answerable to observable reality, to be cognitive or meaningful. Emotivists, for instance, believe that ethical utterances have only emotive, and not cognitive, meaning – that is, they merely report how the speaker *feels* about a certain moral issue at a given time.[76] Given that ethical utterances are non-cognitive, emotivism, in effect, diminishes the significance of ethical statements, which in turn makes light of the importance of ethics as a normative and regulative discipline for human activity. For instance, consider one who truly thinks that the utterance *Abortion is killing* does no more than reflect one's affective state at the time of the utterance. Now it would seem strange for this person to believe this and yet campaign vigorously against abortion, as the only rationale one could give is this: I want others to *feel* as I do about this issue. Vigorously campaigning against abortion only makes sense when one is convinced that, say, abortion *really is* the needless taking of a human life. Thus, endorsement of non-cognitive views of ethical claims leads to ethical lethargy and ethical irresponsibility.

Third, there is the liberal tendency today to privilege individuals over institutions axiologically in both political and ethical philosophy. In liberal political philosophy, especially in the neo-Kantian tradition,[77] persons are thought to be perfectly unencumbered and autonomous selves, who are not constituted by any of the experiences that shape their lives and not bound by communal ties. Persons are individuals in that they are perfectly free-choosing organisms and such selves, free of all encumbrances, certainly cannot be agents capable of self-knowledge.[78] In liberal ethical thinking, following Hume and Mill, individuals are thought to be essentially pleasure-seeking organisms, whose reason functions merely as an instrument of desire. Mill has gone so far as to argue that the freest expression of our impulses, untrammeled by social ties, is just what it means to be an individual. Such a conception of ethical agency, bereft of character, is incongruent with a conception of agents, who are capable of self-discovery.

All of this contrasts greatly with the Classical Greek view, where people were deemed 'political animals' and there could be no conception of self-knowledge outside of a community of community-oriented people. For Plato and Aristotle, reason functioned as the regulative principle of proper conduct – that is, as a tamer of the passions – and humans were believed to be incapable of happiness – the fullest expression of their humanity – outside of their *polis*.

With a focus on cultivating and maintaining excellence of character and evaluating the justness of an act by the goodness of the person committing that act (i.e. just desert), Classical Greek thought placed a premium on responsibility – guided both by a conception of justice as an ethical and political legislative principle and by a conception of individual, constituted by his choices and experiences, that is morally bound to his community and those in it.

Philosophers like Plato and Aristotle had, I believe, a broader and grander philosophical vision than politicians and philosophers generally have today. Theirs was an integrative ideal of binding people together happily for the common good. The first step to this process was self-integration and self-integration was essentially a rational process. Individuals were said to belong to political institutions by nature and there was no moral divide between institutions and individuals. What a person did that impacted on none other than himself was deemed just as much a moral action as an act that impacted on others. As Socrates in *Crito* states, 'All through my life, in any public activity in which I have participated, I am the same man as I am in my private life.'[79] This vision contrasts starkly with the divisive tendencies of the liberal/empirical ideal today or the Great Divide, which runs contrary to the Delphic ideal of personal integration.

Overall, I believe the Classical Greek notion of personal integration as a type of psychical harmony deserves reconsideration today. The chief merits of such views are the privileged position of reason in determining right action, the rejection of the notion that ethical claims are meaningless or non-cognitive, the idea that all actions (both personal and public) are ethically relevant to shaping one's character, and the conception that humans cannot find happiness outside of a community of people.

Let me now turn briefly to some comments concerning the Delphic integrative ideal and the three prominent figures in the second part of this chapter. Of these three, only Plato's Socrates seems genuinely interested in ethical improvement through genuine psychical stability. For Socrates, excellence of character is a matter of the pursuit of knowledge or wisdom and this very pursuit, Socrates tends to think, results not only in self-betterment, but also the betterment of others.[80] Socrates adds that he has devoted his life to this divine calling and his extreme poverty is a witness to his obedience to the god.

Notwithstanding the political instability of his time, Socrates' withdrawal from political activity and insistence that one can best 'fight for justice' by leading a private life[81] seems plainly absurd. Were it applied straightforwardly to the Athens of his day, it would have led to cessation of political activity and, thus, paralysis. Yet paralysis was not an option, for Athens was at war with Sparta for 28 of Socrates' final 33 years of life and wholesale self-reflection within the *polis* would not have been desirable, to say the least.

What Socrates is suggesting, and this is a point as relevant today as it was during his time, is that each person should attend first and foremost to developing excellence within him and place this ahead of all other concerns, for, in this way, political corruption would cease and events like Greek fighting against Greek would seem bootless. I return to the drunken Alcibiades (see Chapter 1), an Athenian general during the Peloponnesian War of dubious character, who illustrates this point while eulogizing Socrates at the end of the *Symposium*:

> He (Socrates) always traps me, you see, and he makes me admit that my political career is a waste of time, while all that matters is just what I most neglected: my personal shortcomings, which cry out for the closest attention. So I refuse to listen to him, for, like the Sirens, he could make me stay by his side till I die.[82]

Thus, the real lesson of Socratic dialectic is this: To live a good life, a happy life, one must begin by turning inward.[83]

The failures of Diogenes and Alexander, in contrast, were failures of personal integration. Both men had incredible capacities for goodness that went unrealized, as each had a soul with inharmonious parts. For Alexander, it was his unstinted, pathological desire for conquest and an unregulated inclination toward immoderation. Diogenes, in contrast, perhaps made himself the victim of a self-dislike projected outward that resulted in disdain for everything around him. The tragedy of such failures is doubly felt. For as Plato says in *Republic*, 'the best nature fares worse, when unsuitably nurtured, than an ordinary one'.[84]

Notes

[1] That is, allowing for periodic release of id impulses.

[2] Sigmund Freud, *The Ego and the Id* (New York: Norton, 1960), 15.

[3] *R.* 434d–444e.

[4] *R.* 435d.

[5] From the Greek word, *logos*, which is generally translated as 'reason', but has numerous other meanings. Plato's choice of *to logistikon* is, of course, intended to convey other meanings of *logos* – such as 'command', 'proportion', and 'ratio' – which 'rational soul' cannot.

[6] *R.* 435c–441c, esp. 437a–439b.

[7] *Phdr.* 246a–b and 253d–254e.

[8] Overall, Freud is certainly more honest about the probability of any one person attaining psychical balance, given our psychical constitution. See *Civilization and Its Discontents*, 'Timely Thoughts and War and Death', and 'Why War?'

[9] *R.* 443d–444a (Grube translation). Plato, *Five Dialogues: Euthyphro, Apology, Crito, Meno, Phaedo,* trans. G. M. A. Grube (Indianapolis: Hackett, 1981).

[10] See Chapter 2 as well as *EN* VI (1139a6–18).

[11] *EN* 1102a15–1103a4.

[12] *EN* 1166a10–30 (Irwin's translation of *EN* used in this section). Aristotle, *Nicomachean Ethics*, trans. Terence Irwin (Indianapolis: Hackett, 1985). Cf. Epicurus *PD* XXXIII–XXXVIII.

[13] *EN* 1166b2–23.

[14] We cannot really know that Plato's depiction of Socrates is accurate. Two other contemporary writers offer different, less praiseworthy, accounts. Xenophon's characterization is not as laudable as that of Plato. The playwright Aristophanes refers to Socrates in four of his surviving works – the *Clouds* being entirely about Socrates and showing him as a buffoon. Aristotle, writing years after the death of Socrates, adds insight to the philosopher in comments scattered throughout his corpus.

[15] The charge at 17b–c is that Socrates is a student of all things in the earth and sky (i.e. an atheistic natural philosopher who attempts to explain everything without the agency of the gods) and one who makes the worse argument the stronger (i.e. a Sophist).

In *Euthyphro*, Socrates is accused of being a maker of gods: One who creates new gods and does not believe in old ones (3b). *Crito* says that Socrates studies things in the sky and below the earth (18b–c, 19b and 23d), makes the worse argument to be stronger (18b-c, 19b and 23d), does not believe in the gods (18c and 23d), creates new gods without believing in the gods of city (24b and 26b), and teaches these things to others (19b).

[16] An Athenian general and one of the three generals sent on the disastrous Syracusean expedition. He was Socrates' favorite pupil and one whose character could not seemingly be tamed.

[17] Plato's uncle and the leader of the 30 tyrants, who temporarily toppled the Athenian democracy in 411 B.C. This tyranny lasted only four months.

[18] *Ap*. 21c–e.

[19] *Ap*. 22b–c.

[20] *Ap*. 22d–e.

[21] *Ap*. 23a–b.

[22] *Ap*. 23b (Grube's translation). See Plato, *Five Dialogues*, 1985.

[23] Socrates offers up his poverty as a proof that he was sent by the gods (23b and 31c).

[24] The dialectical focus of Plato's *Euthyphro* is piety.

[25] *Ap*. 24b–27e.

[26] Instead of the usual manner of proceeding in the court.

[27] That is, from the perspective of Socrates' (or Plato's) own thought. *Ap*. 25b–26c.

[28] Clearly the most contentious claim in the argument, yet one to which Socrates consistently adhered. See *Ap*. 26a, *Prt*. 345d, 358c–d, *Meno* 77, 78, *Grg*. 466e, 467b, *Laws* 688b, 731c, 734b, 860d, *R*. 382a, 413a, 492e, 577e, 589c, *Phlb*. 22b, *Sph*. 228c, 230a, and *Ti*. 86d.

[29] *Ap*. 26b.

[30] See, for example, Aristophanes' *Wasps*, 563–71.

[31] *Ap*. 34c–35c.

[32] *Ap*. 29a–b.

[33] Ap. 32a–d.

[34] *Ap*. 29c–30b. Cf. *Phd*. 60e–61b, where Socrates, in prison, relates a recurring dream where he is enjoined to cultivate music (i.e. philosophy).

[35] *Ap.* 35d.

[36] *Ap.* 36b–e. A magistrates' hall, where dignitaries and victors of athletic festivals were lavishly fed and entertained.

[37] The equivalent of 100 *drachmae*. Six *drachmae* was the average pay of a daily laborer in late fifth-century Athens.

[38] *Ap.* 38b. After each side made its case, there was no formal discussion by the jurors on the issues and no judge to mediate proceedings. Each juror made an immediate decision, which was decided by a majority of votes. Either the prosecution won or the defendant; there was no compromise allowed. Buckley gives a fine account of such Athenian courts of law (1996: 265–73).

[39] *Ap.* 39c–d.

[40] *Ap.* 40a.

[41] For other references to Socrates' *daimonion*, see *Ap.* 26b–28a, *Euthd.* 272e–273c, *Alc.* I.103a, *Thg.* 128d–129e, and *Smp.* 202e.

[42] *Ap.* 40a–c.

[43] *Ap.* 42a.

[44] *Ap.* 26c.

[45] *An.* I.12 (Sélincourt's translation). Arrian, *The Campaigns of Alexander* (New York: Penguin Books, 1971).

[46] Plutarch mentions ethical and political instruction as well as instruction in Aristotle's esoteric works, medicine, and literature. *Vit.* (Alexander, 7–8).

[47] If this is the case, it was not a lasting lesson. For Alexander often, especially in the later years of his campaign, showed a predilection for Persian dress and custom, much to the dislike of his Macedonian soldiers (e.g. *An.* VII.6).

[48] *Vit.* (Alexander, 8).

[49] His biographers (perhaps unwittingly) generally exaggerate greatly the extent to which Alexander was outnumbered in each of his major campaigns.

[50] *Hist.* VII.viii.12–20. Quintus Curtius Rufus, *The History of Alexander*, trans. John Yardley (New York: Penguin, 1984).

[51] *An.* V.26.

[52] *An.* V.26.

[53] *Hist.* VII.viii.12–20. This, of course, may have been a means of trying to integrate Persians into his army and secure peace in the Persian regions he had captured.

54 *An.* VII.1–4.
55 *An.* VII.2.
56 *An.* VI.24–26.
57 This march might also have been undertaken so as to punish his troops for their mutinous decision not to continue the eastern campaign.
58 With, of course, the aid of the technology of his time (e.g. engineers, cartographers, scouts, siege engines).
59 Victor Davis Hanson, *The Wars of the Ancient Greeks* (London: Cassell, 2000), 189–90.
60 According to mythological tradition, Icarus had waxen wings fashioned for him by him father Daedalus in order to escape from Crete. Failing to heed the warning of his father, he flew too high above the earth and the hot sun melted the wax and caused him to fall to his death.
61 *An.* IV.8. Curtius tends to attribute Alexander's successes to extraordinary strength of character and good fortune and his downfall to youth and excessive good fortune.
62 *Hist.* IX.vi.19.
63 Socrates too. *Vit.* VII.91.
64 The father of Cynicism.
65 *Vit.* VI.3 (Hicks' translation). Diogenes Laertius, *Diogenes Laertius: Lives of Eminent Philosophers*, vols i and ii, trans. R. D. Hicks, Loeb Classical Library (Cambridge, MA: Harvard University Press, 1991).
66 *Vit.* VI.22.
67 It may also be that Cynics acquired their name because they would meet at the *Kynosarges*, a gymnasium outside of Athens for those not of pure Athenian blood.
68 *Vit.* VI.73.
69 *Vit.* VI.70.
70 *Vit.* VI.71.
71 *Vit.* VI.42.
72 *Vit.* VI.38.
73 *Vit.* VI.32.
74 *Vit.* VI.46 and 69.
75 *Vit.* VI.66.

[76] And this feeling is conveyed emotively to others in order to evoke a similar emotive response on this issue.

[77] E.g. see especially John Rawls' *A Theory of Justice* (Cambridge, MA: Harvard University Press, 1971), but also Ronald Dworkin's *Sovereign Virtue* (Cambridge, MA: Harvard University Press, 2000) and Robert Nozick's *Anarchy, State and Utopia* (New York: Basic Books, MA, 1974).

[78] See Michael Sandel, 'Justice and the Good', *Liberalism and Its Critics*, ed. Michael Sandel (New York: New York University Press, 1984), 172.

[79] 33a.

[80] Familiarity with the Platonic corpus reveals that Socrates' method of verbal exchange is often less-than-friendly to interlocutors. See Richard Robinson, 'Elenchus', *Philosophy of Socrates*, ed. G. Vlastos (Cambridge: Cambridge University Press, 1971), 91.

[81] *Ap.* 32a.

[82] *Smp.* 216a.

[83] *Laches* shows that Socratic elenchus really reduces to self-knowledge. Nicias states that dialectic begins with some topic or other, until it turns to personal questions. He suggests that such self-illumination is painful, since it discloses one's ignorance, but it is ultimately worth pursuing. 'For me there is nothing unusual or unpleasant in being examined by Socrates, but I realized some time ago that the conversation would not be about the boys but about ourselves, if Socrates were present' (187e–188c). In *Charmides*, Socrates adds that his method of dialectical examination is not directed only at self-betterment, but also at the betterment of others. Socrates says: 'Oh come, how could you possibly think that even if I were to refute everything you say, Critias, I would be doing it for any other reason than the one I would give for a thorough investigation of my own statements – the fear of unwittingly thinking I know something when I do not. And this is what I claim to be doing now, examining the argument for my own sake primarily, but perhaps also for the sake of my friends. Or don't you believe it to be for the common good, or for that of most men, that the state of each existing thing should become clear?' (166c–d) See Plato, *Laches and Charmides*, trans. Rosamond Kent Sprague (Indianapolis: Hackett, 1992).

[84] *R.* 491d.

6
Happiness and 'Political' Integration

> Is there any greater evil we can mention for a city than
> that which tears it apart and makes it many instead of one?
> Or any greater good than that which binds it together and
> makes it one?   Plato, *Republic*

THE FOCUS IN THE PREVIOUS CHAPTER was personal integration as a necessary condition for moral excellence and
a happy life. In this chapter, I extend this notion and
argue that happiness essentially involves not only personal
integration, but also political integration. By 'political',
however, I do not mean the narrow, modern sense of the
word as it relates to the affairs or conduct of government.
Instead I offer a definition more in keeping with the ancient
Greek notion of the word. By 'political', let us understand
'of or relating to active participation in the betterment of
the affairs of one's community'.

    After some remarks about the nature of the Greek *polis*
in Classical Greece, I look at the final days of Socrates in
Plato's *Crito*. Drawing from *Crito*, I argue that Socrates is

not only a model for personal integration (see previous chapter), he is also a model for political integration. I then examine Plato's tripartitioning of the *polis* in *Republic* and how his three-part soul lines up isomorphically with his three-part *polis*. Next, I draw from Books VIII and IX of Aristotle's *EN*, which deal with friendship and different levels of 'friendly' relationships within a *polis*. Last, I summarize the Classical Greek view of a person's relationship to and role in his political community and offer some suggestions about what we might learn from it today.

People and *poleis*

During the Dark Age (c. 1200–c. 776 B.C.), ancient Greece was predominated by kingships. When the Dark Age ended, there was an explosion of people on mainland Greece. There was massive expansionism across the Aegean into Ionia and the Black Sea region and even westward to Italy. Greeks acquired an alphabet from the Phoenicians. Literature began to flourish. Philosophy and science emerged and took root. Geometry was introduced into art. New tools made agriculture easier. Laws were codified, then reformed. This was the age of poets (Homer, Hesiod, and Aeschylus), historians (Herodotus), politicians and statesmen (Draco, Solon, and Cleisthenes), and philosophers (the Milesian philosophers, Pythagoreans, Heraclitus, and Parmenides). This was the age of the Greek city-state or *polis*.

Poleis were large civic units that emerged during the eighth century B.C. and thrived until roughly the death of Alexander of Macedon (323 B.C). In general, a *polis* consisted of primary citizens (usually males only), females and youths (being protected under the law, but being without say in the law), and secondary citizens (free-born natives without influence in government, resident aliens, and slaves). While the first *poleis* were generally political aristocracies, most of these evolved into democracies or oligarchies.

As a *polis* was an independent political unit with its own laws and customs, it was more the norm than the exception that there would be fighting among *poleis*. Therefore, it is wrong to think of Greek *poleis* as parts of a unitary Greek nation-state as one might think of the 50 states being parts of the United States or even the European nations as parts of an economic community of nations. Still, in time, proximity, utility, common language, common ancestry, and in some cases sheer necessity exacted kinship or amicable relationships between some *poleis* and others, if only temporarily.

By the fifth century B.C., the Athenian *polis* had evolved from a political entity, based on political alliances between like-minded aristocratic factions that centered on the Areopagus, to one where political power was rooted in an appeal to the people. The 'people', however, meant male, Athenian citizens and this was some small subset of the Athenian populace. Moreover, though each citizen in principle was allowed equal access to political participation, many citizens, like farmers, could not practice this, due to the demands of their daily life.

In contrast to Athenian democracy, Sparta was an oligarchic *polis*, whose power was in the hands of 30 elders (of whom, two were kings), an ecclesiastical council, and five ephors (who functioned in many governmental capacities and were elected from the citizenry itself).

Notwithstanding the differences between *poleis*, by Classical times, so entrenched was the notion of each *polis* as a relatively self-sufficient political unit that philosophers like Socrates, Plato, and Aristotle could not imagine anything smaller or larger having any sort of stability, vigor, and longevity.

Plato on persons and *poleis*

There is no finer picture of this unitary notion of *poleis* given from antiquity than that left to us by Plato in *Republic*. He states: 'Is there any greater evil we can mention for a city than that which tears it apart and makes it many instead of one? Or any greater good than that which binds it together and makes it one?'[1] For Plato, political stability is best achieved when the various parts of a *polis* each work for the good of the *polis* as a whole.

To get clear on just what Plato has in mind here, let us return to the tripartite model of the human soul in Book IV of *Republic* that we examined in the previous chapter. When a human organism is functioning properly (i.e. when a person is just), each of the three parts of the soul – the rational, spirited, and appetitive parts – work together for the good of the person as a whole. The key here is regard for and cultivation of reason.

The situation with *poleis* is the same, he thinks, as persons and *poleis* are remarkably similar both structurally and functionally. Like a person, a *polis* is an organism of sorts.[2] He writes in an exchange between Socrates and Glaucon. Socrates begins:

> [W]hen one of us hurts his finger, the entire organism that binds body and soul together into a single system under the ruling part within it is aware of this, and the whole feels the pain together with the part that suffers. And the same can be said about any part of a man, with regard either to the pain it suffers or to the pleasure it experiences when it finds relief. . . .
>
>   Certainly. And, as for your question, the city with the best government is most like such a person.
>
>   Then, whenever anything good or bad happens to a single one of its citizens, such a city above all others will say

that the affected part is its own and will share in the pleasure
or pain as a whole.
  If it has good laws, that must be so.[3]

Like the human soul, a *polis* too is tripartite: to the rational
soul, there corresponds in a *polis* the complete guardians
(Gr. *panteleis phylakes*) or rulers; to the spirited soul, there
corresponds the guardians (Gr. *phylakes*); and to the appetitive soul, there corresponds the laborers (Gr. *demiourgoi*[4]).
  In addition, the primary virtues that characterize individuals with excellent character – wisdom, courage, self-
control, and justice – are also attributes of the *polis* and the
three types of people living within. The complete guardians, with the responsibility of ruling a *polis*, must possess
wisdom.[5] The guardians, who preserve the laws and fight
on behalf of the *polis*, must be courageous.[6] Self-control,
which is a mastery of sorts of pleasures and desires, must be
an attribute of both those who rule and those who are ruled
in a well-running *polis*.[7] Last, justice, roughly understood as
'the having and doing of one's own', must also be possessed
by each class. Justice, which is what *Republic* is principally
about, is then a matter of each class functioning for the
good of the *polis*.[8]
  Plato's point is that, as all parts of a person's soul must
work together for the psychical well-being of that person,

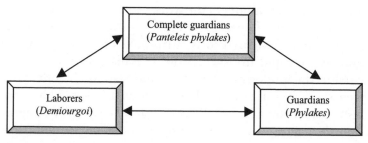

Figure 6.1 Plato's tripartite *polis*

so too in a *polis* must all persons do their part for their *polis* to be well and thrive. The type of political community that Plato describes is one in which individuals live and work principally for the good of their *polis*, not for themselves. In other words, individuals exist for the sake of the *polis*, not the converse (which seems to be the received view in today's free societies). In such a manner, a *polis* flourishes and, though no one group within a *polis* will be outstandingly happy, each will be as happy as it can in a healthy political community.[9]

Socrates' love of Athens

Plato's *Crito* is one of Plato's best illustrations of the principle of organicism at work. Like *Apology*, *Crito* is one of Plato's most studied philosophical works. Here Plato again gives us a vivid portrait of Socrates, but this time he focuses on his political, not his personal, side – his dutiful attachment to Athens.

The dialogue centers on a visit by Crito to Socrates, who sits in prison, a few days prior to his death. It can be readily broken into two parts: a series of arguments by Crito (44b–46a), attempting to prove to Socrates that the latter should escape from prison, and Socrates' response to these arguments in the remainder of the work (46b–54e). In stark contrast to Socrates' measured reply to them, Crito's many arguments, condensed in text from 44b to 46a, are given quickly, in rapid-fire succession, as if his goal was to overwhelm the philosopher rather than persuade him with well-thought-out reasons. Plato tells us that Crito has often visited Socrates in prison before,[10] so we can easily imagine that they have had similar conversations on several occasions. Crito's haste, then, is best explained by desperation: He is throwing out argument after argument in an almost

futile attempt to see whether there is anything at all that he
can say to convince Socrates to escape. Some of the reasons
that Crito spews out are these.

(R_1) I shall lose a friend whom I can never replace (44b).
(R_2) I shall be disgraced in the eyes of others, for many will
        think that I am unwilling to spend money to save you
        (44b–c).
(R_3) No harm will come to us, if we help you escape (44e).
(R_4) There is money enough for you to escape (44e–45a).
(R_5) Men will love you in other places (45b–c).
(R_6) You are playing into the hands of your enemies by
        willingly going to your death (45c).
(R_7) You are betraying your children (45c–d).
(R_8) You profess virtue in all actions, yet you choose the
        easiest (non-virtuous) path (45d).
(R_9) You will bring shame upon yourself and us by not
        escaping (45e–46a).

Socrates goes on to dismiss most of Crito's reasons as
being based on the opinions of the majority, who persuade
more by strength of voice, than by strength of evidence.
Only the opinions of the wise (i.e. experts) should be
valued. The many, in contrast, are foolish and lack understanding.[11] At 48d, he specifically mentions questions relating to money (R_2 and R_4), reputation (R_5 and R_9), and
upbringing of children (R_7) and categorizes these as opinions of the many. Socrates, however, does latch on to one
of Crito's arguments. He says:

> For us, however, since our argument leads to this, the only
> valid consideration, as we were saying just now, is whether
> we should be acting rightly in giving money and gratitude to
> those who will lead me out of here, and ourselves helping
> with the escape, or whether in truth we shall do wrong in
> doing all this.[12]

Here Socrates says flatly that only reason eight deserves consideration: whether it is right for him to escape when the Athenians have voted that he should be put to death. Whether or not he should die is of no importance, for it is not life, but the good life that is to be desired, and the good life, the beautiful life, and the just life are one and the same.[13]

From 49b–e, Socrates puts forth the following argument. At each step, Crito agrees. Formally presented:

(P₁) One must never do wrong.
(P₂) Returning wrong for wrong is wrong.
(P₃) So, one must never return wrong for wrong (P₁ and P₂).

Socrates stops here, but he does so with the understanding that Crito will implicitly conclude, from proposition three and what had been said earlier, the following:

(P₄) So, if escaping from prison is wrong (or returning wrong for wrong) [for one sentenced by law to imprisonment], then Socrates should not escape ((P₁ or P₂) and P₃).

The rest of the dialogue is, in some sense, an investigation of whether antecedent of this conditional is true.[14]

Next, Socrates attempts to show that he has the greatest regard for the laws of Athens and that he is contractually (and morally) bound to obey them.[15] What I call the 'Main Argument' is sketched at 49e and filled out from 49e to 53a. It concerns Socrates' 'agreement' with his *polis* and may be simply spelled out as follows.

(Q₁) One should fulfill every agreement (49e).
(Q₂) Socrates has an agreement with his *polis* (many arguments in support of this from 49e–53a).
(Q₃) So, Socrates should fulfill his agreement with his *polis*.

Socrates, then, has this to say concerning all that his *polis* has given him. Athens has brought Socrates into the world, nurtured him, and educated him. So, as an offspring (and servant) of his *polis*, Socrates is not on equal footing with it. In other words, he has no more right to ruin his *polis* than he would to ruin his father. Yet a *polis* is more to be revered than one's parents, even one's ancestors, and it counts higher among the gods and all wise men. Therefore, Socrates has a moral duty to obey Athens (or persuade it of its wrongdoing[16]), but he cannot disobey it.[17]

At 52a–d, Socrates gives several reasons to show that he was certainly aware of his agreement with Athens while he lived in Athens. He asserts that he has been the most consistent citizen of all Athenians (since he has never left Athens, except when on military duty), that he has never spent time in another *polis*, and that he has never had any desire to know another *polis* or its laws. Furthermore, Socrates states that he so loves Athens that he could have but did not assess his punishment as exile when he was found guilty.

Still of all the arguments that Socrates gives, the most compelling is surprisingly stated quite casually.[18] This argument is a natural extension of the Main Argument presented above. It may be (charitably) fleshed out as follows:

(R$_1$) All who break an agreement with their *polis* are destroyers of laws.

(R$_2$) All who destroy laws corrupt the young and the ignorant.

(R$_3$) So, all who break an agreement with a *polis* are corrupters of the young and the ignorant (R$_1$ and R$_2$).

Consequently, if Socrates should break his agreement with Athens, he reasons, he would prove the jury's verdict true: he would be a corrupter of youth.

At the end of the dialogue, as if to clear up any possible doubts that might remain, Socrates addresses some of Crito's other arguments for escape. These, recall, Socrates dismissed as arguments of the many. Should Socrates escape, his friends would likely be driven into exile and lose their Athenian citizenship (with all of its benefits), or at least lose their property. Moreover, Socrates himself would become an enemy of any *polis* he enters, as he, being one who disobeyed the sentence of the jury, would be perceived as a destroyer of laws. In addition, as a destroyer of laws, it would be disgraceful for him thereafter to practice philosophy. Furthermore, escaping and moving his children to another *polis* would deprive them of the many benefits of their Athenian citizenship, one of which is the opportunity for the best possible education.[19]

In summary, this dialogue shows that Socrates has the highest regard for Athens and the excellence of its laws. He realizes that he can never equitably repay the benefits that he has received from his *polis*, though he has devoted his life to its betterment. In the end, he must pay back as best he can, even if this means giving his very life.

This summary, however, does not seem to sit well with what Plato says about Socrates' defense trial in *Apology*. In *Apology*, Socrates clearly believes that he was wrongly accused and wrongly convicted of corrupting the youth of Athens. Recall, for instance, that he proposes as his fine free meals at the Prytaneum.[20]

Yet, let us assume that Socrates has been wrongfully accused and convicted by the *polis* (i.e. the jury). So long as the *polis'* error is one of ignorance – and it must be, since no one can knowingly do wrong[21] – the apposite remedy is knowledge or truth. Thus, Socrates has no right to punish Athens or disobey its decrees.[22] Instead, he must try to persuade the *polis* of its wrongdoing. Failing to do so, he can only obey its decrees.[23]

In going to his death, however, Socrates both obeys and persuades. He is telling every Athenian that he is willing to obey the decrees of Athens, even if it costs him his life. This is excellence of character in its highest form: civic and political duty before personal gain. Moreover, Socrates is reminding all Athenians that it is the *polis* that is ultimately responsible for all that is truly good in their lives and that each person has a sacred duty to obey it at whatever price.

Friendship in Classical Greece

Before concluding, since this is a chapter on political integration, it is fitting to say something about one of the most important types of 'political' bonds in antiquity as well as today – the bond of friendship (Gr. *philia*). Here I return to Aristotle's *Nicomachean Ethics* (*EN*), which arguably contains the richest philosophical account of friendship ever composed.

The significance of this special bond for Aristotle for leading a politically integrated life is shown by noting that, of the ten books of his *EN*, he devotes two of the books, Books VIII and IX (roughly, one-fifth of the work), exclusively to an account of *philia*. Scholars generally translate *philia* as 'friendship', though the word also connotes 'affectionate ties' or 'a binding of discordant elements'. I follow the customary translation of 'friendship' for *philia* throughout, with the understanding that this translation is not suitable for many instances of the Greek word as Aristotle employs it in the *EN*.

Aristotle tells us that friendship is a virtue that is indispensable for a good life. The rich and poor need friends and affection, and so do the young and old. Even animals, in a way, share friendship.[24]

Friends are 'the greatest external good', because men, as he is wont to say, are naturally political.[25] In addition, the pursuit of happiness is an activity and even the most god-like and seemingly solitary activity, contemplation, is bettered when it is shared with friends. Moreover, even the most virtuous person needs someone upon whom to confer benefits.[26]

At VIII.2, he elaborates three necessary conditions for friendship. First, he says, the object of one's filial affection must have a soul. Second, this ensouled object of affection must itself be capable of affection and must return it. Last, each party must be aware that the friendship is reciprocated.[27]

There are, he says in VIII.3, three kinds of friendship: that of pleasure (Gr. *hēdonē*), that of utility (Gr. *chrēsimon*), and that of goodness (Gr. *agathon*). Friendship based on utility, he argues, is transitory, for what is deemed useful changes over time. Thus, such filial bonds, found especially among the old, dissolve as soon as the cause of their friendship is removed. Likewise, friendship based on pleasure, found especially among the young, is fickle and perhaps even less durable than that of pleasure. Friendship based on goodness, though, is based on the inherent goodness of each party and, as what is good is unchanging, such friendships are among equals and endure.

Now friendships may occur among those who are equal in excellence and those who are unequal – the former types of friendship being more durable than the latter. Friendships among virtuous people are rare, however, because excellence of character is rare, but, when such friendships occur, they are complete. He describes complete friendship as follows:

> [C]omplete friendship is the friendship of good people simi-lar in virtue; for they wish goods in the same way to each other insofar as they are good, and they are good in their own right. Now those who wish goods to their friend for the

friend's own sake are friends most of all; for they have this attitude because of the friend himself, not coincidentally. Hence these people's friendship lasts as long as they are good; and virtue is enduring.[28]

Moreover, at VIII.8 he adds:

Equality and similarity, and above all the similarity of those who are similar in being virtuous, is friendship. For virtuous people are enduringly [virtuous] in their own right, and enduring [friends] to each other. They neither request nor provide assistance that requires base actions, but, you might even say, prevent this. For it is proper to good people to avoid error themselves and not to permit it in their friends.[29]

By implication, friendships based on pleasure and utility are coincidental; complete friendship is based on the excellence of the other's character and, consequently, it is more capable of lasting. Unlike friendships based on utility or pleasure, complete friendship endures because what is good is its cause and what is good is enduring.

Consistent with what Plato says in *Symposium*, good friends aim at loving more than being loved, and this love is proportional to the character of a friend.[30] Thus, Aristotle adds, friendships take time to form. Quick friendships, in contrast, dissolve easily, for they bind without love and form without reason.[31]

Since true friendships, nurtured by love and reason, can only flourish with time, the number of truly good friends cannot be many. In such a manner, true friendships are similar to erotic relationships:

[I]ndeed it even seems impossible to be an extremely close friend to many people. That is why it also seems impossible to be passionately in love with many people, since passionate erotic love tends to be excess of friendship, and one has this for one person; hence also one has extremely close friendship for a few people.[32]

Moreover, it is extraordinarily difficult, because of limited personal resources, to be good toward many people at the same time.[33]

How many friends, then, should one have? The number of friends, Aristotle says, is like the amount of seasoning on one's food. Just as too much seasoning on food overwhelms its taste, many friends are superfluous and a hindrance to good living. A few friends are sufficient for a good life, 'just as a little seasoning on food is enough'.[34]

At VIII.7 and 11–12, Aristotle discusses friendship among unequals: ruler and ruled, parents and children, man and wife, brother and brother (presumably, older and younger), and master and slave. He argues, almost algorithmically, that the affection in a relationship among unequals must be proportional to the relative excellence of character of each person. In other words, for such an implausible relationship to succeed for any amount of time, the better person must be loved more than the one who is inferior. Only in this way can such friendships occur and have any chance of enduring.[35]

Nevertheless, making a just return according to one's comparative worth in such friendships, especially for the inferior parties, is rarely possible. Inferiors must do all that they are capable of doing, though this will generally fall short of the better person's due.[36]

Not surprisingly, those most worthy of love are philosophers. What they give us, he says, cannot be measured by money.

> And it would seem that the same sort of return should also be made to those who have shared philosophy in common with

us. For its worth is not measured by money, and no equivalent honor can be paid; but it is enough, presumably, to do
what we can, as we do towards gods and parents.[37]

Relevance for today

From what we have seen in this and in prior chapters, one of
the most distinctive features of Classical Greek ethics, epitomized by Plato and Aristotle, is its communitarianism – its
subordination of duty to oneself to duty to the *polis* or, in a
manner of speaking, its subordination of ethics to politics.[38]
For Plato and Aristotle, personal value makes sense only
insofar as persons are responsible and contributing members of their *polis*, which is deemed to have a worth that
exceeds or is independent of the particular individuals in it
at a given time. The order and justice in a *polis* are not acci-
dental. A *polis* is just not because it happens to have at some
time certain citizens in it who are just, but because justice
requires (perhaps even constitutionally) that it have in it a
certain number of just citizens, whosoever they might be, at
all times to ensure order and stability – that is, to ensure
happiness.

The situation is otherwise in many, if not most, free societies today. The strength of a state or nation is deemed principally a matter of its economic stability and the purchasing
power of the individuals in it. Ever increasingly, economic
considerations drive politics and a consumerist ideology
drives economics. The underlying morality of consumerist
political ideology is radical individualism, where a state or
nation exists *only* to meet the needs of each of the individuals
in it, however unnecessary these 'needs' may be. People are
content to refrain from all talk of good and bad, virtue and
vice – perhaps because of the atrocities committed by tota-
litarians, who waved the flag of virtue and who paid lip

service to communitarian ideals while they viciously slaughtered countless thousands of people and imposed solidarity by dictatorial or tyrannical means. In fact, it has become passé to speak of any goods being universal or even species-specific. On the consumerist model, the goodness of something is determined wholly by the demand for it, which is ever-changing, not by some property intrinsic to that thing.

In America, for instance, liberty was a good in the early republic as a moral and democratic standard of communal strength, based on the character of the individuals in that community. This was a rational and perfectionist ideal insofar as people strove to better themselves as persons in order to solidify themselves and their communities. Today this perfectionist ideal – a freedom, guided by reason, to pursue betterment of character, what may be called *freedom to* – has been supplanted by an anti-perfectionist notion of freedom – the liberty both to get one's own share of the available goods and to be left in peace to enjoy them in private, what I call *freedom from*. Radical individualism or *freedom from*, if what I have said about happiness as integration is correct, is an unstable, degenerative ideal. This is liberty without regard for the *community* of individuals.

Of course, recognition that the radical individualism of certain free societies today is a degenerative ideal is not to say that Classical Greek communitarianism is without defect. Classical Greek communitarianism suffers from axiologically privileging *poleis* at the expense of the individuals in them. Avoiding the mistake of radical individualism – thinking of human institutions as existing primarily, if not only, to serve the needs of each and every institutionalized person – it makes the contrary mistake of thinking that individuals exist principally to serve the needs of human institutions. On such a view, the chance for human flourishing, through plurality and equality of resources and freedom of opportunity, seems unhealthily restricted.

Both extremes, then, are wrong. The correct relationship between individual and community, *freedom to* above, is something in between the extreme individualist philosophy implicitly endorsed by many democratic societies today and Classical Greek communitarianism. This middle ground is proper political integration. Civilized communities today are collections of individuals with common interests and aims and these individuals thrive only insofar as each person recognizes that his own good is inextricably tied to the good of every other person in his community.

In this regard, I have tried to show in this chapter that Socrates, as depicted in Plato's *Crito*, is the embodiment of a politically integrated citizen of Athens. R. E. Allen has this to say about Socrates' concern for the betterment of self, others, *polis*, and even cosmos:

> Virtue and justice imply concern for the good of others. Diotima (in *Symposium*) will claim that the works of Eros issue in education; Socrates, in the *Euthydemus* (275a), says he desires that Cleinas should become as good as possible, and this, indeed, defined Socrates' peculiar mission to Athens: 'I go about doing nothing but persuading you, young and old, to care not for the body or money in place of, or so much as, excellence of soul' (*Apology* 30a). If the pursuit of happiness is inherently self-regarding – in one's own interest – it is also inherently other-regarding – in the interest of others: concern for one's own good is implicated, not accidentally but essentially, with the common good. ... Moral psychology has a metaphysical foundation; self-interest implies community, and community, universality.[39]

Before finishing, there is another, greater issue – challenging the Classical Greek notion of political health and stability – that I would like to address next, since it pervades much of contemporary thought on the limits of human happiness in 'civilized societies' and it ties in neatly with radical individualism's insistence that each person's happiness is a matter of fulfilling as many of their desires as possible within the constraints of institutionalization. In 1930, the eminent psychoanalyst Sigmund Freud wrote a groundbreaking work, *Civilization and Its Discontents*. In this work, Freud claims to have made a monumental discovery: a civilization flourishes *at the expense of* the health and happiness of each of the individuals in it.

Freud – beginning with the philosophical question, *What is the meaning of life?* – turns away to the more scientific and accessible question, *What do we perceive to be the meaning of life?* The answer, he states, is hardly in doubt: we strive to be happy.[40]

With Freud, as with Epicurus, happiness is freedom from pain and access to pleasure. Pleasure, Freud adds, is simply the gratification of the needs of our most primitive, sexually disposed mental apparatus – the id. Freud writes, 'What we call happiness in the strictest sense comes from the (preferably sudden) satisfaction of needs which have been dammed up to a high degree, and it is from its nature only possible as an episodic phenomenon.'[41] With the maturation of our mental apparatus, other agencies (i.e. the ego and the superego) develop that function to delay or frustrate opportunities for pleasure through a regard for reality and morality. This leads to unhappiness.

Tracing back human phylogenetic development, Freud argues that civilization arose both to protect men from the sometimes violent forces of nature and to regulate the relations of humans.[42] Here a paradox arises: civilization protects us and regulates our mutual relations at the very expense of our own happiness. Society demands that we live by rules, but these very rules promote order by suppressing our most primitive and vital instincts – our libidinal or sexual instincts. The tension seems irremediable: the demand by individuals for freedom of libidinal expression versus the regulations of civilization that prohibit this expression.[43] The upshot is that society thrives at the very expense of the psychical health of the individuals in it.

This problem, Freud thinks, may not be solvable. We 'get by' through deflection strategies or intoxication, but these merely mask the growing underlying tension and afford little, if any, comfort. The only viable strategy is sublimation, which allows us some outlet for our libidinal energy. Sublimation thrives on renunciation and displacement of these hedonistic impulses, which is most appropriately directed toward a sexual bond with another human being. We divert sexual energy, for instance, into philanthropy, artistic creation, scientific study, religion, and even philosophy.

Civilization itself is a product of this displaced libidinal energy. Sexual energy is used to build social bonds, whose very rules function to suppress libido. This, Freud believes, is a poor exchange: Individuals have a goal of happiness; civilization has a goal of unification. Thus, while civilization thrives, the individuals in it become increasingly neurotic and unhappy. We are willing, it seems, to exchange our happiness for the security society gives us.[44] Put bluntly, civilization is a product of the need for security, not happiness.

The problem that Freud brings to our attention is intriguing. Yet that it may not be solvable is, I think, false. First, the Freudian sense of 'happiness' is based on the assumption that we are fundamentally impulse-driven animals, whose impulses by nature are sexual and asocial.[45] Aristotle of course disagrees, stating that we are not impulse-driven but political (and rational) by nature. If Aristotle is correct, and I believe that he is, then Freud's very model of the human psyche, like many similar models today, may be called into question. We form bonds, not just for security, but because it is our nature to do so.

Moreover, the Freudian definition of 'happiness', though it works well for *his* model of the mind, seems much too narrow. There are types of happiness that all people experience that have nothing to do with satisfaction of dammed-up impulses. There is the happiness one experiences when looking at and taking in an extraordinary work of art. There is the happiness of knowing that you are loved. There is happiness of finally coming to understand something that formerly perplexed you. Each of these experiences, as illustrations of episodes of happiness, ties in better with the Greek conception of happiness as a type of psychical stability or harmony.

Freud's dilemma – that people willingly sacrifice true happiness, release of libidinal tension, for the security of society – readily dissolves when we reject the claim that happiness is just periodic sexual release of built-up libidinal tension. Instead, true happiness, I maintain, is *integration,* and integration, at least up to this point of the unfolding of my thesis, has both personal and political components.

Notes

[1] *R.* 462a.

[2] The better the *polis*, the more it is like a living organism. *R.* 435a–e and 462c–d.

[3] *R.* 462c–e (Grube's translation).

[4] The very word Plato uses for his creator of the cosmos in *Timaeus* (see Chapter 7).

[5] *R.* 428a–429a.

[6] *R.* 429a–430c.

[7] *R.* 430c–432a.

[8] *R.* 432b–434c.

[9] *R.* 42b–421c.

[10] *Cr.* 43a.

[11] *Cr.* 47a–48a.

^{12} *Cr.* 48c–d (Grube's translation).

^{13} *Cr.* 48b.

^{14} Depending upon which version of the conclusion (P_4) one adopts, there are two distinct arguments that Socrates could be offering. Let us call these 'Version A' and 'Version B'.

> *Version A*
>
> A_1. If escaping from prison is returning wrong for wrong, Socrates ought not to escape from prison (P_4).
>
> A_2. Escaping from prison is wrong (several arguments in *Crito*).
>
> A_3. Socrates was wronged (strong evidence for this in *Apology*).
>
> A_4. Returning wrong for wrong is wrong (P_3).
>
> A_5. So, escaping from prison is returning wrong for wrong (A_2, A_3, and A_4).
>
> A_6. So, Socrates ought not to escape from prison (A_1 and A_5).
>
> *Version B*
>
> B_1. One must never do wrong (P_1).
>
> B_2. Escaping from prison is wrong (several arguments in *Crito*).
>
> B_3. So, Socrates ought not to escape from prison (B_1 and B_2).

The problem here is that Socrates seems to be putting forward Version A from 49a–d, when Version B much more simply establishes the claim, 'Socrates ought not to escape from prison'. Nothing Socrates says hereafter requires Version A.

^{15} *Cr.* 49e–53a.

^{16} Roughly the same argument that Socrates uses against Meletus in *Apology* (26a–b).

^{17} *Cr.* 50c–51e.

^{18} *Cr.* 53b–c.

^{19} *Cr.* 53a–54a.

^{20} *Ap.* 37a.

^{21} *Ap.* 26a.

^{22} Of course, if Socrates had been guilty of corrupting the youth and this crime was acknowledged to be a crime of ignorance, the appropriate penalty, in keeping with Athenian law, would have been remedial education, not death.

^{23} Recall Socrates' discussion with Meletus in *Apology* (25b–26c). Socrates, of course, could not persuade the Athenian jury, representatives of Athens, of his innocence.

^{24} *EN* 1155a5–23.

[25] *EN* I.7 (1097b12), IX.9 (1169b19), *Pol.* I.2 (1253a3–4), and III.6 (1278b20).

[26] *EN* 1170b25–31.

[27] *EN* 1155b34.

[28] *EN* 1156b6–13 (Irwin's translation).

[29] *EN* 1159b3–7.

[30] *EN* 1159a36–b1.

[31] *EN* 1156b25–33.

[32] *EN* 1171a10–14.

[33] *EN* 1158a11–14.

[34] *EN* 1170b26–28.

[35] *EN* 1159a–24–29.

[36] *EN* 1163b14–19.

[37] *EN* 1164b2–6.

[38] MacIntyre maintains that this is a legacy from Homeric times, where an individual could only attain self-knowledge within a society of fellow human beings (2002: 123–4).

[39] 1991: 70.

[40] 1989: 23–5.

[41] Ibid., 25.

[42] Ibid., 42.

[43] Ibid., 49 and 59–60.

[44] Ibid., 68–73 and 106.

[45] Not to say that sexual activity is itself not a social activity, but merely to emphasize that for Freud the aim is periodic libidinal satisfaction. With this in mind, society is basically structured to frustrate individuals sexually.

7

Happiness and Cosmic Integration

Remember that you are an actor in a play, which is as the playwright wants it to be: short if he wants it short, long if he wants it long. If he wants you to play a beggar, play even this part skillfully, or a cripple, or a public official, or a private citizen. What is yours is to play the assigned part well. But to choose if it belongs to someone else.   Epictetus, *Handbook*

THAT HAPPINESS INVOLVES PERSONAL INTEGRATION and some sense of political integration may seem relatively uncontroversial to many, but that it also involves some kind of universal or cosmic integration may not seem so obvious to most. Consequently, my aim in this final chapter is to show that complete happiness requires in addition some sense of cosmic integration.

I begin rather straightforwardly in the first half by looking at some of the best-known cosmologies in Classical and Hellenistic antiquity. Each of these is illustrative of Greek teleology and holism. I start with the cosmologies of Plato and Aristotle. I then turn to the cosmological thought of another, rival school in antiquity, Stoicism – the principal focus of this chapter. In the second half of this chapter, I critically analyse, in cosmological perspective, Stoic ethics as depicted by the Grecophile and Roman slave Epictetus.

At chapter's end, I sketch out a non-teleological approach to cosmic integration, significantly impacted by Greek thought, that completes the argument of the previous two chapters. Fully integrated persons are those who are not only personally and politically integrated, but also cosmically integrated to their fullest capacity. Complete happiness, I conclude, is identical to complete integration.

Plato's crafted cosmos

Plato's ontology, depicted by the famous illustration of a divided line at the end of *Republic* VI, comprises two realms: the visible and the intelligible. Visible things, of which there are primary and secondary entities, are not true realities or proper objects of knowledge, but instead mere objects of opinion. Not having a claim to being – since they come into being, change, and are destroyed over time – Plato calls these visible entities 'becomings'. Concerning the primary visible objects (C, see Figure 7.1), there exist animals, plants, and artifacts. At the lowest level of visible things (D) are entities that have the least claim to reality. These are the tenuous representations of primary visible objects, such as shadows, images, reflections, or pictures.

Ascending to the level of intelligible things or 'beings', for each kind of object at C, there corresponds a Form. Such Forms (B [and A?]) are non-spatial, non-temporal, eternal, unchanging, and insensible. For example, for all temporal and mutable visible-world cats, there exists apart from them an immutable and invisible form – Cat. Thus, Forms are intelligible realities and the true objects of knowledge. Nonetheless, these too are ontologically inferior (in some sense) to an even higher reality, the Form of Forms or the Form of the Good (top of A) – what all forms have a share of.[1] Given *Republic's* account of the relative ontological unimportance of visible things, it should be clear that

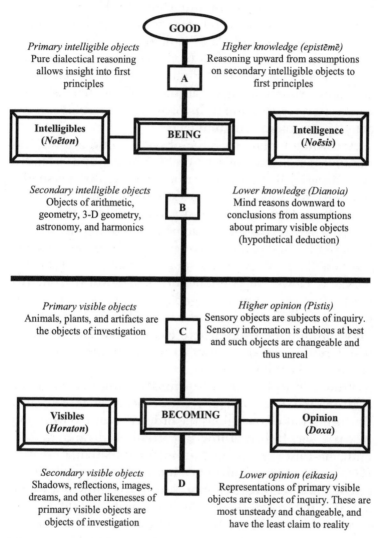

Figure 7.1   Plato's divided line

speculation about the cosmos, since this is a visible thing, was not a matter of utmost importance for Plato.

However, the generation of the sensible, physical cosmos is the topic of one of Plato's dialogues, *Timaeus*, a dialogue generally thought to have been written not much later than *Republic*. Here Plato has his main character Timaeus propose a 'likely account' of the genesis of the world (Gr. *ouranos*) that involves the interplay of two causal principles at different levels.[2]

According to Timaeus, the physical world is a result of the mixed influence of Reason (Gr. *Nous*) and Necessity (Gr. *Anagkē*). Being the superior force, Reason persuaded Necessity to fashion the greatest part of generated things toward the best end. Necessity then molded the primal chaos, a material soup of elements, into a copy of what is eternally and unalterably real, and it aimed to make the best likeness, given the matter available. Hereafter, Timaeus views the construction of the world from two levels: from top-down, a 'god's-eye' perspective, where the works of Reason are most sensible and directly at play;[3] from bottom-up, where Reason puts Necessity, the wandering or errant cause, to work for the majority of coming-to-be things.[4]

From 29d to 47e, creation unfolds by means of a divine craftsman (Gr. *demiourgos*), whose being is as eternal as the forms and who fashions the ordered, sensible world out of what was before visibly discordant and random. The craftsman uses as a model an intelligible, living creature (Gr. *zōon*), of which all other living creatures[5] are living parts. This creature, as a model for the cosmos as a whole, is reality in the highest degree. The sensible world, being a copy of this intelligible being and put together in the best possible manner, is then given intelligence.[6] It too needs to possess the sundry forms that intelligence does in the eternally living creature. Therefore, the *demiourgos* creates the earth, all the creatures that dwell on or around it, and the heavenly gods.[7]

Section 47e–69a of *Timaeus* gives us the bottom-up perspective of creation. Reason persuaded Necessity to fashion the 'greatest part of things' in the best manner possible.[8] With space as the receptacle of all becoming,[9] Necessity imposed geometric form on the primal chaos of inchoate matter to be used as the elements of all visible things.[10]

The final section deals with the parts of the body and soul,[11] the substances of the body (like bone and flesh),[12] growth and diminution,[13] diseases of the body and soul,[14] and other such things.

Plato's story of creation in *Timaeus* – though given only as a 'likely account', since it deals with entities about which one can have opinion and not knowledge – nicely illustrates cosmic organicism and cosmic teleology. Plato, so steeped in teleological thinking, could only think of the cosmos as an organic entity of the sort that was the product of an eternal and well-intentioned intelligence. Human beings, as intelligent animals, were parts of this cosmic organism and one of the greatest goods of creation.

Aristotle's proper-place cosmos

Unlike Plato, Aristotle does not regard sensible objects as objects ontologically inferior to intelligible realities (i.e. otherworldly Forms). Sensibles, for Aristotle, are the ultimate realities of his cosmos and the forms related to these sensibles are not, as we shall see, otherworldly.

Aristotle's cosmos is a plenum – that is, it is completely filled with objects that are in principle sensible. Each sensible object, for Aristotle, comprises matter and form. Yet Aristotle differs from Plato in that he thinks that form inheres *within* each sensible object and that it gives shape, function, and essence to that object, which, considered otherwise, is merely a mass of matter. Form, then, is the essence or defining characteristic of a thing. To identify something's form is to know its definition, purpose, or function. All entities, both living and non-living, have a particular form and, presumably, all entities of the same kind have the same form (i.e. every penguin has the form or essence of penguin). Matter, easily enough, is an entity's material composition. Matter determines the possibilities of something's use, for the kind and quantity of matter determine just what forms it can acquire. From a block of marble, for instance, one cannot make a soft sphere or a sphere that is larger than the block. Things of the same form appear and are different only insofar as they have different matter. So, as form is a principle of taxonomic identification, matter is a principle of individuation (see hylomorphism, Appendix B).

Aristotle's cosmos, unlike that of Plato, is a teleological system where there are two main realms – both of which concern visible things. The dividing line of these two realms is the sphere of the moon: All things above the sphere of the moon are perfect, divine, and unchanging; all things below this sphere are generated, destroyed, and changeable.

The physical principles regulating both realms, which I derive mostly from his *Metaphysics*, I summarize below:

1. *Nature=df*: nature is a principle of change (i.e. motion)[15] or remaining unchanged (i.e. unmoved) (*Ph*. II.1–2 [192b8–193a3]).
2. *Principles of motion*
   PM_1: motion cannot come to be or perish (*Metaph*. 1071b7 and *Ph*. VIII.6 [258b10]).
   PM_2: an everlasting motion is initiated and sustained by an everlasting mover (*Metaph*. 1073a28).
   PM_3: a single motion is initiated by a single mover (*Metaph*. 1073a29).

3. *Principle of potentiality*: what has a potentiality need not actualize it (*Metaph*. 1071b19).
4. *Principle of determinism*: nothing is moved at random (*Metaph*. 1071a35).
5. *Principle of change*: Whatever is moved can be otherwise (*Metaph*. 1072b5).

Below the sphere of the moon, all things are an admixture of the material elements – fire, air, water, and earth – each of which has an active (hot or cold) and passive (dry or wet) capacity (Gr. *dynamis*) and has its own proper sphere to which it naturally tends (see Figure 7.2, below). Fire (hot and dry) moves by nature away from the center of the cosmos and to the outermost sphere of the sublunary realm, bounded by the sphere of the moon. Air (hot and wet) also moves away from the center and finds its proper place just under the sphere of fire, as air is light, but not so light as fire. Earth (cold and dry) is the heaviest element and moves toward the center as do all heavy things. Water (cold and wet) is also heavy and tends toward the center of the cosmos. Yet being lighter than earth, its proper place is just above the earth and below the sphere of air.[16] Thus, the sphere of the moon is a boundary for the motion of light elements, while the center of the cosmos is a limit to natural downward motion. What prevents the elements from settling in their proper spheres in homogeneous masses is the circular motion of the sun and, to a lesser extent, that of the moon. These motions mix the elements and enable them to form homogeneous and heterogeneous masses as parts of living things.[17]

Above and including the sphere of the moon, there are some 55 concentric spheres[18] that account for the stars and planets, as well as the initiating and sustaining cause of all motion – the prime mover. Each of these spheres is considered to be a divine body.[19] Outside of this last sphere exists

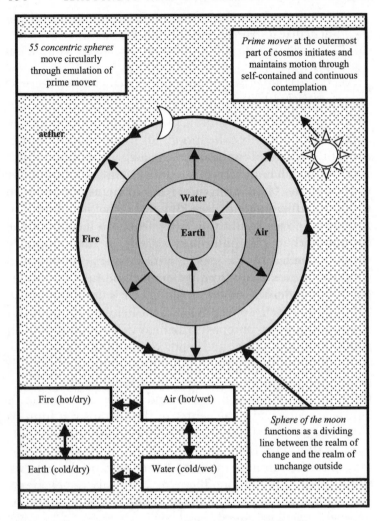

Figure 7.2   Aristotle's cosmos and conversion of the elements
Above is an illustration of the superlunary and sublunary realms of
Aristotle's cosmos. Lower left is a depiction of how Aristotle conceived
of conversion of the element in the sublunary realm. Note that only
those elements that have one 'contrary' (hot, cold, wet, or dry) in
common are directly convertible into each other

the prime mover, which is the most divine substance. Being pure actuality and pure form (i.e. wholly devoid of matter), the prime mover initiates and maintains the motion of the spheres through constant and self-objective thought.[20] The realm outside of the sphere of the moon is filled with an unchanging fifth material element that is endemic to that region – *aether*. All motion in this region is unending and circular.[21]

In all, Aristotle's cosmological account, like that of Plato, aims to explain how the cosmos itself possesses the good. He offers, by way of analogy, a picture of how the order in an army of men is good. The good of this order is some actualized potentiality of the men that is realized not because of the men themselves, but because of the general in charge of the men. Similarly, the good of the cosmos, he invites us to conclude, is caused by the most divine first mover as governor of all order. He writes:

> All things – fishes, birds, and plants – are joined in some order, but not all in the same way. Nor are they unrelated to each other, but they have some relation; for all things are joined in some order in relation to one thing. (It is like a household, where the free members are least of all at liberty to do what they like, and all or most of what they do is ordered, whereas only a little of what slaves and beasts do promotes the common [good], and mostly they do what they like.) For the nature of each sort of thing is such a principle [that aims at the good of the whole]. I mean, for instance, that everything necessarily is eventually dissolved, and in this way there are other things in which everything shares for [the good of] the whole.[22]

Stoic cosmology and ethics

Stoicism[23] was a major school of thought in the Hellenistic period that was founded in Cyprus by Zeno of Citium

(c. 350–258 B.C.), son of Mnaseas. Like Epicureanism, Stoicism blended empiricism with rationalism in that it built its theory of knowledge around certain sensory impressions, kataleptic impressions (see Chapter 4), that were taken to be unshakeably true. Like Cynicism, it modeled ethical living on Socratic frugality and its unconcern for worldly things. Like Platonism, it drew ethical sustenance from Socrates' tireless search for truth and uncompromising indifference to anything other than this pursuit.

The earliest Stoics were chiefly cosmologists.[24] The Stoic cosmos itself was believed to be both a plenum and an animal (Gr. *zōon*),[25] and nature (Gr. *physis*), regarded universally, was a generative force, responsible for all growth, life, and order within the cosmos.[26] As an animate body, the same principles that were responsible for animal vitality were deemed responsible for the life of the cosmos, which continually came to be and passed away in recurrent cycles. Behind the vitality of this phoenix universe were two material principles: god, a fiery and powerful active force,[27] and a type of watery matter without attributes that the active force fashioned.[28] These two material principles were not separable natures; they described two aspects of the same material thing.

Like a human embryo, for Stoics the cosmos was thought to develop at various stages over time. At the first stage, a fiery god acted on the precosmic water. This interaction then resulted in the generation of the four elements (fire, air, water, and earth) that were arranged in spherical tiers in the circular universe.[29] With the birth of the elements, the cosmos came into being.

Pervasive throughout the cosmos and vitalizing it throughout all of its cycles, there is a tenuous matter called *pneuma*, a vital breath or wind of sort (the same sort of breath that permeates and vitalizes the body as soul).[30] *Pneuma* is entirely a material principle that is responsible for coherence and order in the cosmos. A later Stoic Chrysippus (280–206 B.C.), son of Apollonius, tells us that *pneuma* does this by effecting a certain tension (Gr. *tonos*) within the cosmos.

Chrysippus appeals to the analogy of a spider and his web to describe human tension: when any insect lands in the web, the tension of the web conveys this motion to the spider.[31] This tensional force was deemed responsible for seeing, hearing, moving, sleep, death, and even desire in humans. Given the similarities between the cosmos and humans,[32] it is likely that Chrysippus thought this spider-web analogy could facilitate understanding of the cosmic tension as well.

As a result of the cosmic tension, there is vital, material unity and coherence to the cosmos as there is with all things that are its parts. Animals have a soul (Gr. *psyche*). Plants have an analogous binding agency (Gr. *tonos*). Even inorganic things have a fiery principle (Gr. *hexis*) that, turning back toward itself, holds them together. Because of this, even the most lifeless of things, like rocks, were likely thought to be vital in some sense.

In time, the cosmos matures to such a developed state that the fiery god is in perfect command and what is moist is entirely absent. The cosmos is now wholly ablaze, a complete conflagration. Yet in such conflagration are the seeds for regeneration of all past, present, and future things. Until such time as a new cosmos is born, all evil is vanquished. The cycle is eternal.[33]

Early Stoic ethics was a matter of recognizing and contemplating truth within this cosmic framework. This exacted awareness of the harmony or order of the universe and a willingness to cooperate as much as possible in facilitating and maintaining this harmony. Yet when Stoicism was moved to Rome after the death of the Stoic philosopher Posidonius (135–51 B.C.), ethical speculation took on less of a cosmological slant. Roman Stoics like Seneca, Aurelius, and Epictetus, focused on development of virtue or excellent character, though such development was always (at least implicitly) understood to occur within the larger framework of the cosmos itself.

Throughout their long history, the Stoics never wavered on the notions that virtue is knowledge and that the kataleptic impression, being essentially propositional, was foundational for attaining wisdom. As I mention in Chapter 4, for Stoics, wisdom comes through assenting only to those impressions that are kataleptic or grasping in nature – that is, those that reveal their cause with utmost clarity such that no mistake about their truth is possible. The Stoic model for attaining knowledge here is essentially that of Aristotle at *Metaphysics* α.1. From raw perceptions, we form memories from collections of perceptions and experiences from groups of these, until finally we arrive at knowledge. Assenting carefully to the simplest kataleptic impressions, a person can thus build up a store of knowledge and attain wisdom.

Overall, virtues – prudence, justice, courage, and self-control[34] – are the sole goods and are sought insofar as they are goods, not for their effects. Each is choice-worthy in the greatest possible sense and admits of no change. In contrast, foolishness, injustice, cowardice, and lack of self-control are bad and to be avoided. All other things – like life, health, pleasure, beauty, strength, wealth, reputation, noble birth – exist between virtue and vice. They are 'indifferents', in that a wise person's attitude toward them ought to be one of complete indifference.[35] For happiness does not depend on these, though a good person will use these and not their opposites (i.e. death, disease, etc.) in beneficial ways and prove their value to him, while the bad person will likely come to greater harm with them. So, such indifferents are 'preferred', while their opposites are 'dispreferred'.[36]

Of the Stoic conception of excellence, Diogenes Laertius writes:

> Virtue is a consistent character, choice-worthy for its own sake and not from fear or hope or anything external. Happiness consists in virtue since virtue is a soul which has been fashioned to achieve consistency in the whole of life.[37]

All persons have a capacity to be virtuous. One wise person possesses excellence to the same extent that does another,[38] while all that are not wise are vicious to the same extent. Plutarch writes:

> 'Yes', they [the Stoics] say, 'but just as in the sea the man an arm's length from the surface is drowning no less than the one who has sunk five hundred fathoms, so even those who are getting close to virtue are no less in a state of vice than those who are far from it. And just as the blind are blind even if they are going to recover their sight a little later, so those progressing remain foolish and vicious right up to their attainment of virtue'.[39]

In the end, happiness was perceived to be 'living in agreement with nature'. For the Stoic Chrysippus, this meant in accord with one's own nature and that of the cosmos, right reason, or Zeus.[40] Cicero in his *Tusculan Disputations* writes of the Stoic sage:

> It is a peculiar characteristic of the wise man that he does nothing which he could regret, nothing against his will, but does everything honorably, consistently, seriously, and rightly; that he anticipates nothing as if it were bound to happen, is shocked by nothing when it does happen under the impression that its happening is unexpected and strange, refers everything to his own judgement, stands by his own decisions. I can conceive nothing which is happier than this. It is an easy conclusion for the Stoics, since they have

perceived the final good to be agreement with nature and living consistently with nature, which is not only the wise man's proper function, but also in his power. It necessarily follows that the happy life is in the power of the man who has the final good in his power. So the wise man's life is always happy.[41]

Overall, happiness for Stoics is complete integration, both personally and cosmically, through excellence (fulfilling one's own nature) and living according to providence (agreement with cosmic nature). What binds virtue-driven persons to providence is what both persons and providence share – reason.

In stark contrast to the wise person stands the vicious person, who is ruled by four irrational, disobedient-to-reason, or contrary-to-nature movements: distress, fear, appetite, and pleasure. Distress is a fresh opinion that some ill is present, while fear is an avoidance of some anticipated ill. Both of these are irrational, bodily contractions of sorts. Appetite is pursuit of some anticipated good, while pleasure is a fresh opinion that something good is present. Both of these are irrational, bodily swellings of sorts.[42] These four passions are only genuine passions when they are impulses – that is, passions that have the soul's assent. Given this, even a sage will be sometimes moved by passions – fortuitous impressions concerning sexual arousal, sorrow, or a brightening of the eyes – but he will not assent to these and he will quickly gain composure. So, though a sage will sometimes be temporarily moved by passions, failing to assent to these, he will not experience genuine passions.[43]

Epictetus' *Handbook*

One example of the Stoic interest in ethical improvement is handed down to us through the words of the first-century

(A.D.) philosopher Epictetus. Born a slave, Epictetus obtained his freedom and settled in Nicopolis (a northwest coastal city in Greece), where he taught philosophy until his death. He wrote nothing, but his pupils put down many of his ideas in works that survive, one of which is known to us today as the *Enchiridion* or *Handbook*.[44]

Perusal of the *Enchiridion* shows that Epictetus was not a penetrating or highly critical thinker, but one whose interests centered on the practical implications of Stoic philosophy. The work itself reads not as a systematic and critical treatise on ethics, as does Aristotle's ethical works,[45] but as a manual of short prescriptions for peace of mind and happiness.

Consistent with early Stoic philosophy, Epictetus viewed the cosmos as a completely material and deterministic system, in which every event was uniquely determined by antecedent causes. He believed, in keeping with stoic fatalism, that people have no control over their bodies and what they do with them, but they do have control over their opinions, desires, impulses, and aversions. The best people can do is tame their desires and aversions so that they are in harmony with natural necessity, which governs all things.[46]

Remember, what a desire (Gr. *orexis*) proposes is that you gain what you desire, and what an aversion (Gr. *ekklisis*) proposes is that you not fall into what you are averse to. Someone who fails to get what he desires *is unfortunate*, while someone who falls into what he is averse to *has met misfortune*. So if you are averse only to what is against nature among the things that are up to you, then you will never fall into anything that you are averse to; but if you are averse to illness or death or poverty, you will meet misfortune. So detach your aversion from everything not up to us, and transfer it to what is against nature among the things that are up to us. And for the time being, eliminate desire completely, since if you desire something that is not up to us, you are bound to be unfortunate, and at the same time none of the things that are up to us, which it would be good to desire, will be available to you. Make use only of impulse and its contrary, rejection, though with reservation, lightly, and without straining.[47]

And again:

Remember that you are an actor in a play, which is as the playwright wants it to be: short if he wants it short, long if he wants it long. If he wants you to play a beggar, play even this part skillfully, or a cripple, or a public official, or a private citizen. What is yours is to play the assigned part well. But to choose it belongs to someone else.[48]

Though he is merely following earlier accounts of Stoic cosmic fatalism, it is difficult to grasp how Epictetus or any of the Stoics could have believed that people have control over their thoughts and beliefs, but no control over their physical actions. Cosmic fatalism implies that all events in the physical cosmos are fated. How then can anyone have command over his states of mind (which themselves are physical)? This is a difficulty that Epictetus does not address.[49]

The overall recipe for happiness leads to cultivating the apposite psychical dispositions to fate: apathy (Gr. *apathē*) and resignation. Epictetus elaborates, 'Do not seek to have events happen as you want them to, but instead want them to happen as they do happen and your life will go well.'[50] A helpful image is that of a woman falling from a steep cliff to immanent death. She could close her eyes and adopt an attitude of naive uncertainty about her future, but, if she desires wisdom, she will not shut out reality and will readily accept her fate.

In spite of the unsolved problem of cosmic fatalism with control over one's states of mind, Epictetus does assert that you can, in some sense, make ethical progress. He tells us it is our manner of thinking about affairs that brings on fear and distress, not the state of affairs itself. It is not lack of property or food that causes fear and distress, but letting our passions affect our judgements concerning external affairs.[51] Correct judgement is merely a matter of releasing from the opinions of others, and letting our opinions accord with nature.

> What upsets people is not things themselves but their judgements (Gr. *dogmata*) about the things. For example, death is nothing dreadful (or else it would have appeared dreadful to Socrates), but instead the judgement about death that it is dreadful – that is what is dreadful. So when we are thwarted or upset or distressed, let us never blame someone else but rather ourselves, that is, our own judgements. An uneducated person accuses others when he is doing badly; a partly educated person accuses himself; an educated person accuses neither someone else nor himself.[52]

Epictetus goes on to give us a list of checks for making progress. One making progress does not praise, censure, or blame another. He is no braggart; instead he is one who blames himself first when things go awry. He laughs at those who praise him and ignores those who censure him. Making his way carefully so as to avoid injury, just as an invalid, he is nonetheless insouciant and free from desire.[53]

The wise person does not get swept away by grief, Epictetus states. He may moan outwardly, but inwardly he stays composed and calm.[54] Weighing all decisions with due measure,[55] he does not put off what is important to another day, for he fully recognizes that his life may come to a sudden end at any moment.[56] He cautions:

> And if you meet with any hardship or anything pleasant or reputable or disreputable, then remember that the contest is now and the Olympic Games are now and you cannot put things off any more and that your progress is made or destroyed by a single day and a single action.[57]

A wise person, thus, willingly accepts the ridicule of others for his piety and apathy,[58] since he knows that what is most important is acquiescence to the will of the gods, who have brought about everything in the cosmos for the best.[59]

In short, like Socrates, the Stoic sage places wisdom, hunger for truth, humility, and hardihood above ostentation and ease of living.[60]

Relevance for today

The Greek notion of cosmic teleology has fallen on hard times today. In place of an ordered universe,[61] where all things exist or come about for what is best, many if not most contemporary philosophers and scientists believe that we live in a universe in which events are not end-directed. No cosmic blueprint or divine decree dictates that any particular event will come about and that it must come about because it is for the best. Instead, given the state of the universe at some particular time and given that the laws of physics are what they are, at the level of visible things, most work under that assumption that things happen because of necessity.[62]

Nonetheless, there is something that we can take from the Greek cosmological perspectives for living a happy life: complete happiness has a cosmological component. My argument for this is difficult to articulate, for, in trying to state just what I mean by 'cosmic', I wish to avoid any unfounded or unintuitive metaphysical assumptions about the exact nature of the cosmos and our relationship to it. I do not posit that the cosmos itself is some sort of living being, that it has some unity of purpose or end to which humans are instrumental, or that the universe itself is under the governance of a divine will. Aside from all of these,

I believe there is a common-sense notion of cosmic integration that I can tease out in what follows.

Most people perceive their lives to be a series of disjointed episodes. There are some important events in each day, some very important events in a lifetime, and then there is the time between those events, which is uneventful – sometimes even monotonously so. Yet on a day-to-day basis, events flow ceaselessly by as they merge into and stream out of each other. Focusing only on a few disjointed events each day and shunning interest in the countless others, people's lives become disjointed, not fluid. In living episodically, they do not experience much of the continual stream of events around them. Living only for the 'significant' events, they, as it were, pop in and out of existence in a life of cosmic disconnectedness.

John Dewey captured this same idea many years ago in a distinction he made between sensationalizing and intellectualizing events. 'Events are sensational in the degree in which they make a strong impact in isolation from the relations to other events that give them their significance.' In contrast, an intellectual response to an event is one in which the event is seen in its relations to other things.[63] The intellectual response, he maintains, is the proper response to events.

To experience life fully, we need to expand our interests to experience much more of what is readily around us. We need to regard life as whole and become increasingly a part of the flow of events. Bertrand Russell in *Conquest of Happiness* writes:

> Through ... [external] interests a man comes to feel himself part of the stream of life, not a hard separate entity like a billiard ball, which can have no relation with other such entities except that of collision. All unhappiness depends upon some kind of disintegration or lack of integration; there

is disintegration within the self through lack of coordination between the conscious and the unconscious mind; there is lack of integration between the self and society, where the two are not knit together by the force of objective interests and affections. The happy man is the man who does not suffer from either of these failures of unity, whose personality is neither divided against itself nor pitted against the world. Such a man feels himself a citizen of the universe, enjoying freely the spectacle that it offers and the joys that it affords, untroubled by the thought of death because he feels himself not really separate from those who will come after him. It is in such profound instinctive union with the stream of life that the greatest joy is to be found.[64]

Russell also uses this metaphor of a stream elsewhere in *Conquest of Happiness*. He asserts that we flow into the future in two ways: in an instinctive way and in a hypercivilized way. Instinctively, we strive to procreate. The hypercivilized manner is through work – the creation of something that extends on indefinitely into the future.[65] He is certainly following Plato in *Symposium* here and perhaps the Stoic Zeno, who defined 'happiness' as a 'good flow of life'.[66]

In short, happiness at the cosmic level is a vision both of the interconnectedness of things and of one's own part in this flow. It is the recognition that we are an integral part of the course of events – not a separate entity that chances to collide periodically with other entities.

The notion of cosmic integration that I sketch implies cosmic responsibility. We measure the worth of a person through words and deeds, though we have no sure means of gauging their precise impact. Yet they do certainly impact on others and the world around us. The most trivial words that we utter and the smallest actions we perform influence the world in which we live for better or otherwise. Thus, deliberation before deed is not only a wise policy, it is our moral responsibility.

One event, in particular, has indelibly impressed upon me the extent to which what we say and do affect those around us. As I walked toward a bookstore one late summer morning, a middle-aged woman, some twenty feet ahead of me, waited by the door to hold it for me. As I reached the door, I thanked her and complimented her on her kindness. Suddenly I saw the most radiant smile that I had ever seen. It seemed almost to consume her face. She then said (and I remember her precise words), 'That's the nicest thing anyone's ever said to me'. I smiled, said something in return, and then we went our separate ways.

For the rest of the day, this episode stayed in my mind. Her smile – almost Cheshire cat-like in breadth – came from nowhere. It took a while before it occurred to me that *I* was responsible for that smile. I also realized that she was likely to spread around good cheer to others with whom she would interact throughout the day and that these others too might act similarly. Moreover, the catalyst for all of this was one short sentence. I paused to consider the conceivable effects of all the sentences that I could utter and all the actions I could perform in a single day, and how these would add up over a lifetime. This suggested to me that I must be more circumspect about what I do and say in the future. It also made me wish that I had been more circumspect concerning what I have done and said in the past.

Here, as I reflect on this incident, one philosopher in particular comes to mind – Aristotle. Aristotle often reminds his audience that one action does not make a person virtuous; excellence, instead, is a state that requires a conditioned base of the right sort of actions that are done at the right time, toward the right people, in the right manner, and for the right reasons.[67] In this manner, the happiest life is a lifelong commitment to virtuous activity in *all* of one's actions – both public and private. It is also in some measure integration with the cosmos itself.

I wish to conclude this chapter with some brief comments on the Stoic notions of fate, resignation, and apathy.

For the Stoics, all events were deemed completely determined by antecedent causes and the whole cosmic web of events was foreordained by divine intelligence for the best possible end. And so, just as most people today tend to think that what has once passed has passed and cannot be altered, the Stoics believed that what is to be is to be and cannot be altered. Thus, all events – past, present, and future – are completely outside of our control. Given this sense of providential fatalism, resignation and apathy seem quite reasonable (if these, at least, are within our control).

Most of us, I assume, work on the assumption that strict determinism is false – that some part of the things we do on a daily basis is 'up to us'. In short, we have some capacity for self-determination through deliberation and choice. If this is the case, and I certainly think that it is, then the Stoic notions of fate, resignation, and apathy taken *en tout* are unserviceable.

Still there are some lessons we can extract from Stoic ethics concerning living a happy and good life. Though some actions are within our power, many others, though we may be tempted to think otherwise, are simply not. Suppose, for instance, that a young woman from a poor family in Kutztown has a consuming dream of earning a scholarship to attend the University of Michigan. She works ceaselessly, intelligently, and efficiently at realizing this dream. Yet at some point, whether the dream comes true or not is not up to her anymore. It is in some sense 'up to fate', or at least up to powers outside of her. So, once she has done all that she could have done to matriculate at Michigan, thereafter it seems sensible that she should adopt an attitude of resignation concerning what eventually happens.

Additionally, the Stoic goal of impartiality toward ethical issues is, in some respects, an important advance from the provincial, *polis*-based views of both Plato and Aristotle. For the latter thinkers, though happiness is a non-subjective state of an agent's soul, considerations of a person's excellence do not seem to extend beyond his *polis*. Therefore, what is in a person's best interest is what is in his *polis'* best interest. Happiness requires partiality. The Stoics, in contrast, begin with the notion of humans as imbedded in all that exists – god or the cosmological web of events.[68] Furthermore, they maintain that passion is confusion within the soul that prohibits correct judgements about reality and, thus, impedes the path toward excellence. So, the most desirable ethical disposition, one that leaves judgement unclouded, is one of strict impartiality toward all things.

Yet is strict impartiality a needed ingredient of a sound ethical theory today? It is not that ethical decision-making today requires strict impartiality, for instance, through demanding that friends and loved ones are given no preference in one's life. What the Stoics have shown is that strict impartiality toward all things is a better starting point than is *uncritical partiality* – for example, the type with which Aristotle begins (in assuming, for instance, both that friendship is an unqualified virtue and that we are by nature disposed to seek friends). Honest ethical reflection necessitates critical analysis in some measure of all ethical tenets we take to be true or foundational. To this end, Stoic ethics marks an important development in ethical theory.

Notes

1. *R.* 509d–511e and 532a–534a.
2. *Ti.* 29c–d.
3. *Ti.* 29d–47e and 69a–92c.
4. *Ti.* 47e–69a.
5. Presumably, the Forms.

6   *Ti.* 29b–30c.

7   *Ti.* 39e–40c.

8   *Ti.* 48a.

9   *Ti.* 48e–49a.

10 *Ti.* 53c–55c.

11 *Ti.* 69a–73a.

12 *Ti.* 73b–76e.

13 *Ti.* 80d–81e.

14 *Ti.* 81e–87b.

15 All change was seen to be a type of motion. Aristotle's word is *kinesis*, which translates best as 'motion'.

16 *GC* II.3 (330b22–28).

17 *GC* II.2 (329b26–33) and *Cael.* III.6.

18 *Metaph.* XII (1074a7–14).

19 *Metaph.* XII (1074a15–16 and 1074b1–13).

20 *Metaph.* XII (1071b22–3 and 1074b23–7).

21 *Metaph.* XII (1071b7–12).

22 *Metaph.* XIII (1075a11–25).

23 So-called, most likely, because they lectured at a Stoa, a covered colonnade near the market area. Stoicism was prominent for over 500 years and made a natural transition to Roman politics.

24 It is only when Stoicism was transplanted to Rome that the interest in cosmology began to wane.

25 *SVF* II.633.

26 *SVF* II.1132.

27 *SVF* II.1045.

28 *SVF* II.300–1.

29 Similar to the Aristotelian cosmos, except that all four of the elements had a natural tendency toward the center of the cosmos – both bodies without weight and especially heavy ones (*SVF* II.555).

30 *SVF* I.135–8.

31 *SVF* II.879.

32 *SVF* III.220.

33 *SVF* I.98, 102, II.604, 606, and 1052.

34 For Stoics, these are the four primary virtues.

35 In contrast to Aristotle, who said these too were goods, though of a lesser sort.

[36] *Vit.* VII.101–5. I use the translation of Long and Sedley throughout this section.

[37] *Vit.* VII.89.

[38] Cleanthes maintained that a wise person's excellence was unshakeable, while Chrysippus could slip away from excellence by intoxication or depression. *Vit.* VII.127.

[39] *SVF* 1063a–b.

[40] *Vit.* VII.87–9.

[41] *Tusc.* V.81–2.

[42] *SVF* III.391.

[43] *On Anger* II.iii.1–2.

[44] White's translations throughout.

[45] Both Aristotle's *EN* and *EE*.

[46] *Ench.* §1, 26, 27 and 49.

[47] *Ench.* §2.

[48] *Ench.* §17; see also §33.

[49] The notions that all events are completely fated, a type of fatalism consistent with determinism, and that human will can either choose to accept things as they must play themselves out or refuse to do so are patently inconsistent. In general, Stoics maintained that all events were determined according to nature (Gr. *kata phusin*), while what was bad (one's refusal to accept events as they must play themselves out) was something contrary to nature and within one's control (Gr. *para phusin*).

[50] *Ench.* §8.

[51] *Ench.* §12–13.

[52] *Ench.* §5; cf. §20.

[53] *Ench.* §48.

[54] *Ench.* §16.

[55] *Ench.* §29, 34, 42, 44, and 45.

[56] *Ench.* §7.

[57] *Ench.* §51.

[58] *Ench.* §22.

[59] *Ench.* §31.

[60] *Ench.* §5, 32, 46, and 51.

[61] Recall that the Greek word, *kosmos*, literally means 'order'.

[62] Of course, those who insist that humans are in some sense in control of their lives (and I am one) must reject this strict determinism.

[63] John Dewey, *Freedom and Culture* (Amherst, NY: Prometheus Books, 1989), 39–40

[64] Russell 1996: 191.

[65] Ibid., 154.

[66] Long *et al.* 1990: 63a.

[67] *EN* II.6 (1106b21–5).

[68] This does not exclude normal human relationships with genuine concern for others. See, for instance, *Vit.* VII.85–6 or Stobaeus' *Treasury* LXXXIV.23.

Postscript

Is Happiness a Puzzle?

IN THE PREFACE TO THIS BOOK, I maintain that happiness is one of the most seductive and puzzling issues concerning human existence: Everyone wants to be happy, but few seem to know what happiness is or how to acquire it.

Using Greek ethical views as a guide, I have argued that to be happy one must seek personal, political, and cosmic integration. If this nested three-part model is correct, it explains why true happiness is very elusive. Only those persons who devote themselves to a lifetime of personal discovery and growth and who place themselves within and at the service of their community as well as within the larger context of the cosmic flow of events can find the equanimity and can achieve the stability of character that is distinctive of all happy people.

Happiness is elusive. This is not however because it is a dispensation of the gods that is meted out to a few privileged people. Just like the acquisition of any skill, procuring happiness takes planning, focus, discipline, and persistence. It takes a *rational* commitment toward integrating oneself with oneself, one's community, and even everything that exists.

Yet, with all of this, it is probable that one may still fail to achieve happiness in a lifetime. For, as Aristotle noted centuries ago,[1] external circumstances also factor into the equation. A little luck helps. At least, it does not hurt *not* to be continually plagued by one random misfortune after another. This is perhaps why the Greek word for happiness, *eudaimonia*, has its etymological roots in 'being blessed by a good god'.

And so I leave off where I began: acknowledging the elusiveness of happiness. But is this really a puzzle? Why should the road to happiness not be long, steep, and treacherous? As Hesiod in *Works and Days* says:

> In truth, inferiority can be gained easily and in abundance,
> The road is smooth, and it lies very nearby.
> Yet, in front of excellence (Gr. *aretē*), the immortal gods have placed sweat,
> And the path toward it is far-stretching and steep, and rough at first.
> But when one has reached the top, then it becomes easy, for the difficulty.[2]

And for all who undertake this arduous journey, I can give no assurance that you will ever reach the top and find happiness. Still you will have as your guides the ancient Greek philosophers, who know best the rocky terrain and the numerous obstacles along the way. Moreover, the quest for happiness, I suspect, will likely offer numerous opportunities for enlightening adventures and enlightened reflection on the nature of happiness. It is an odyssey that, I hope, will lead to peace, within and without.

> Athena raised her voice aloud, and made every one pause. 'Men of Ithaca', she cried, 'cease this dreadful war, and settle the matter at once without further bloodshed'.
>
> On this, pale fear seized every one; they were so frightened that their arms dropped from their hands and fell upon the ground at the sound of the goddess' voice, and they fled back to the city for their lives. But Odysseus gave a great cry, and gathering himself together swooped down like a soaring eagle. Then the son of Kronos sent a thunderbolt of fire that fell just in front of Athena, so she said to Odysseus, 'Odysseus, noble son of Laertes, stop this warful strife, or Zeus will be angry with you'. Thus spoke Athena, and Odysseus obeyed her gladly. Then Athena assumed the form and voice of Mentor, and presently made a covenant of peace between the two contending parties.[3]

Notes

[1] *EN* I.8 (1099a31–3).
[2] *Op.* 287–92.
[3] *Od.* 530-fin.

Appendix A
Important Names

Aeschylus (c. 524–c. 456 B.C.): the first of the three great tragedians. Aeschylus fought at Marathon and perhaps also at Salamis,
Artemisium, and Plataea. He wrote some 90 plays, of which only
seven survive. His last three plays form part of the trilogy *Oresteia*,
which contains *Agamemnon*, *The Libation Bearers*, and *The Kindly Ones*.

Apuleius (fl. 2nd century A.D.): Ancient Latin writer whose novel
Golden Ass is the only novel from antiquity to survive in entirety. He
also wrote *On the Philsosophy of Plato* and *On the God of Socrates*.

Cicero, Marcus Tullius (106–43 B.C.): the greatest of Roman ora-
tors, he was also a noted politician and a compiler of philosophical
information. His philosophical works are invaluable sources of information concerning the philosophical climate of Greek and Roman
antiquity.

Cleisthenes (fl. 510 B.C.): as head of the family Alcomaeonidae, he
became ruler of Athens in 506 B.C. and initiated democratic reforms
to weaken the aristocratic political substructure of Athens.

Diogenes Laertius (fl. 3rd century A.D.): biographer who wrote a ten-volume work on the lives of eminent Greeks. This work is a helpful, though sometimes inaccurate, source of information on these ancients.

Dionysus: Greek god of wine, fertility, and religious ecstasy, and enthusiasm. Dionysus entered Greek culture as early as 1200 B.C. He is often contrasted with Apollo, the god of reason.

Draco (fl. 621 B.C.): the first Greek to codify the customary Athenian laws.

Furies: the Greek goddesses of vengeance. They especially avenged blood crimes within a family.

Heraclitus (c. 535–c. 475 B.C.): Ephesian philosopher who taught that the only reality was change itself. He tended to identify this ongoing flux with the material element fire, whose very substance seemed to change eternally. Heraclitus had a strong impact on Plato and the Stoics.

Herodotus (c. 485–c. 420 B.C.): born in Halicarnassus in southwest Asia Minor, he is called the world's first historian in that he wrote a detailed account of the Persian Wars (490–479 B.C.), where the Greeks successfully fended off the mighty Persian army. This account is extraordinarily valuable yet, by today's standards, is tremendously shoddy history. It is fraught with numerous digressions, false causes, and fabrications that make disentangling fact from fantasy virtually impossible.

Hesiod (late 8th century B.C.): next to Homer, the earliest Greek author whose works survive. We have two poems of his: *Works and Days* and *Genealogy of the Gods (Theogony)*.

Homer (fl. 800 c. B.C.): the greatest Greek poet and believed to be the author of the two greatest poems in antiquity, *Iliad* and *Odyssey* (not all scholars agree that he wrote both). These poems describe a time long gone: the events of the Trojan War (c. 1250 B.C.) and the ten-years-long journey of Odysseus homeward after the war. These poems had a grip on Greek culture (in a manner not unlike that of the Bible in Christian culture) in that they not only entertained, but they served as a basis for morality and gave boys and girls gender roles for which to strive.

Milesian philosophers (fl. 6th century B.C.): see Appendix B.

Parmenides (c. 515–c. 440 B.C.): Parmenides lived in the Greek city of Elea, in southwest Italy, where he founded a school. He proposed in his poem *On Nature* that there are two paths: one of reality and one of appearance. Concerning reality, Parmenides says that what is is and must be; what is not is not and must not be. Given the oneness of what is, he concluded, what is must be ungenerated, indestructible, unchangeable, indivisible, and motionless. Concerning the way of appearance (unreality), Parmenides states that the myriad variety of shapes and images are the result of two unreal forms: Light and Dark. The influence of Parmenides on Plato is unmistakable.

Plutarch (c. 50–c. 125 A.D.): though a Roman citizen, Plutarch was a moralist and biographer of ancient Greeks and Romans in antiquity. His primary focus was probably not historical accuracy and his work reflects this. Nonetheless, he is an important source of information about history and these important personalities.

Pythagoras (c. 570–c. 500 B.C.): Greek mathematician, philosopher, and mystic who was born at Samos and lived to be about seventy years of age. We know little of him, except through references to him by others. Settling at an important Greek colony in southern Italy, Croton, he set up a cultic society and attained the status of celebrity.

There were two teachings of his that profoundly influenced Plato: the importance of numbers and the transmigration of souls. Concerning the former, Pythagoras believed that numbers were the key to unlocking the hidden truths of the cosmos. For instance, he deemed '10' to be an important number because the sum of the first four integers – one, two, three, and four – equals 10. Moreover, we can literally see this magical relationship by mounting three horizontally related dots over four such dots, then two dots over the three, and last one dot over the two.

Next, Pythagoras believed that souls do not pass on into the underworld, but they pass into new bodies. Each transmigration is determined by the degree of a soul's pollution. One who is corrupt may come back as a beast, while a purified person may come back as a politician.

There were certain rules of good conduct characteristic of Pythagorean cultic lifestyle that seem to be to us today more superstitious than sensible. For example, a disciple was forbidden to discuss Pythagorean principles in the dark and no one was allowed to eat beans (presumably because of the disturbance of the soul caused by flatulence).

Solon (c. 630–c. 560 B.C.): responding to an early sixth-century B.C. crisis in Athens (c. 594 B.C.) concerning aristocratic abuse of power, Solon proposed critical economic and political reforms. On the economic side of things, first, those who lost their land through debt to aristocrats got their land back. Second, those slaves who were sold abroad were brought back to Athens. Third, he cancelled all public and private debts. Last he encouraged olive-oil production, the investment in skilled craftsmen, and nonagricultural employment. On the political side of things, Solon abolished good birth as a criterion for holding office, and made wealth the deciding factor. He then divided the Athenians into four economic groups based on wealth. He created a Council of 400 for discussing preliminary issues regarding the *polis*. On the legal side of matters, Solon prohibited all loans where a person used himself as collateral. He also made it possible for anyone wronged to prosecute and to appeal a decision to a 'People's Court'.

As a result of these reforms, aristocrats suffered politically and financially. There ensued factionalism between three main rival parties: Men of Coast under Megacles, Men of Plain under Lycurgus, and Men of Hills under Peisistratus. Judged by their immediate results, Solon's reforms were unsuccessful. Nonetheless they were an important first step toward curbing the aristocratic self-interest and corruption.

Theophrastus (370–287 B.C.): born on Lesbos, Theophrastus was a pupil of Aristotle and his eventual successor upon Aristotle's death. He wrote on an array of topics and is best known for his *Characters*, a work on abnormal personality types.

Appendix B

Important Terms

apotropaism: the early Greek view that one must do whatever one can in order not to incur the wrath of the gods through actions designed to placate them.

Areopagus: a special court of law that dictated judicial, executive, and legislative matters in Archaic Athens. In the Classical Period, the Areopagus was drastically reduced in power to handling deliberate homicides, woundings, and arson.

aristocracy: literally, the rule of the best, those of noble birth. Most such small groups of ruling aristocrats monopolized wealth and land, while they assumed full control over religious, military, and political affairs. Aristocracy came into prominence after the Homeric kingships and slowly declined when prosperous merchants gained some share of political control in city-states.

Classical Greece: roughly, the period in Greek antiquity from the Persian Wars beginning at 490 B.C. to the death of Alexander the Great in 323 B.C.

communitarianism: the theory that the ties of a political community are based on affection and common purpose. For Greek thinkers like Plato and Aristotle, these ties form naturally, because of the belief that cities are indissoluble units (or nearly so) that are more divine than or of greater ontological status than the individuals in them.

consequentialism: the view that an action is to be judged right or wrong by reference to its perceived consequences.

cosmopolitanism: literally, the view that the cosmos itself is one's *polis* or community. This was a key feature of Stoic throughout

Dark Age: the period of time in Greek antiquity that covered roughly 1200–776 B.C. The Dark Age was characterized by massive depopulation of Greek lands and great devastation of property. There is substantial disagreement about the causes of these events.

democracy: rule of the people, usually male citizens only. This form of government first appeared in ancient Athens in the late sixth century B.C.

determinism: the theory that every event is sufficiently brought about by a cause or causes. In a deterministic universe, for instance, given a precise knowledge of the state of the universe at any one time and having knowledge of the laws of physics, one would be able to predict (or retrodict) every future (or past) event.

egalitarianism: roughly the view that all humans are equal and deserving of the same liberties, rights, or opportunities.

egoism: the view that each person ought to act so as to seek his own self-interest.

egoistic hedonism: the view that each person ought to act so as to seek his own pleasure.

empiricism: the view that all knowledge is rooted in sensory experience. Radical empiricists maintain that only one's own sensory data are objects of knowledge.

epistemology: the branch of philosophy that studies knowledge. What is knowledge? How do we come to know? To what extent can we know? These are some of the questions of epistemology.

ethnocentrism: that which is centered on the people, a tribe, or a nation.

etiology: an account by appeal to antecedent causes.

fatalism: the view that events are necessitated in such a manner that we cannot avoid or prevent them from happening thus. For instance, in the Greek tale of Oedipus, it was foretold by the oracle that the hero would at some time kill his father and marry his mother. No matter what precautions were taken to prevent this from happening, things happened just as they were portended.

Hellenistic Greece: roughly the period in antiquity from the death of Alexander the Great in 323 B.C. to the Roman conquest of Greece in 164 B.C. It is so-called because the conquests of Alexander 'Hellenized' much of the civilized world.

Hippocratic medicine: the dominant school of ancient medical thought in antiquity that emphasized that physical health was a matter of a balance of material elements (humors) within the physical body. These elements were said to be the primary substances in the human body. Some Hippocratic authors (and Galen much later) thought these to be four in number – bile, black bile, phlegm and blood – though there was much disagreement on this. According to this model, illness was an imbalance of these substances. Treatment of illness consisted principally of restoring balance back to the body, especially through excesses of bile and phlegm. For instance, bile in the brain was believed to be the cause of frenzy and phlegm was perceived to cause epilepsy. Treatments consisted of emetics, purgations, exercise, rest, and nutritional remedies. Though substantially modified through the years, humoral medicine was still the basic physiological theory of physical health up to the eighteenth century.

homoeroticism (following up on Chapter 1): homoerotic relationships, in keeping with the stratification of Greek society, were asymmetrical by their very nature, though mutually beneficial. This is because the relationship was thought to be essentially 'educative' – helping the boy in athletics, military aptitude, and readiness for manhood. First, the boy strove to resist the advances of the lover. Once won over, the boy would grant the adult sexual favors, while he merely passively engaged in the sex. He was expected not to enjoy sex, but to look upon the adult lover with 'cold sobriety'. In contrast, the lover, in full enjoyment of the sexual experiences, was expected to educate his beloved in readiness for manhood.

As the lack of reciprocity in the sexual experience shows, Greeks, in general, viewed sex as a form of power: submissiveness was construed as a form of inferiority; aggressiveness, characterized especially through penetration, was a symbol of manliness.

Though we may never know precisely why male homoeroticism was practiced, there are many social factors that conduced towards it. First, there was the role of women in Greek society. Women were socially suppressed and males often needed other sexual outlets. A woman's job was household management (*oikonomia*) and this in itself proved to be an impediment to normal sexual relationships in hetero-sexual society. (We must not think of household management as some small or servile task. All things eaten and worn were produced at home, under the supervision of the wife. The wife was like the head of a small factory. Consider also the significance of Hestia in Greek mythology.) In aristocratic circles, women were segregated even more from men.

Second, though men were expected to marry a female citizen, marriage was seldom for love. Most men were probably not in love with their wives and would seek other amorous outlets. Men were legally free to seek alternative partners (slaves, prostitutes, etc.), but not among equals. Women, in contrast, had no such alternative.

Third, there was the risk of unwanted births. Men likely practiced anal intercourse with women and intercourse between thighs. This itself might have led to homoeroticism.

Last, not unrelated to the role of women in Greek society, there was female inferiority. Females were regarded as gross subordinates. Pericles himself said, 'the greatest glory of a woman is to be least talked about by men, whether they are praising you or criticizing you'. Young boys would, at least, grow up to be men in time, and this provided males with a loftier form of romance.

hylomorphism: for Aristotle, hylomorphism (Gr. *hulē* is matter and *morphos* is form) means that almost all realities are admixtures of matter and form. Take, for instance, an axe. Its matter consists of iron and wood, while its form is its essence or defining feature: being a thing that chops. These are also two of the celebrated four 'causes' of all things. There are also 'efficient' and 'final' causes of things. The efficient cause of axe is the work of the axe maker in creating the axe. The final cause is the actualization of the axe – that is, the axe as it is actually chopping.

This ties in importantly with Aristotle's account of potentiality (Gr. *dynamis*) and actuality (Gr. *energia*). A human at birth *potentially knows* (P_1) in that he is the type of organism that has a capacity to acquire knowledge at some later time. Once he has acquired knowledge, he *potentially knows* (P_2) in the sense of having but not presently using knowledge, which is, at the same time, a primary sense of *actually knowing* (A_1). When a person actualizes the knowledge that he has, he is said to know actually in the most complete and divine sense (A_2).

isomorphism: a one-to-one structural correspondence between any two things. For example, the three parts of Plato's *polis* are presumed isomorphic to the three parts of the human soul.

material equivalence: two statements are materially equivalent if and only if both are true under the same circumstances and false under the same circumstances.

metaphysics: the attempt to give a comprehensive, consistent, and coherent account of reality. More narrowly, the study of Being in itself. In this latter sense, metaphysics is synonymous with ontology.

Milesian philosophers: the first philosphers and natural scientists came from Miletus: Thales (c. 610–c. 540 B.C.), Anaximander (c. 610–c. 545 B.C.), and Anaximenes (c. 585–c. 525 B.C.). They sought to demythologize the world by offering naturalistic instead of theological explanations of observable phenomena. All were monists, in that they believed all things are (come out of or are reducible to?) one material thing. Thales was the first philospher and he is known to have said that all things are water. Anaximander posited that the primary material principle is 'the indefinite' or 'the boundless'. Last, Anaximenes stated that the true matter behind all things is air, and change occurs due to condensation and rarefaction.

naturalism: the view that moral properties are equivalent to or derived from natural properties. Moral justification here becomes a scientific enterprise in that the question of how I ought to behave is merely a matter of scientifically disclosing my natural dispositions toward actions.

nomological: lawlike.

normativism: having to do with what ought to be the case, instead of what is the case (naturalism). Inferences from 'ought' to 'is' or, conversely, from 'is' to 'ought' are therefore generally thought to be invalid.

oligarchy: rule of a few, usually wealthy noblemen.

ontology: *see* metaphysics.

oracle of Delphi: religious sanctuary in honor of the god of prophecy, Apollo. This was the wealthiest and most prestigious sanctuary in Greek antiquity. It was likely in existence as early as the eighth century B.C. and it came into prominence by the sixth century B.C.

There were both priests and a priestess at the oracle. The priestess, called *Pythia*, was the mouthpiece of Apollo. She was past middle age and of upstanding virtue. At dawn, she would purify herself in the water of the Castalian spring. Then the priest would sacrifice a goat to test for whether or not the day would be auspicious. If so, the Pythia would enter the sanctuary of the inner temple and ascend upon a sacred tripod in order to receive any message from Apollo.

When suppliants came (there were only nine consultations per year), they purified themselves in the Castalian spring, offered a cake outside the temple, and then sacrificed a goat inside the temple. Conducted to the inner sanctuary, they were told to think holy thoughts and speak words favorable to a good omen. The priest would then give the suppliant's question to the Pythia and she would return a response, given to the suppliant in verse. Such responses were not always free of ambiguity.

pancratium: this was a very popular competitive sport at religious/athletic festivals of antiquity like the Olympic Games. Pancratium combined elements of ancient boxing and wrestling, but was more brutal than either sport in that there were very few restrictions about what one could do to defeat an opponent.

Peloponnesian War, Second: a bitterly exhausting series of battles between Sparta and its allies and Athens and its allies that lasted from 431 B.C. to 404 B.C. The Spartans, who had a great advantage on land, developed principally a land strategy. The Athenians, who had a tremendous naval advantage, decided upon and implemented a naval strategy. Along the way, there were periodic breaks, intrigue, scandals, and miscalculations. Athens even suffered a major plague that decimated one-third of its population. There were major turning points during the war, but neither side could ever seem to muster up enough reserve to turn the tide. It was ultimately Persian intervention, mostly through resources, that decided the war in Sparta's favor. When Athens surrendered in April of 404 B.C., the tension and fighting between the two *poleis* continued on for many years thereafter. This is generally referred to as the Peloponnesian War, though there was a prior war between the two, as it were, Greek superpowers that lasted from 460 to 445 B.C.

phylogeny: the origin or genesis of the phylum or species.

Plato's Forms: Forms are immaterial, nonspatial and atemporal entities that have a reality greater than visible objects.

Plato's theory of Forms is a confluence of Parmenidean, Heraclitean and Pythagorean thinking. He combines Heraclitus' view that all things are in flux and that what is ultimately real is flux or change; Parmenides' notion that reality is one, unchanging, ungenerated and indestructible; and the Pythagorean emphasis on the importance of geometry and number in understanding nature.

To understand his theory of Forms, we must look at Plato's ontology. Let us divide 'reality', provisionally understood, into two realms, one accessible to the senses and one accessible to reason. What is perceived through the senses, as both Parmenides and Heraclitus noticed, is in flux and continually changing, and so, following Parmenides, it is no proper object of knowledge. Strictly speaking, this realm is not real. The objects of intelligence, such as the objects of geometry, are stable, permanent and unchanging. Thus, they are proper objects of knowledge and not graspable by any appeal to sensation or imagination (which is visible in nature).

Consider the nature or Form of triangle as opposed to any visible or imaginative representation of it. Formally: all (Euclidean) triangles are three-sided figures whose interior angles, summed, equal 180 degrees. This definition is unalterable and it is graspable only by intelligence (pure thinking), not any appeal to sensation or any faculties associated with sensation. All the various Formal types of Triangle without exception perfectly fit the definition or Form. It is by virtue of the Form, Triangle, that we have knowledge of its properties. Moreover, by an appeal to the Form (not any visible representation of it), I can *discover* qualities of triangles that I had never known to exist. This is true reality.

Consider, next, any visible manifestation of the Form, Triangle: this is only an imperfect representation of Triangle. Such visible manifestations nowise answer to the definition given by the Form. This is apparent reality.

Plato believed that there were Forms not only for mathematical objects, but also for most visible things – such as Maple Tree, Human Being and Chair – and even ethical 'realities' – such as Virtue and Goodness.

polis: the basic political unit for the ancient Greeks after the demise of the kingships that populated Greece prior to 800 B.C. A *polis* consisted of proper citizens (usually males only), females and youths (being protected under the law, but being without say in the law), and secondary citizens (such as free-born natives without influence in government, resident aliens, and slaves). The many *poleis* (pl.) that existed in Greece, roughly from 800 B.C. to the aftermath of Alexander's campaigns (c. 300 B.C.), were independent political units that, through utility or kinship, formed ties with other *poleis*. While the first *poleis* were mostly aristocracies, most of these evolved into democracies (i.e. Athens) or oligarchies (i.e. Sparta, Corinth, and Thebes).

rationalism: the view that reason predominates or is the exclusive tool in the acquisition of knowledge.

relativism, ethical: the view that values differ from person to person or, more popularly today, society to society. The relativist is committed to maintaining that there are no universal ethical principles. The first form was made famous by the Greek sophist Protagoras, who wrote, '[Each] man is the measure of all things: of things that are, that they are; of things that are not, that they are not'. Social relativists argue that truth is determined merely by agreement within a given society.

Socrates' demon: Socrates often asserts that an inner voice or *daimōnion* warns him about impending evil. This is perhaps best understood to be a spirit or lesser god.

Socratic elenchus: a method of inquiry that begins usually by an interlocutor stating a view on some topic (*Prt.* 331c), and then having it exposed to dialectical analysis. Socrates, through dialectical refutation, attempts to show that his interlocuter does not know what he thought that he knew. At each stage of the argument as it unfolds, Socrates attempts to refine or rebut definitions, opinions and even concessions through skilful elenchtic refutation by means of counterexamples. His interlocutor ends up contradicted and confounded, and winds up in a state called *aporia*. Prior to this, there was a state of undiagnosed ignorance. Now, the interlocutor's ignorance is disclosed or diagnosed. In the best possible scenario, an interlocutor realizes his ignorance and commits himself to eradicating it by seeking the truth and not pursuing any activities on which his ignorance may have some bearing. In a less-than-favorable scenario, an interlocutor will admit to frustration but not to ignorance, and so he will continue to do those things about which he is ignorant. This is not the proper aporetic state, conducive to knowledge. This, as a kind of mental gymnastics, is a necessary condition for learning.

Sophists: itinerant philosophers in ancient Greece who flourished during the fifth and fourth centuries B.C. Sophists (from the Greek word *sophia* or 'wisdom') purported to be able to teach a willing pupil whatsoever he desired to know, but specialized in topics such as rhetoric, logic, politics, morality, mathematics, grammar, and natural science. Their art boiled down to being able to teach students to argue persuasively on any topic, but Plato tells us (*Prt.* 318d–319a) that their main aim was to prepare people for active public life. So, instead of truth or knowledge, they aimed at craftiness in argumentation or persuasiveness. Though early on they ranked as men of wisdom, by the time of Aristotle they were generally held in contempt. Noted Sophists were Protagoras of Elis, Gorgias of Leontini, Prodicus of Ceos, and Hippias of Elis.

syllogism: at *APo.* I.2, Aristotle tells us that real science is a knowledge of causes (71b9–11). Knowing the cause of some event takes shape as an explanatory demonstration in the form of a syllogism (preferably with universal and affirmative statements), whose premises must be true, primitive, and immediate as well as more familiar than, prior to, and explanatory of the conclusion (71b17–24). In addition, the deduction, if it is to be properly a demonstration, must say more than *that* something is the case; it must tell *why* something is the case. In short, the middle term of the syllogism, the term common to both premises, must be causal, not just descriptive.

To illustrate, Aristotle has us consider two deductions. The first is a deduction of the fact. Here we argue for the proposition, '*Being near* belongs to *planets*', because '*Not twinkling* belongs to *planets*' and '*Being near* belongs to *not twinkling*'. Schematically:

P1: All *planets* are *things that do not twinkle*.
P2: All *things that do not twinkle* are *things that are near*.
C: All *planets* are *things that are near*.

In this syllogism, our middle term, *things that do not twinkle*, is supposed to be a cause of why *things that are near* is attributable to *planets*. Yet, the causal explanation is the other way around: *planets* are *things that do not twinkle* because they are *things that are near*. Consequently, a proper demonstration, a deduction of the reason why, would go like this.

P1: All *planets* are *things that are near*.
P2: All *things that are near* are *things that do not twinkle*.
C: All *planets* are *things that do not twinkle*.

Here, *nearness* gives the reason why planets do not twinkle.

symposium: an all-male, after-dinner drinking party hosted by aristocrats that was essentially of a sexual-intellectual nature. There were sesame cakes and other appetizers, but drinking of wine was the focal point. Servers and entertainers were generally young male and female slaves, chosen for their beauty. *Hetairai* (party friends as prostitutes, servers, dancers, and flute girls) presided over the party.

Each symposiast would recline on a couch, propped up on his left elbow, Phoenician style. There were usually between seven and fifteen couches, with two men to a couch. One of the symposiasts was appointed *symposiarchos* and presided over the night's events, especially the drinking.

Symposiasts drank from a wide and shallow vessel (Gr. *kulix*), nicely suited for the reclined drinking of wine. Wine was diluted with water (1/3 or 1/4 wine–water ratio), an admixture prepared in a large mixing bowl (Gr. *kratēr*) and distributed by slaves. The ratio might change during night, but drinking undiluted wine was generally frowned upon.

Kottabos, flicking dregs of wine at a specified target, and competitive singing were often featured. Often philosophical or political (mostly right-wing) discussion occurred. It is certainly at such symposia that subversive, antidemocratic sentiment took root. As the evening 'progressed', the *hetairai* might climb on to couches or symposiasts might start a *kōmos*, a drunken torchlit procession in honor of Dionysus.

teleology: study of phenomena that are goal-directed, orderly, designed, purposive, or dispositional. In particular, the notion that certain things are designed for or function toward some end or good. This view is prevalent in Plato, Aristotle, and the Stoics. For instance, Aristotle thought that the parts of a body function for the good of the organism as a whole, while the human organism itself acts because of some perceived end.

trope: from the Greek word *tropos*, which means 'turn', 'direction', 'manner', 'mode', or 'way of life'. 'Trope' is probably best understood in any of the last three senses.

tyranny: an abusive form of one-person rule. Tyrants, as described by Plato and Aristotle, rule by consuming passions, instead of regard for good or what is best for all.

Further Reading

General

Annas, Julia (1993) *The Morality of Happiness*. New York: Oxford University Press.

Buckley, Terry (1996) *Aspects of Greek History: A Source-Based Approach*. New York: Routledge.

Dover, K. J. (1974) *Greek Popular Morality in the Time of Plato and Aristotle*. Oxford: Blackwell.

Everson, Stephen (ed.) (1998) *Companions to Ancient Thought* 4: *Ethics*. Cambridge: Cambridge University Press.

Frankena, William 'A Critique of Virtue-Based Ethical Systems', in Louis Pojman (ed.), *Ethical Theory: Classical and Contemporary Readings*. New York: Wadsworth, 334–9.

Freud, Sigmund (1989) *Civilization and Its Discontents*. New York: W. W. Norton & Company.

Herodotus (1931 [1920]) *Histories*, Vol. i, trans. A. D. Godley. New York: Putnam.

Hesiod (1982) *The Homeric Hymns and Homerica*, trans. Hugh G. Evelyn-White, The Loeb Classical Library. Cambridge, MA: Harvard University Press.

Irwin, Terence (1995) *Plato's Ethics*. New York: Oxford University Press.

Konstan, David (1997) *Friendship in the Classical World*. New York: Cambridge University Press.

Long, A. A. and D. N. Sedley (1990) *The Hellenistic Philosophers*, Vol. 1. New York: Cambridge University Press.

Nussbaum, Martha C. (1986) *The Fragility of Goodness: Luck and Ethics in Greek Tragedy and Philosophy*. New York: Cambridge University Press.

Price, A. W. (1989) *Love and Friendship in Plato and Aristotle*. Oxford: Clarendon Press.

Russell, Bertrand (1996) *Conquest of Happiness*. New York: W. W. Norton & Company.

Plato

Primary sources

Plato (1989) *Symposium*, trans. and comm. Alexander Nehamas and Paul Woodruff. Indianapolis: Hackett.

Secondary readings

Adkins, Arthur W. H. (1996) 'The "Speech of Lysias" in Plato's *Phaedrus*', R. Louden and P. Schollmeier (eds), *The Greeks and Us: Essays in Honor of Arthur W. H. Adkins*. Chicago: University of Chicago Press, 224–40.

Allen, R. E. (1991) 'Comment', *The Dialogues of Plato*, Vol. II: *The Symposium*. New Haven, CT: Yale University Press, 3–109.

Brentlinger, John A. (1970) 'The Cycle of Becoming in the *Symposium*' and 'The Nature of Love', in *The Symposium of Plato*, trans., Suzy B. Groden. Amherst, NY: University of Massachusetts Press, 1–31 and 113–27.

Burnyeat, M. F. (1977) 'Socratic Midwifery, Platonic Inspiration', *Bulletin of the Institute of Classical Studies* 24: 7–17.

Cornford, F. M. (1950) 'The Doctrine of Eros in Plato's *Symposium*', in *The Unwritten Philosophy and Other Essays*. Cambridge: Cambridge University Press, 68–80.

Dover, K. J. (1978) *Greek Homosexuality*. New York: Random House.

Edelstein, Ludwig (1971) 'The Role of Eryximachus in Plato's *Symposium*', in *Ancient Medicine: Selected Papers of Ludwig Edelstein*. Baltimore: The Johns Hopkins University Press, 153–71.

Gould, Thomas (1963) *Platonic Love*. London: Routledge and Kegan Paul.

Hackforth, R. (1950) 'Immortality in Plato's *Symposium*', *Classical Review* 64: 42–5.

Luce, J. V. (1952) 'Immortality in Plato's *Symposium*', *Classical Review* 66: 137–41.

Markus, R. A. (1971) 'The Dialectic of Eros in Plato's *Symposium*', in Gregory Vlastos, *Plato: A Collection of Critical Essays*, Vol. II, 132–43.

Moravcsik, J. M. E. (1971) 'Reason and Eros in the Ascent-Passage of the *Symposium*', in John Anton and G. L. Kustas (eds), *Essays in Ancient Greek Philosophy*. Albany, NY: State University of New York Press, 285–302.

Morrison, Donald (2001) 'The Happiness of the City and the Happiness of the Individual in Plato's *Republic*', *Ancient Philosophy* 21: 1–24.

Neumann, H. (1965) 'Diotima's Concept of Love', *American Journal of Philology* 86: 33–59.

Plochmann, G. K. (1963) 'Hiccups and Hangovers in the *Symposium*', *Bucknell Review* 11: 1–18.

Rosen, Stanley (1968) *Plato's Symposium*. New Haven, CT: Yale University Press.

Vlastos, Gregory (1981) 'The Individual as an Object of Love in Plato', in Gregory Vlastos, *Platonic Studies*. Princeton, NJ: Princeton University Press, 3–37.

White, F. C. (1989) 'Love and Beauty in Plato's *Symposium*', *Journal of Hellenic Studies* 109: 149–57.

Aristotle

Primary sources

Aristotle (1985) *Nicomachean Ethics*, trans. and comm. Terence Irwin. Indianapolis: Hackett.
—— (1995) *Selections*, trans. and comm. Terence Irwin and Gail Fine. Indianapolis: Hackett.

Secondary readings

Annas, Julia (1999) 'Aristotle on Virtue and Happiness', in Nancy Sherman (ed.), *Aristotle's Ethics: Critical Essays*. Lanham, MD: Rowman & Littlefield, 35–56.

Anscombe, G. E. M. (1958) 'Modern Moral Philosophy', *Philosophy*, 33.

Barnes, Jonathan (ed.) (1995) *The Cambridge Companion to Aristotle*. New York: Cambridge University Press.

Broadie, Sarah (1991) *Ethics with Aristotle*. New York: Oxford University Press.

Burnyeat, Myles (1999) 'Aristotle on Learning to Be Good', in Nancy Sherman (ed.) 1999: 205–30.

Cooper, John M. (1980) 'Aristotle on Friendship', in Amélie Oksenberg Rorty (ed.), *Essays on Aristotle's Ethics*, Berkeley: University of California Press, 301–40.

—— (1999) 'Friendship and the Good in Aristotle', in *Aristotle's Ethics: Critical Essays*, Nancy Sherman (ed.). Lanham: MD: Rowman & Littlefield, 277–300.

Everson, Stephen (1998) 'Aristotle on Nature and Value', in Stephen Everson (ed.), *Companions to Ancient Thought* 4: *Ethics*. New York: Cambridge University Press, 77–106.

Hutchinson, D. S. (1995) 'Ethics', in *The Cambridge Companion to Aristotle*. Cambridge: Cambridge University Press, 195–232.

Lear, Jonathan (1988) 'Ethics and the Organization of Desire', in *Aristotle: The Desire to Understand*. New York: Cambridge University Press.

MacIntyre, Alisdair (2002) *After Virtue*. Notre Dame, IN: University of Notre Dame Press.

McDowell, John (1998) 'Some Issues in Aristotle's Moral Psychology', in Everson (ed.) 1998, 107–28.

—— (1980) 'The Role of *Eudaimonia* in Aristotle's Ethics', in Amélie Oksenberg Rorty (ed.), *Essays on Aristotle's Ethics*. Berkeley: University of California Press, 359–76.

Meyer, Susan Sauvé (1998) 'Moral Responsibility: Aristotle and After', in Everson (ed.) 1998, 221–40.

Rorty, Amélie Oksenberg (ed.) (1980) *Essays on Aristotle's Ethics*. Berkeley: University of California Press.

Sherman, Nancy (ed.) (1999) *Aristotle's Ethics: Critical Essays*. Lanham, MD: Rowman & Littlefield.

Wolz, H. G. (1999) 'Aristotle on Virtue and Happiness', in Nancy Sherman (ed.), *Aristotle's Ethics: Critical Essays*. Lanham, MD: Rowman & Littlefield, 35–56.

Epicurus

Primary sources

Epicurus (1994) *The Epicurus Reader: Selected Writings and Testimonia*, trans. and ed. Brad Inwood and L. P. Gerson. Indianapolis: Hackett.

Secondary readings

Annas, Julia (1993) 'Epicurus on Agency', in Jacques Brunschwig and Martha C. Nussbaum (eds), *Passions and Perceptions: Studies in Hellenistic Philosophy of Mind*. New York: Cambridge University Press.

Asmis, Elizabeth (1984) *Epicurus' Scientific Method*. Ithaca, NY: Cornell University Press.

Nussbaum, Martha (1994) 'Epicurean Surgery: Argument and Empty Desire', in *The Therapy of Desire: Theory and Practice in Hellenistic Ethics*. Princeton, NJ: Princeton University Press, chapter 4.

Rist, John M. (1972) *Epicurus: An Introduction*. Cambridge: Cambridge University Press (see esp. chapter 7).

Sedley, David (1998) 'The Inferential Foundations of Epicurean Ethics', in Everson (ed.) 1998, 129–50.

Striker, Gisela (1993) 'Epicurean Hedonism', in Jacques Brunschwig and Martha C. Nussbaum (eds), *Passions and Perceptions: Studies in Hellenistic Philosophy of Mind*. New York: Cambridge University Press.

Skepticism

Primary sources

Galen (1985) *Three Treatises on the Nature of Science: On the Sects for Beginners; An Outline of Empiricism;* and *On Medical Experience*, trans. Richard Walzer and Michael Frede. Indianapolis: Hackett.

Sextus Empiricus (1985) *Selections from the Major Writings on Scepticism, Man, and God*, ed. Philip P. Hallie. Indianapolis: Hackett.

Secondary readings

Annas, Julia (1996) 'Scepticism, Old and New', in M. Frede and G. Striker (eds), *Rationality in Greek Thought*. Oxford: Clarendon Press, 239–54.

Hallie, Philip P. (1985) 'Classical Scepticism – A Polemical Introduction', in Sextus Empiricus, *Selections from the Major Writings on Scepticism, Man, and God*. Indianapolis: Hackett.

Holowchak, M. Andrew (2002) *Ancient Science and Dreams: Oneirology in Greco-Roman Antiquity*. Lanham, MD: University Press of America.

Mill, John Stuart (1985) *On Liberty*. New York: Penguin Books.

Nussbaum, Martha (1994) 'Skeptic Purgatives: Disturbance and the Life without Belief', in *The Therapy of Desire: Theory and Practice in Hellenistic Ethics*. Princeton, NJ: Princeton University Press, chapter 8.

Wittgenstein, Ludwig (1969) *On Certainty*, ed. G. E. M. Anscombe and G. H. von Wright. New York: Harper & Row.

—— (1984) *Culture and Value*, trans. Peter Winch. Chicago: University of Chicago Press.

Socrates

Primary sources

Plato (1983) *Five Dialogues: Euthyphro, Apology, Crito, Meno, Phaedo*, trans. G. M. A. Grube. Indianapolis: Hackett.

Secondary readings

Benson, Hugh H. (ed.) (1992) *Essays on the Philosophy of Socrates*. New York: Oxford University Press.
Brickhouse, Thomas C. and Nicholas D. Smith (1992) 'The Formal Charges Against Socrates', in Benson (ed.) 1992, 14–31.
Irwin, Terence (1998) 'Socratic Paradox and Stoic Theory', in Everson (ed.) 1998, 151–92.
—— (1995) *Plato's Ethics*. New York: Oxford University Press.
—— (1992) 'Socrates the Epicurean', in Benson (ed.) 1992, 198–219.
McPherran, Mark L. (1992) 'Socratic Piety in the *Euthyphro*', in Benson (ed.) 1992, 220–41.
Penner, Terry (1992) 'The Unity of Virtue', in Benson (ed.) 1992, 162–84.
Reeve, C. D. C. (1989) *Socrates in the Apology: An Essay on Plato's Apology of Socrates*. Indianapolis: Hackett.
Robinson, Richard (1971) 'Elenchus', in *Philosophy of Socrates*, ed. G. Vlastos. Cambridge: Cambridge University Press.
White, James Boyd (1996) 'Plato's *Crito*: The Authority of Law and Philosophy', in *The Greeks and Us: Essays in Honor of Arthur W. H. Adkins*, R. Louden and P. Schollmeier (eds). Chicago: University of Chicago Press, 97–133.

Stoicism

Primary sources

Epictetus (1983) *The Handbook*, trans. Nicholas White. Indianapolis: Hackett Publishing Company.

Long, A. A. and D. N. Sedley (1990) *The Hellenistic Philosophers*, Vol. 1. New York: Cambridge University Press.

Secondary readings

Edelstein, Ludwig (1980) *The Meaning of Stoicism*. Cambridge, MA: Harvard Unversity Press.

Frede, Michael (1980) 'Stoics and Skeptics and Clear and Distinct Ideas', in *Doubt and Dogmatism*, Myles Burnyeat and Jonathan Barnes (eds). New York: Oxford University Press, 151–76.

Irwin, Terence (1998) 'Socratic Paradox and Stoic Theory', in Stephen Everson (ed.), *Companions to Ancient Thought*, 4: *Ethics*. Cambridge: Cambridge University Press (1998), 151–92.

Lapidge, Michael (1978) 'Stoic Cosmology', *Phronesis* 18: 161–85.

Long, A. A. (1996) *Stoic Studies*. Berkeley: University of California Press.

Nussbaum, Martha (1994) *The Therapy of Desire: Theory and Practice in Hellenistic Ethics*. Princeton, NJ: Princeton University Press, chapters 9 and 10.

Rist, John M. (1978) 'The Stoic Concept of Detachment', in J. M. Rist (ed.), *The Stoics*. Berkeley: University of California Press, 259–72.

Alexander of Macedon

Primary sources

Arrian (1971) *The Campaigns of Alexander*. New York: Penguin.

Rufus, Quintus Curtius (1984) *The History of Alexander*. New York: Penguin.

Secondary readings

Green, Peter (1992) *Alexander of Macedon*. Berkeley: University of California Press.

Hanson, Victor Davis (2000) *The Wars of the Ancient Greeks*. London: Cassell.

Lane Fox, Robin (1994) *Alexander the Great*. New York: Penguin.

Diogenes the Cynic

Primary sources

Diogenes Laertius ([1925] 1991) *Diogenes Laertius: Lives of Eminent Philosophers*, vols i and ii, trans. R. D. Hicks. Loeb Classical Library. Cambridge, MA: Harvard University Press.

Secondary readings

Dudley, Donald R. (1967) *A History of Cynicism*. Hildesheim: Georg Olms.
Krueger, Derek (1996) 'The Bawdy and Society: The Shamelessness of Diogenes in Roman Imperial Culture', in R. B. Branham and Marie-Odile Goulet-Cazé (eds), *The Cynics: The Cynic Movement in Antiquity and Its Legacy*. Berkeley: University of California Press, 222–39.
Moles, John L. (1996) 'Cynic Cosmopolitanism', in R. B. Branham and Marie-Odile Goulet-Cazé (eds), *The Cynics: The Cynic Movement in Antiquity and Its Legacy*. Berkeley: University of California Press, 105–20.

Index